What Others Say About the Book

Those who read this book will encounter many unexpected, rewarding and pleasant surprises. I certainly did.

There are many, many books written by parents of autistic children. None are like this. There are very few autistic individuals like Krishna, the primary subject of the book. I say "primary" because the book, written as a journal covering April 1997 through March, 1998, concerns much more than Krishna. Jalaja Narayanan's title From a Mother's Heart: A Journal of Survival, Challenge, and Hope is aptly chosen. Krishna, in his twenties, is the focal point of the story, but the charm of the volume lies in its clear and comprehensive exposition of what goes on in the heart—and in the mind—of his highly intelligent, highly articulate, very well read, and totally devoted mother.

Be prepared for excursions into literature, poetry, history, science, current affairs, politics and a vast array of other topics that Jalaja guides us into and through her world. One does not have to be addicted to autism to enjoy and benefit from this opportunity to share Jalaja's thoughts and experiences. Her perceptions of the world as a mother and an Indian woman living in America are insightful and fascinating.

Then there is the paradoxical, frustrating but also fascinating Krishna. A severely autistic, very difficult young man, with only marginal ability to communicate, Krishna displays amazing abilities in physics and mathematics (mathematics, not just calculation). Jalaja and her extraordinarily patient husband Nan, a Ph.D. in electrical engineering, have, like many of us parents of autistic children, explored almost every available modality of treatment in their desperate, dedicated attempts to help rescue Krishna from autism. There is much to be learned from their experiences.

You will find reading this book a rewarding adventure.

Bernard Rimland, Ph.D.
Director, Autism Research Institute

"This poignant book describes a mother's emotional journey during which she struggles to understand the inconsistencies in her autistic son's behavior and abilities, to identify professionals and treatments to help him and to advocate for his happiness and a more normal life. This is a memoir which in many ways reflects the lives of all parents of children with special needs. It chronicles a parent's attempts to deal with frustration, resignation and hope. But the primary message of this book is the triumph of the human spirit when faced with adversity. It describes the need for determination despite selfdoubt, the power of believing in one's self and one's child and the certainty that life can be better for those who are labeled "disabled" and for whom society seems to have little hope.

This is a book that should be required reading not only for all families involved in the care of a child with special needs, but for health care professionals, educators and those establishing public policies which will substantially impact on the lives and future of all individuals with handicapping conditions."

Dr. Margaret L. Bauman, MD
Pediatric Neurologist
Director, LADDERS
Harvard Medical School
Massachusetts General Hospital

"This book, "From a Mother's Heart" is the story of a journey fueled by love, guided by wisdom and revealing remarkable persistence in the face of adversity. The book can be readily understood both as a narrative of every day events and as a source of the sort of knowledge that is only achieved by a family that is deeply devoted to finding the "Truth". Readers will gain much insight into the nature of autism, family dynamics and heroism."

Dr. Martin A. Kozloff
Watson Distinguished Professor
Watson School of Education
University of North Carolina

From a Mother's Heart

A Journal of
Survival, Challenge, and Hope

Jalaja Narayanan

Vite Publishing, Inc.
Andover, Massachusetts

From a Mother's Heart
A Journal of Survival, Challenge and Hope
By Jalaja Narayanan

Published by:
Vite Publishing
P.O. Box 1632
Andover, MA 01845 U.S.A.

Order from:
BookMasters, Inc.
30 Amberwood Parkway
Ashland, OH 44805
order@bookmaster.com

Copyright © 2001
First Printing 2001

Printed in the United States of America

Publisher's Cataloging-in-Publication
(Provided by Quality Books, Inc.)

Narayanan, Jalaja
    From a mother's heart: a journal of survival, challenge, and hope/
    Jalaja Narayanan.—1st ed.
        p.   cm
      ISBN: 0-9706541-0-3
      1. Autistic children—Family relationships   2. Parents of autistic
    children   3. Autism—Psychological aspects   I. Title
    RJ506.A9N37   2001
    618.92'8982 QBI00-1097

Dedication

To my Mom
Who taught me to dream with commitment.

To my son Krish
Who proved that commitment fulfills dreams.

Foreword

"It is a humbling experience to read "From a Mother's Heart," humbling for a professional who has worked with children and families affected by autism for the past 30 years, humbling in several ways.

First, even though I know from discussions with many hundreds of families what daily life can be like for a family with a child severely affected by autism, seldom have I read or heard an account with such illuminating detail about how the disorder impacts every aspect of daily life. Sleeping, waking, dressing, eating, making needs known, communicating with strangers, behaving in public, let alone the more complex skills of sharing interests and communication with family, and finding constructive activities to use and stimulate Krishna's superior intellect—all were (and sometimes continue to be) challenges for Krishna and his family. How easy for professionals, who see a client for an hour or a morning, to put out of our minds the realities of coping with problems and maximizing constructive activities for 24 hours a day.

More humbling still is observing the insight that caring and sensitive parents achieve about some of the underlying processes in individuals with autism and about the best ways to improve their abilities and behavior. Krishna's mother discovered for herself that "his actions do not match his understanding. There is little correlation between his intellect and his behavior." This is the basic idea behind the eminent Russian neuropsychologist Luria's "second signaling system," namely language and its control over behavior, and how in some neurological disorders, there is a pathological disconnection between language and intellect and behavior. Krishna's mother also arrives at some of the most important principles of behavior modification such as positive reinforcement and the importance of total consistency in applying it. And finally, she arrives at the conclusion that Krishna's difficulties have motivational abnormalities as their root cause, a theory that has become popular in the last decade or so, among psychologists and psychiatrists who study autism. Many fundamental ideas about core processes, genetic links, and possible treatments with regard to autism and other developmental disorders have been developed by concerned and involved parents. It is salutory for professionals to be reminded from time to time just how important it is to take parents' ideas as worthy of serious investigation.

For parents of children with autism who are young or recently diagnosed, a cautionary note about Krishna's story is in order. Krishna is unusual among people with autism. Although many individuals with autism suffer from anxiety, Krishna's anxiety is expecially marked. When I saw Krishna, it was quite apparent that this extreme anxiety prevented him from showing many of the skills he had. He is also quite unusual in the degree of discrepancy he shows between his remarkable intellectual ability and his severe behavioral difficulties. Most children and adolescents with normal or superior intellectual ability do not have the same degree of difficulty in using or applying those skills, even though their behavior or social style may remain atypical. It must also be remembered that Krishna was a young child 25 years ago. Early intervention and education have come a long way since then, and the prospects for young children today must be regarded as better than those that Krishna faced.

There are universal themes in this book that will touch all parents, whether their children have disabilities or not. Letting go of preconceptions about who our children should be, and accepting them as they are even while demanding the most from them, is something faced by every parent. Imposing discipline when we would rather soothe and comfort is difficult for all of us. And how to balance the needs of our children, our partners and ourselves is faced by all parents on a daily basis, as Krishna's mother and father had to decide how best to balance his care and education with the other demands in their lives.

Finally, an aspect of the book that touched me deeply, even though it is hardly discussed explicitly, is the obvious support and devotion between Krishna's parents. Every marriage faces hardship, whether from economic troubles, illness, loss, or other tribulations. I have seen many marriages dissolve under the stress, disappointment, or disagreements that can result from having a child with a disability. In other cases, as here, the partners' trust and love for each other seems strengthened by adversity, and this obviously carries over to the family devotion and affection showed by Krishna's sister. The unwavering solidarity of this family will inspire all parents."

Dr. Deborah Fein,
Professor of Psychology
University of Connecticut

Like a turtle
I withdraw my limbs
Of pain and strain
Stress and distress
Madness and sadness
Dejection and depression,
To concentrate upon
A cause named Krish,
With selfless love,
And tender care.
With blazing faith,
And mystic serenity.
With lightning hope
And thunderous vitality.
I serve my beloved,
Each day and every night,
Like a melting wax
In the burning heat,
With peculiar obsession,
And indifferent expectation.
For what I receive or reject
For what I lose or gain
Is beyond me, the ignorant
But for Thy Divine Will.

By Jalaja Narayanan

Preface

I wrote this book as the mother of an autistic son, a mother who has lived with her son for over two decades. The ultimate reality of living with an autistic on a day-to-day basis is brought forth in a diary form. It is a one-year snapshot of the last twenty-five years of joys and sorrows, triumphs and failures.

This book is not a treatise on autism. It deals with the unpredictability of autism and how one tries to cope with it. Coping with autism is coping with unpredictability.

Here, one witnesses the poignant roller coaster of emotions from hope to dismay, joy to sorrow, anger to tranquility, disbelief to belief, boredom to creativity, sanity to insanity. No one day is the same. Every day is fight or flight for survival. As is surely so also of other life-altering illnesses. This is what every family teetering on survival with a serious illness, whether it be mental, physical or emotional is dealing with.

Families having children with challenging problems such as autism, Down's Syndrome, cerebral palsy, and many other devastating syndromes will find this book useful because the purpose of this journal is to share my feelings, thoughts, emotions, trials, and joys with others. Sharing as a healing force does wonders for the aching soul. They will find solace in feeling that they are not alone. We all have seen the therapeutic effects of Alcoholics Anonymous and similar organizations on people's lives. What's more, families facing very serious, life-threatening illnesses such as heart disease, cancer, brain tumors, and AIDS will find this book to be of value.

When I was groping in the dark, the book *For the Love of Anne* gave me some direction. It was my candle in total darkness. I derived so much strength and solace from that book. If this journal of mine can provide some light of hope, however faint it may be, to someone in his or her total darkness of desperation and hopelessness, then I have achieved one of my goals for writing. What good is life without mental strength? Control of mind gives such happiness and peacefulness that it surpasses all riches, fame, and power.

One of the great saints of India says that with shoes, one can walk even over thorny bushes and stony slopes. You are protected from it all. We don't need to cover the whole world with leather in order for us to walk safely. Similarly, I don't need to make Krish's autism go away for me to be happy. All I need is a pair of shoes to walk over the thorny fields; that is, I need a change of attitude, a strong, controlled, poised mind.

To win the mind is to win all, just as to one who is wearing shoes, the whole world is covered with leather. The simple truth is if you change, the whole world will change.

Acknowledgments

My daughter, Malini, for her unshakable faith in my storytelling ability. I couldn't have written this book without her constant prodding for more than a decade.

My editor, Robert Fiske, who read my manuscript and gave me valuable suggestions to make it a finished book.

My dear friend, Toshiko, who saw the possibility for a book in my relentless work and believed in this book even before it got started.

My husband, Nan, who never got tired of my irrelevant, dumb questions regarding publication of this book and answered them with kindness.

This list of acknowledgments is incomplete without thanking Victoria Perry, who typed my illegible handwritten manuscript into readable material.

Jalaja Narayanan
North Andover (MA)

April 1997

April 1, 1997

I am holding Krish so tightly to my chest that he is gasping for breath. I fear it is the last time I will ever see him. This cannot be happening. He is my baby. Please, God, I'll do anything—he doesn't have to be like everyone else; he doesn't have to be normal; he never has to talk; he can even die so long as they don't take him from me. Where they are taking him, what they will do with him, I do not know. Please, God, where are you?

Three uniformed men dressed in black are approaching us. I cannot yet see their faces, but they look surly and unpleasant. They are walking toward us. My poor baby, what will he do without me? We should run. Should we run? Are they pointing guns at us? Is death better? Whatever did I do wrong? Wasn't I God fearing? Didn't I treat Krish well? Didn't I devote myself to him?

Maybe when they see my tears, they will soften and let me keep him; maybe they will not separate us. I hold Krish still tighter. I see now their faces; I see that my tears mean nothing to them. They are cold, unfeeling.

Two of the men grab my arms and hold me firmly. The third man pulls Krish away. As they take Krish from me, I am crying, screaming, "No, he is my son! Let me come!" They throw me to the ground, but I get up and start running toward them. I am chasing them, but my feet are heavy, as if made of iron. I am too slow, too old. I can no longer see my son's face. He is gone.

After I awoke from my nightmare, my body was shaking and I was disoriented. I went to see whether Krishna was all right or not. I was relieved to find him sleeping peacefully.

My deep feelings about placing him in a residential program must have surfaced. I am sure no matter how difficult it is to care for a child at home, putting him or her in a residential program must be the most excruciating decision for the family. To me, a permanent residential program is almost like giving my child a life sentence. It means I as a parent have failed. The very thought always creates enormous guilt and incurable sadness in me. It is like a young mother giving up her baby for adoption. She would certainly go through a heart-wrenching roller coaster of emotions before any such decision. Will my baby be loved? Will he grow up to be normal? Who is going to protect him from abusers, physical as well as emotional?

If I place him in a residential program, I will feel as though I had abandoned him for my own comfort and lifestyle, even though that is not the case. The major concerns I have about residential programs are that good-quality care may not be available, and he may be drugged for easy management. To me personally, my success in life is keeping Krish at home. If I can achieve that, I am a successful person.

The nightmare also is the reflected image of the extreme fear and anger I felt about an incident my friend Nancy Johnson told me. She told me this story in horrifying detail.

When Krish was thirteen, he was having difficulties at school. Since his teacher had a number of children with special needs, we felt he needed an aide or a teacher to take him for a walk outside whenever he felt overwhelmed in the classroom. But the school system turned down our request since no money was available for an aide. Because Krish's behavior was getting worse, I pulled him out of school and kept him at home.

We couldn't find any program we liked in Massachusetts. At this time, we came to know about a school in Japan. It sounded excellent. I liked the school's philosophy. When I talked to the principal, I was very impressed with her attitude. She sounded very much like me, and believed Krish would grow up to be normal. She also believed me when I said that Krish was smart.

So we took Krish to Japan and enrolled him in school. I met Nancy Johnson on my first visit to the school with Krish. She was very kind and spoke to me only for a few minutes because she was on her way home from school with her son, Joe, who was also attending the program for the autistic.

In the two years of our stay in Tokyo, Nancy and I became very good friends. She has a daughter who is only a year younger than my daughter, and they became very good friends. Later, when the school opened a branch in the United States, Krish and Joe attended it. Both our family and Nancy's moved back to the United States. Joe used to feel that he was Krish's big brother at school. When Joe's school years ended, he returned home to Washington to attend a program.

According to Nancy, the program in Washington was not good. Joe started to regress, and he was having difficulties with his aggressive behavior. Because Nancy and her husband needed some help to contain Joe's angry outbursts, she made an appointment with a psychiatrist, hoping to get some medication to help Joe with his aggression.

As Nancy told me, there was a long wait in the doctor's office. Joe was becoming restless, and his behavior started getting worse with the long wait. Joe asked for food many times, not only because he was hungry but also because the waiting room was crowded. Every time my friend asked the receptionist whether it was okay for her to go to the cafeteria, she was told that the doctor could call her in at any time, and that it was not advisable for her to leave. So she waited and waited, but the doctor never called her name. My friend tried to explain her situation to the receptionist several times, that Joe needed to get out of the crowded room, but her words fell on deaf ears.

By this time, Joe's behavior had escalated to a point where he became angry, frustrated, and aggressive. Without informing Nancy, the doctor called the police. When two policemen arrived, they hand-cuffed Joe, dragging him to the police car, while Nancy stood there horror stricken.

Her son, whom she nursed as a baby, cherished as her precious gift from God, and loved as her very own self, was being abducted from her before her eyes. Her own doctor instigated the kidnapping. She felt as if her rights as a mother were being violated. She felt victimized. "How can such an atrocity take place in broad daylight in a doctor's office?" she wondered. "Is there any justice in this world? What have we done to deserve this?"

No one in the waiting room came to her rescue because it wasn't anyone else's business. They went on reading about how Ted Turner and Jane Fonda spent a weekend in the Far East and the latest events in Madonna's life. It is not fashionable to get involved in others' business. It is not cool. I, too, wanting to be accepted, would have done the same thing, that is, nothing. This would probably not have happened in a less civilized world. In a less civilized world, people would be more caring and compassionate toward one another.

The boy resisted with all his might. He was on the floor, kicking and screaming. Two policemen were dragging him out while he was screaming; they dragged him all the way to the police car. "Mom, I am scared. Don't send me away. I will be good," he cried with tears streaming down his face. The police said that they were taking him to the station to put him in jail, and Nancy should come to court in the morning. This autistic son of hers spent the night in jail all alone. I cannot comprehend how a professional in a mental health field could call the police on an autistic person who was waiting in his office.

First of all, the doctor should not have let him wait that long. He should have known what waiting for an hour or two can do to an autistic. Second, the police obviously should not have been called in. The doctor's third, and perhaps most reprehensible, mistake was that he testified against Joe and wanted him institutionalized. The police also testified against Joe. Nancy was crying hysterically. She pleaded with the judge to let him go home. The judge was more compassionate than either the doctor or the police, and trusted her enough to let her take her son home. But he warned her, "Please leave this town. Move to another town where you have no problem with the police." That, a few months later, is precisely what she did.

This story shook me up thoroughly. I have been trying to grapple with the facts of this incident since I heard it. The doctor's despicable behavior leads me to believe he should lose his license to practice. No one so insensitive and thoughtless deserves to call himself a psychiatrist. I am still violently shaken by this.

April 3, 1997

Today, my husband insisted that I write about the infant years of Krishna from the very beginning. Reluctantly, and with a dreary and sad disposition, I began to write the most trying period of my life.

The joy I felt the day he was born cannot be expressed in human language. I had so many dreams for him. I wanted him to become a great scientist. I wanted him to become a neurosurgeon. At times, I thought he could be both.

He was a very quiet baby in his first year of life, although he was not doing any of the normal activities of a one-year old. He didn't walk; he didn't say mama or papa; he didn't show interest in toys; and he didn't like being held or cuddled. He started regressing slowly around the age of two. He showed very little interest in food. He didn't sleep well. He was awake most of the night and slept only three or four hours a day. He also displayed a lot of bizarre behaviors, such as looking at his hands, flapping his hands, rocking, hitting his head against the wall, tapping his chin, playing with his urine and saliva or the toilet water, screaming and crying, displaying fear at the sight of strangers, and pulling his hair as well as others' hair when throwing a tantrum.

His screaming tantrums were unpredictable and caused enormous stress, gripping confusion, and debilitating anxiety in the family. This extreme unpredictability in his behavior and his moods kept us terrorized and immobilized day in and day out. Will he sleep or not? Will he eat or not? Will he behave or not? Will he be constipated or not? Will he throw a tantrum or not? Will he be stressed or not? I couldn't plan anything around him. I was always waiting for some crisis to happen. Something was terribly wrong.

When Boston Children's Hospital told us he was autistic, I misunderstood what it meant. I took *autistic* for *artistic*. My first reaction was one of elation; maybe Krish would be our next great artist like Van Gogh. Even after learning about the implications of autism, I still didn't understand the term. Even today, it is still an unfolding enigma.

The doctors were very bleak about his prognosis. They said, "We know very little about this syndrome. Children with autism don't communicate as normal people do, and they will never interact. They will always remain loners. We do not know much about the prognosis. But usually they do not do well." One physician said, "You may want to place your son in a residential program." I felt as though my child was given a death sentence. They were extremely pessimistic and had scant hope for his future. But I can't find fault with them either since the syndrome in those days was even more of a mystery than it is now. As parents, we got little help, a good deal of confusion, and an infinite amount of worry. There was no prescription for cure and only a vague description of what autism is.

My positive spirit and my love for him wouldn't allow me to accept their prognosis. In an angry, quaking voice, with tears in my eyes, I told them, "You can't write off a child at three or four, and you can't assume the role of God by saying that he will never make it. The Creator of this universe can make him a prodigy if He wills it. You are not above God."

After the Children's diagnosis, nothing made sense any more. Nothing prepared me for such emptiness. My whole life was coming apart at the seams. No motivation. No energy. No desire. No interest. Any and every activity became pointless. My whole being, my whole existence, ceased to exist. Out of sheer practice and habit, using every ounce of self-discipline I possessed, I forced myself to do my basic duties as a young mother. I was so numb with total exhaustion that it was an effort even to worry. That took too much out of me, I guess. All I wanted to do was curl up in a corner and do nothing. You could call me practically dead. I was a mindless, walking corpse.

In those early days of the diagnosis, I doubted whether I would ever pull myself together. There were many days when I saw the sky, the stars, the moon, and the trees all crying with sadness for me. In my imagination, I even saw the ocean become more turbulent because of my presence. This perception of Nature's sympathy for my state comforted me.

Those were the days I couldn't bring myself to express my feelings to anyone, nor could I get in touch with myself. All of my spiritual background in my upbringing as a Hindu didn't come to my aid. After a month of initial shock and mourning, something strange started to happen.

Usually, I keep a clean, meticulous house. Everything had to be in order. But now I no longer cared. Clean for what? My son was doomed. I saw my house become disorganized. The sink was filled with dirty dishes, and dirty clothes were piling up. What's more, my daughter, Malini, was asking me to play with her, but I could only look distantly into space. I had no joy left with which to play with her. Every week we were seeing top neurologists in New York, Pennsylvania, or Washington who confirmed this dreary diagnosis. Life was so chaotic. My husband was affected to such an extent that he was unable to make a career-enhancing presentation to a top executive.

I finally saw the destructive side of my depression, which was touching and affecting everyone around me. That single revelation put me on the road to recovery. I cannot lose everything good in my life to autism. I started to go below the layers of being a weak, vulnerable, scared self. When my secret trap door to my innermost sanctum sanctorum opened, I caught a glimpse of what I am really made of. An awareness to my true self dawned on me. I was not this weak, scared self, but a very strong, optimistic, intelligent self sparked by the divinity of God. He would certainly guide me through this monumental struggle.

I wondered, can night stay on forever without the follow-up of day? Doesn't birth guarantee our looming death? Everything in Nature is subject to change. Therefore, my sad feelings also will yield to sunny thoughts. I have to believe this too shall pass. This hopeless and dejected feeling also will give rise to hope and joy. The lines I memorized as a teenager often came to my rescue:

> Drive my dead thoughts over the universe
> Like withered leaves to quicken a new birth!
> And, by the incantations of this verse,
> Scatter, as from an unextinguished hearth,
> ashes and sparks, my words among mankind!
> Be through my lips to unawakened earth
> The trumpet of a prophecy! O Wind,
> if winter comes, can spring be far behind?
> from Shelly's "Ode to the West Wind"

April 5, 1997

I have been thinking about the transformation that has taken place in me, also, over the past twenty years. Before Krishna, I was a sweet, gentle, innocent person. I tried so hard to please people. Above all, I loved to have fun. I invited more than 120 people to Krish's first birthday party. They were all my friends. I invested a lot of time in nurturing my friendships with people.

Then came Krish's autism. That changed my outlook on life. It was not my wish. Irrespective of my wish, I was given this precious little boy with a rare syndrome that even specialists didn't know much about. Krish's autism took everything out of me. Many days, I wasn't aware what day it was. I was so involved in Krish's problems, I forgot who I was and what my needs were. Soon, I became a recluse. I was being transformed from a social butterfly to a loner.

April 6, 1997

What was Krishna like when he was two years old? He looked very healthy and very handsome. He had an enticing smile with twinkling eyes. But he also had many symptoms of autism that had to be dealt with daily, some of which I am dealing with still today.

As a baby, he was unresponsive to love. He never even raised his hands in anticipation of being picked up. If left alone without intervention, he would rock in a corner for hours at a time while hitting his head on a wall. He would stare into space, never giving eye contact, and he would scream with all his might whenever he was held or hugged. He ferociously rejected love and affection. Every time he was picked up, his body started trembling visibly. When strangers approached him, he screamed at the top of his lungs as if his very existence were threatened.

In those early days, he slept very little. He would rock and whine all night. And that doesn't mean that he had a good nap in the afternoon. He seemed too tense to fall asleep. Almost every night, my husband, Nan, and I took turns being with him, so as to give him company. When we patted him rhythmically or stroked his back gently, he slept for a few hours. But the minute I withdrew my hand from his body, he woke up with a violent shake. So most of the nights I stayed with him until 4:00 in the morning. For years, I was sleep deprived. I never had more than four hours of sleep a day.

As an autistic person, Krish suffered from an eating disorder. Around this time, he was drinking only milk from the bottle. Occasionally, he ate applesauce. The first project I took upon myself was to eradicate his bizarre food habits. I told myself, "If I can't change a two year old, how can I hope to change a fifteen year old?" If a habit is left to take its own course, it becomes a fixation, and thus an obstacle to development. A Spanish proverb says it well: "Habits are at first cobwebs, then cables."

The first breakthrough came after six weeks of intensely hard work to make him take a sip of juice from a glass. From that moment, changing his food habits became much easier. In fifteen months, he was eating rice, bread, crackers, soup, and so on. In the same way, we were gradually able to teach him to bite and chew his food. Every small breakthrough meant a bar in his cage was lifted. From a very tiny seed grows a very large banyan tree. An invisible atom produced the atom bomb that destroyed Hiroshima and Nagasaki. In my opinion, nothing in life is too small or too trivial to ignore.

Krish was very much developmentally delayed. He sat at seven months, crawled at ten months, and walked at one year and seven months. He had a lot of coordination problems. At three, he couldn't go up and down the stairs; he didn't know how to jump or roll a ball. He had a lot of difficulty in picking things up. We did immense work with him in developing his gross and fine motor skills by teaching him to ride a tricycle, jump on a trampoline, throw a ball, and so on.

His ability to touch, smell, and taste was adversely affected. Likewise affected were his abilities to hear and see, understand gestures, and mimic movements. How could he understand and relate to the world around him when he had no comprehension of it through his five senses? No wonder he was terrified and suspicious of everything new; no wonder he was filled with fear.

April 7, 1997

My whole existence revolved around Krishna. My intense life with Krish had cost me my friends and relatives. When he was young, we used to go to close friends' houses for dinner, as a family. But I was never able to sit and have a decent conversation. I was always managing him and his behavior. So I never enjoyed my outings with him, nor did my friends.

I always ended up trying to explain his behaviors to others, and at the same time, dealing with him, trying to stimulate and structure him. No matter how much I explained, my friends couldn't understand. Everyone always had more questions. It was too much to handle all at once—trying to handle them as well as Krish. Sometimes, my aloofness created a lot of misunderstanding.

I started to shudder at the thought of visiting my friends with him. I didn't like to leave him home with a babysitter for hours just so I could have some fun with a friend. It was extremely hard to find any babysitter who could pull him out of his shell and structure his time and attention meaningfully. I dreaded the thought that he might be rocking or engaged in some bizarre self-stimulating behavior in a corner, lost in himself for hours. It wasn't fair to Krish when he was fighting for his survival with autism.

It was the same with inviting people over to my house. It meant I had to stop structuring Krish's behavior for much of the day. He was left wholly unattended while I was cleaning the house and cooking for my friends. There, too, I felt as though I wasn't being fair to him. What's more, the day following the entertaining and commotion was seldom productive for either of us: either I was too tired or he was not in the mood to learn. It became too much of a trial. So I stopped inviting people over.

Slowly, visiting with my friends became less and less frequent. It wasn't a deliberate decision. I simply had no time for anyone else except Krish. He was a full-time job. I couldn't leave him alone for a minute lest he engage in unwanted, self-stimulating, destructive behaviors. I was his primary teacher.

Since my husband was very involved in his career, I was the one who took Krish to the doctor, to the therapist, to teachers' meetings, and so on. I was, and I still am, his principal advocate. He cannot advocate for himself. I also had to make sure all of his needs were taken care of. To this day, every person I meet with and every phone call I receive or make is directly or indirectly connected to Krish. Time management was and still is an overwhelming factor in my life.

My identity has gotten lost in this ordeal. All of my relatives and friends ask me, "How is Krish?" when they see me or call me, not how I am doing. They all think that I am identified with Krish and that I, as a person myself, scarcely exist. It is not their fault. It is mine because I had no topic to talk about other than Krishna. My identification with him was complete. It was even as though I, too, became autistic because I practiced what it feels like to be autistic many times in an effort to better understand my son. Certainly, my identity was lost. Gradually, my self-image shattered.

Last year, my husband quit his full-time job in exchange for a part-time job. Next to keeping Krish home, that was the best decision we made in our entire lives. My quality of life has improved immeasurably since Nan resigned his position. Now, I take care of myself. I practice music for an hour or two. I even find time to write my journal. My house is in order. I am able to wash my hair often. I changed my glasses after six years. I even found time to do that! I haven't gone to a dentist or had a physical examination in so many years for lack of time. I am planning to do those straightaway.

The Jalaja in me is asserting herself. The challenge of raising an autistic child has changed me from a sweet, nonassertive person to a determined, assertive, strong-willed fighter. Now, I am applying those skills to develop myself. No longer am I to be known as my husband's wife, or Krish's mother, or Malini's mom. I want to be known as *Jalaja*.

April 8, 1997

The challenge I have been confronted with in raising Krishna is to try to do a superhuman feat when all I have to work with are human failings. Why on earth would I attempt to raise Krishna? No one would find fault with me if I did not want to develop and nurture him. In fact, my father-in-law advised me to place him in a residential program lest I ruin my life.

Keeping Krishna home and working hard to improve him in not simply one area but virtually all areas requires an incredible amount of hard work from me, as it does from Nan, and that means loss of freedom. Should I have friends or not? Is it okay to go to a late movie or not? Should I watch TV or not? Should I have a restful sleep or not? Will I be able to celebrate my birthday or not? Will I be able to celebrate my wedding anniversary? Should I go to Malini's convocation or not? Actually, the day of the convocation, Krishna had no one to be with him. And he wouldn't have survived the huge crowd if we took him with us. So, I didn't go. This is the loss of freedom I am talking about.

But when I saw this baby son of mine doomed to a life of loneliness and despair, all of my desires for a normal life became petty and inconsequential. So what if I don't see a movie? So what if I can't see Malini's graduation? She will survive, but Krishna may not. I was given rotten choices, as was Sophie in the movie *Sophie's Choice;* either my son or I was to be doomed to loneliness. I am the doomed one—or so I feel just now. I traded my freedom for his. I put in 24 hours a day, 365 days a year, for the first 15 years of his life.

I worked tirelessly, day and night, without recognition from the world around me—no recognition even from my own mother, my mother-in-law, my husband, my daughter, my sisters and brothers, and other in-laws. To this day, I remember my mother-in-law wondering why was I sleeping as late as 8:00 a.m. I did not want to tell her my autistic son was awake all night, and I had been patting him to sleep. Even if I had told her, she wouldn't have understood. I was very lonely, indeed. I had no career besides Krishna. He was my career. My silent, lonely, tireless work with my son for years with little or no reward—how could it impress the world around me? There is no trophy, no big promotion to show for it. Isn't success associated with money and recognition? Neither of these did I achieve for myself or for my family with my all-consuming work. Why did I choose a seemingly useless life? Am I not smart?

Over and over I asked myself, what addicts me to such a tough life? The only answer I can come up with is I cannot bear my child living in slavery to autism. My love for Krishna has drawn me to this life like a moth to a flame. Over these past twenty-five years, I have learned that love is extremely powerful. The minute one starts to explain the word *love,* its true meaning disappears. It is much more powerful than the words that try to explain it. We cannot do enough justice to real love by mere words. Love can be expressed only in austerities and sacrifices. The more you explain, the less it becomes clear because words assume more prominence than any inner meaning does. It has to be felt. Love, when felt intensely, will drive people to the edge.

I do know that I still want Krishna unshackled by the slavery of autism. To do that, I myself had to become a slave of autism. What a choice! One of us has to be sacrificed at the altar of autism. At least I had a life before Krishna, but he has known autism every minute of his life. There is no escape, no parole for him. I felt I was pushed to the point of accepting slavery in order to free him, even if only a little.

I recall Tony Morrison's Margaret, the slave woman, who hated slavery as a way of life for her children. First, she tried to escape with her children. But unfortunately, she did not succeed. So she decided to kill them all, one by one. She did not succeed there, fully, either. Let us assume that she had succeeded in killing all of them without being caught; she would have had to live with that secret for the rest of her life. That secret would have been her slavery. She chose emotional slavery for herself in order to free the children.

I often feel life was unfair to me to have such awful choices. But I always countered my negativity with the thought that it was wholly unfair for a child to be sentenced for life to autism, with no parole. Criminals get parole. But an innocent toddler with this syndrome never gets released; he or she can only get better. So I let myself be afflicted with autism by keeping him home. I am acutely aware of his problem when I am teaching him to behave or speak. I know I could have chosen a freer life by being away from him because I live in a country compassionate enough to provide us with fairly decent residential programs. But I chose to turn away from them. Instead, I chose to have him at home to give him every chance to improve. It is my way of showing my love for him.

I didn't write all these years because I didn't want to tell the world how Krishna has been the source of my agony and misery, and how pathetic my life has become over the years. Again, I am feeling miserable and guilty for pointing my finger at Krishna for my horrendously lonely life; it so hurts to do so. How stupid of me to blame him when I know he had no choice or chance at his birth.

At least in war, you can hate the enemy. I can't even hate my son for inflicting this worry on me because it is not he who is doing this. I am always forced to use my intellect to distinguish Krishna, the person, from autism, the affliction. It is very difficult at times not to get upset with Krishna. But I must remind myself that in spite of all these guilty feelings, I must tell the truth. Without the truth, there is no point in writing at all. There is no emotional sharing with other parents in similar situations. No sharing with others means no healing for me. I must always remember one thing: my feelings, my emotions, my ideas, and my faith can be expressed in written words, and those words, put down on paper, can assume a powerful voice if written well. This will connect me with strangers thousands of miles away in oneness of mind; one single thought, one single thread connecting many minds so far apart. Again, this communication without ambiguity can happen only when I am open and honest about my feelings. I firmly believe this sharing can help not only me but others in similar predicaments. That is well worth taking the risk.

We all talk about closure. There is no closure in autism. It is an unending, relentless saga. I get closure only when either I or my child dies. So I am going to be a lifelong parent. Perhaps, through sharing my story, it is the closest I can get to closure.

After years of struggle, I have accepted my lot in life. I don't feel so acutely miserable about my loneliness or loss of freedom right now. The loss of freedom in mundane things is replaced with freedom to contemplate and grow. The ordeal has affected me hugely, with a precious, life-saving lesson. If I let my mind be fettered with negative thoughts, I am fettered. If I let my mind soar high above the external events of my life, I am totally free! This transformation was brought forth step by step from one ordeal to another by my faith in our Creator—and also in the ability of my son. Henry David Thoreau said, "if one advances confidently in the direction of his dreams, and he endeavors to live the life which he has imagined, he will meet with success unexpected in common hours."

It took almost twenty-five years to say this openly to all of you, but to say it so publicly in this format is still heart-wrenching, still hurtful.

April 9, 1997

A few days ago, I wrote about my friend Nancy and her son, Joe. Joe and Krish went to a school in Tokyo for the autistic. My friendship with Nancy grew over the years, even though we saw each other only a few times during that period. She struck me as a very dedicated, hardworking, and caring mother.

A couple of weeks ago, Nancy called from the Midwest to say she wanted to visit me, and a few days later, she did so. She was distressed about her son, who was then attending a residential school. She had a conflict. She wanted her son to stay home and attend a day program, but he is occasionally aggressive, and her husband is suffering from cancer and other ailments. Her husband needed a lot of help from her to take care of his basic needs. She unloaded all of her worries and asked my opinion about what she should do. In my opinion, she couldn't possibly do more than what she has been doing. That is exactly what I told her.

While we were talking, Krish came into the room. He went straight to her, put his arms around her, and held her in that position for a few minutes. In a very gentle, kind voice, he said, "I love you very much, sweetheart. I really do. Don't worry." He sat in a chair next to her and held her hand for ten or fifteen minutes. He didn't let go of it until he said his goodbyes before going to Newton. I felt that he must have heard some of what she confided in me. He must have felt sympathy for her situation. When Krish showed so much love, she broke down. When that happened, he simply hugged her, hugged her so tightly that I myself got very emotional. She was totally overwhelmed with Krish's love. She whispered, "Krishna, I wish Joe could give me a hug like that. He doesn't like to be hugged. He doesn't like to show love with a hug either."

For the rest of the day, she repeatedly told me what a kind man Krish is:

> I can't get over his sensitivity to my troubles. He read my heart and gave me the right medicine, which is love. I really needed that hug and needed to hear those words of his. Through him, God spoke and gave me strength. Now I feel so refreshed and strengthened that I can go on with my life. When I came over here, I was a very sad and tired woman. Now, I feel I am recharged. He touched me with his spirituality.

She is right. Krishna can be very loving and very sensitive. Only in the hands of autism is he sometimes a frustrated, peevish, angry person.

April 21, 1997

This morning, I was thinking about my daughter, Malini, and her husband, Vish. They live in Chicago. Malini is studying medicine at the University of Chicago. She wants to apply for a residency in neurosurgery this year, and she would like us to visit for a few weeks, for moral support. Neurosurgery is a very competitive, male-dominated field. Only one hundred of a much larger number of applicants are selected nationwide. So naturally she is worried.

When I burst into the study room, Krishna was studying with his Dad. I had something very important to tell them. I simply didn't want to wait:

> Nan, why don't we take off this afternoon for Chicago, like teenagers do, in the car? I really want to do this impulsively. Can I do something without planning, without analyzing every minute detail? This trip doesn't need much planning because we would be going by car. We can take a few clothes and fill up the tank and take off. I have always lived extremely seriously. This one time, I want to do this flippantly.

My husband's reaction was one of disbelief and shock. He has never seen me like this. His first reaction was, "Are you okay? Are you having a nervous breakdown? What's going on here? I am worried." I said:

> I am all right. I simply want to be different today. I am tired of always thinking in terms of pros and cons. I simply want to do this before I change my mind. Anyway, Malini and Vish have been begging us to come. When we think too much about something, we don't do it. Let us not make it a big deal. Let's just go.

He reluctantly agreed.

Krishna wrote in the computer, "First time, Mom has a great idea." Nan said, "We can leave tomorrow, not today. I want to see that everything is okay with the car, and I want to make hotel reservations with Marriott." I said, "Fine," and went ahead with my packing.

April 22, 1997

This afternoon, after lunch, we loaded the car and left for Chicago. Malini and Vish were elated about our coming. I was telling Nan, "This is a memory-making time. We will never forget this trip, even when we are rocking in our rocking chairs on the front porch, in our 70s and 80s."

April 24, 1997

Krish was a model traveler all the way to Chicago. When we were stuck in heavy traffic caused by strings of accidents, some minor and some major, Krish endured them with a smiling face, constantly reminding us as well as himself, "Going to see Malini." That gave him the mental strength to be able to put up with any hardship along the way. He loved our stay at the Marriott. He was ecstatic about eating in the room. He made me order room service all evening.

The next day, we visited our friend Nancy in the Midwest. She was extremely loving and attentive toward Krishna. The way he was attracted to her love and kindness was an amazing sight to see.

Later in the day, we went to see Joe at his school. Krish was very anxious and did not want to stay too long. He was virtually running away from the director of the school. He kept his body so far away from the director that he had to strain to extend his hand to give a handshake. He tried to avoid everyone and wanted to get out of the place quickly. There was no sparkle in his eyes and no smile on his face. When we left the school grounds after our short stay and got in the car, Krish smiled and said, "Happy to go home."

Later, when Krish was asked how he enjoyed his visit with Nancy Johnson, and what did he think of the school, he wrote on the pocket computer:

> I enjoyed it very much. I kindled her motherly emotions. I had her undivided, fond affection. The school reminded me of my residential

school. It is a babysitting place with some work. Ultimately, they don't want to teach anything in academics. Yesterday, most of the boys were idle. They were just standing or sitting and doing nothing.

April 26, 1997

When we arrived in Chicago, we didn't have good directions to Malini's house, so when we called her, she said she and Vish would meet us at a nearby gas station. Several minutes later, Krish had spotted their car, and he just went wild. Before anyone could stop him, he was running toward it, still moving though it was. My first reaction was, "Is he crazy? Why is he running through the parking lot toward an oncoming car?" but that was before I recognized the passenger in the car to be Malini. He was much more alert and quicker than either Nan or I. When he is motivated, he excels. Here the motivation was his longing to see his dear sister.

On seeing him running toward her car, Malini stopped in the middle of the gas station and got out. He immediately put his arms around her and hugged her for a long time; it looked like an eternity to me. No, "Hi!" No, "How are you?" He got into her car and put his head in her lap. For a few minutes, the car was parked in the middle of the gas station. We didn't know or care if anyone was waiting behind us. The whole family seemed pinned down by Krish's reaction.

April 27, 1997

When Krish was very young, I prepared a list and hung it on the wall in almost every room. It read:

The Rules for Krishna's Learning to Be Observed by the Family

1. Structure should be given all day to discourage unwanted, repetitive behaviors. Remember, no learning occurs with them. During one's time, one is not even allowed to go to the bathroom without arranging someone to be with him.
2. Never talk about what he cannot do. Talk only of what he can do.
3. Reward and punishment should be used. Punishment in the form of disapproval, indifference, and chiding. Also withhold

his favorite music or food. Reward should always be more than punishment.

4. House should remain organized and clean in order to give orderliness to his disorderly, unfocused, unpredictable, disarrayed, confused, chaotic mind.

5. Never fight, argue, contradict, or create conflicts in his presence. Never be hopeless and unhappy. Always stay assured. Be firm and be a leader.

6. Always believe in his ability to be educated. Don't expect miracles and sudden breakthroughs. Achievement comes in droplets, not in bucketfuls.

7. Never compare him to other children of his age. When you compare Krish, you lose confidence in him.

8. Always reevaluate his progress, however little it may be. This is extremely important for parents to get motivation. We need rewards, too.

9. Play constant mind games to ward off worries about the future.

10. Live one day at a time.

11. Constantly count your other blessings to undermine this tragedy. Otherwise, it will loom larger than life.

12. Cultivate faith in God. He knows best.

13. Never, ever go near people who feel doomed. They will pull you down and the family, too. Also avoid the professionals who have a bleak outlook for autism.

14. Give up on the kid only when he is forty years old, not before. Then you have the satisfaction that you did everything in your power.

15. Be prepared to sacrifice your life for this child. It is not a one-year or five-year course, but a lifetime program.

Every time I strayed away from my goal, I went back to this piece of paper, which had the potential to change my pattern of thinking for that day. It was my sacred book.

Krishna, who seemed deaf and mute at the age of four, is today an entirely different person. Now there is no concept that he doesn't comprehend. He has read *A Tale of Two Cities, David Copperfield,* and *Great Expectations* by Charles Dickens. He also recently read the autobiography of President Reagan. His comprehension in my opinion is better than average. But that doesn't go for his speech. Although he can verbalize his wants, wishes, and needs, he still has difficulty in speaking fluently. He cannot engage in a meaningful conversation, nor can he answer questions appropriately.

He is a warm, sensitive, caring, and loving person. He has an unusual relationship with his sister Malini. He is very protective of her. He also now loves to be with people. He has no problem with strangers or new places. He has no problem in openly expressing his love for us or for people whom he loves. But he is claustrophobic and gets tense in a crowded room.

No longer is he in his shell. He loves to go out with people. He enjoys going to shopping malls, movie theaters, restaurants, science and art museums, and the YMCA. He never likes to stay home for long stretches of time. He is the one who plans our vacations abroad. It is never easy to travel with him because of his hyperactivity and acute, unpredictable tension. But with a meticulously planned trip, he is manageable. Last vacation, he decided we should go to Paris. He loves to see exotic places. The next city he wants to see is Moscow.

Once, I counted twenty-six bizarre, unwanted, stereotypical behaviors in him. Now he has a total of only five: hyperventilating and flexing his hands when he is stressed out, pulling up his socks when he is nervous, jumping up and down while making loud noises when frustrated, and grabbing Nan's shirt when he is angry. His problem behaviors are extensively discussed later in the journal. The rest of his inappropriate behaviors have vanished.

The majority of his unusual fears are gone. We can take the fears away from him by merely talking about his apprehensions. He has great appreciation for logic. Still, he has a few unusual fears, like cutting his hair and nails and going in the water at the beach.

Krish communicates fairly very well on the computer, using only his right index finger. Right now, he is writing about his autism and his early years. He has a good command of language. In our house, he is the dictionary. You can ask for the meaning of a word, and he will write it out immediately. He really has excellent aptitude for learning new words.

His strong suit is academics. He is exceptionally talented in mathematics. Currently, he is studying *Linear Algebra* by Gilbert Strand of MIT, and *Advanced Calculus* by Professor Hilderbrand of

MIT. He has already studied *Probability and Statistics, Elementary Differential Equations,* and *Boundary Value Problems.*

His math ability has helped him learn physics. The books he has completed so far are *Electricity and Magnetism, Introduction to Electrodynamics, Introduction to Quantum Physics,* and *Basic Concepts in Relativity.* In addition, he has done extensive studying in electrical engineering. Right now, he is reading a book titled *Data Base Management.*

Improving Krish's behavior is the last peak of the Mount Everest of autism yet to be reached. Although he has overcome many hurdles on his road to normal behavior, there are quite a few more to overcome. Learning to behave normally is the toughest and the greatest challenge of all for an autistic like Krish. We cannot give up on our hopes and dreams for Krish. A dream lost is a precious life lost. "Awake, arise, stop not until the goal is reached."

April 28, 1997

Malini was working hard on her papers and curriculum vitae, and was busy with her exams. She felt overwhelmed and exhausted. Her personal statement had to be submitted that very day. Krish wrote on the computer, "Let me help you with your personal statement." He wrote a beautiful statement in two hours:

> The essence of surgery is locating the problem area, cutting off the problem part and healing the patient. Highly needed are a problem-solving mind, mental toughness, dexterous hands, and a caring attitude.
>
> The problem-solving mind is what I cultivated at MIT. MIT is the top research institute in the world. The life at MIT was rigorous, intellectually challenging, and ultimately grueling. Highly acclaimed is the electrical engineering department. Judgment of the MIT electrical engineering department has been made. It is ranked number one in the USA. I studied for five years doing an outstanding research project on eyes. This project required innovative, meritorious, terrific research. The research trained my mind to solve problems.
>
> I may be talented in surgery because of the dexterity of my fingers. Great is my yeoman's hand trained in highly grueling, tennis championship tournaments. Ultimate gruel is the rigorous, long tournament.

Three to four years of jogging have augmented my physical stamina. Rigorous is tedious surgery.

I have an autistic brother. I cared for him and loved him. For years, I served him. He had bizarre behaviors that no one, including doctors, could understand. Ubiquitous was his bizarre behavior. The joy and fun we shared when we went sledding! The joy of life is in sharing, and no one can take away that joy. That caring attitude will be demonstrated by me in healing patients.

Ultimate buoyancy is needed for juggling kids in water. In the surgical room, the surgeon has to initiate and monitor ultimate life-threatening procedures. Young and energetic am I. The surgery is filled with bottomless, hazardous pits. The life can be miserable. But I have trained my mind to withstand tough pressures. The life with my brother was traumatic and tough. My mom gave all she had for him. I did not get that much of her attention. Posthumous was I, though my parents were living.

The Ukraine is an unknown country. Yet, it has produced a great and talented star in skating. In a similar vein, I am unknown now, but my future will give rise to a great surgeon.

Nan asked Krishna a question, "Should the essay be so self-praising?" Krishna answered, "I feel that she is competing with the top people, and she is up against male chauvinism. Gone should be modesty. Tough should be the essay."

She took the rough draft to the dean of students, Dr. Olson, who liked it and approved it. This was Krish's first recognition from the outside world. Later, Malini changed it completely and added medical vocabulary to make it her own, before submitting it to medical schools. We were all elated. Can anyone imagine an autistic writing a personal statement for his sister who is studying medicine at one of the most prestigious universities in the country, the University of Chicago, and applying for neurosurgical residency? And on top of it, the statement was approved by Dr. Olson. "What do you think of Dean Olson's preliminary approval of your essay?" I asked Krish. "Great," he replied. "I am thrilled. Ultimate test is Malini's admission."

That night, I couldn't sleep. I am well aware of his capability. But someone like Dr. Olson accepting the statement was enough to send me through a roller coaster of emotions. So many questions crowded my fertile mind. So many ifs. If only he could write like Temple Grandin, who wrote so beautifully in *Thinking in Pictures*. If only he could become motivated.

How can we parents motivate him? We have taught him many skills. The skills he has are enough to make him lead a rewarding and fulfilling life. He is naturally endowed with talent in math and writing. People with less talent are shining more brightly than he is. Even with autism, he can lead a good life, if only he had the motivation. It became very clear to me that he needs motivation to extricate himself from autism. People like Temple Grandin have it. But I cannot compare him with Temple Grandin because in my opinion, they are only mildly autistic in comparison to Krishna. And they have normal speech, whereas Krishna is severely speech impaired. One can be weird and bizarre looking, deaf and dumb, or mentally retarded and physically disabled and still have a meaningful and contributory life, provided that he or she is motivated. Maybe it is different with autism. Maybe the more autistic a person is, the less motivated he or she is. Maybe the level of motivation is directly influenced by the degree of autism.

With motivation, it seems to me, anything is possible, and without motivation, nothing is possible. But how can I motivate him? We are giving him lots of love. We are giving him lots of opportunities. We constantly teach him new skills. Every year, we give him three months of ayurvedic treatment in India. He is structured and taught electrical engineering, physics, and math. We supply him with audiotapes on great world leaders to motivate him. I cook nourishing food every day and make sure his health is excellent, with megadoses of vitamins, like B complex and C. He has people to take him out into the community every day for four hours. They are all men near his age, not older men, so he can feel that he is not left out and without friends in life.

I try very hard to keep my house spotless so that his mind is not scattered. Even the house we live in is dictated by his needs. Nan is working part time in Newton, which is nearly an hour away. We would like to move to Newton so that Nan could be closer to work, but a comparably sized house in Newton costs around two million dollars. Krish always writes, "I need a big house, not a fancy house." For him, space is very important. His behavior changes for the worse in a small place. He feels crowded and gets tensed up. I really don't know what else we can do to trigger his motivation.

Is motivation an innate quality a person is born with, like black hair or blue eyes? Nobody forced Thomas Edison at gunpoint to conduct more than two thousand experiments, day and night, to invent a light bulb. No one forced Gandhi to forgo his illustrious career to work for India's freedom. What triggered them to such heights of excellence? Motivation. Motivation. Motivation. But how do I trigger it in Krish?

April 30, 1997

Krish has been studying well here at Malini's. He has two young role models that are burning the midnight oil. Malini is writing papers one after the other, often until 2 a.m. She gets up at 5 a.m. and is off to the hospital by 6. Vish, who is a cardiology fellow, goes to bed around midnight and also leaves for the hospital by 6 a.m. They are extremely hard working and survive on very little sleep. Krishna has been studying late into the night, too, until 11 p.m. He has been studying for six hours a day. I can't believe he is so motivated, but I am delighted that he is.

The other day, I was worrying about his motivation level. Now, without any fight or confrontation, he is inspired to study. He is becoming so studious and hardworking. He is motivated. All he needs is his sister and Vish. We, his parents, are decidedly motivated and hard working, but the age difference between us is too great. He is not influenced by Nan and me, whereas he is influenced by his sister, who is so much closer to him in age. Maybe the solution is living with Malini.

May 1997

May 4, 1997

Today, he worked on his book about autism. He has been writing about his condition since October of last year, not regularly, but now and then. This morning, he wrote, "We can leave the old text alone. I want to move forward. Ultimately a book should read cogently. The book should be rewritten. Previously, I was not writing a book. I was communicating to Mom and you."

I was watching him, mesmerized. Here is my autistic son, taking charge of his book. He has his own ideas about how it should read.

When he was three, he did not recognize his name. He did not turn his head when his name was called. Around this age, specialists told us that he would never be able to attach sound to an object. That means that he didn't have the capacity to comprehend the spoken language.

They were right. He would turn his head toward the telephone when it rang. He would hear the doorbell. But to my words, there was no response. When I said, "Sit," he walked away. When I said, "Come," he stayed still. Either he didn't hear or he didn't care. The response was one and the same.

I started teaching him to understand language by breaking the skill into small steps. In the beginning, I used the same word over and over for the entire week. When I said, "Eat," I mimicked eating. Other words I tried to familiarize him with were "sit" and "jump." As soon as I said the word, I would demonstrate its meaning by sitting or jumping. When he started understanding single words, I went on to two-word phrases like "Come eat" and "Drink milk." I never used articles, adjectives, or adverbs. I didn't even use conjunctions like "and." I wanted to limit his confusion. The more numerous the sounds, the more confused he became. After eighteen months, he started to understand sentences with three or four words.

I always had to keep in mind that his retention was not very good. He seemed to have a short-term memory problem. I always spoke very slowly, tried to pronounce words very deliberately, and made sure he understood by repeating the same phrase or sentence a few times. This kind of careful, slow, deliberate speech was very hard on me since I talk a lot in a very short time, always rushing to cover more. I also spoke loudly to attract his attention and still his wandering mind.

I tried to put a lot of emphasis on words, for example, "dinner-r-r," "soup-p-p." I tried to focus his attention on what I was saying. Every word had to be taught. He picked up nothing on his own. If I taught him ten words, he knew ten words, no more.

At the age of four, he could not make speech sounds. He had no imitation skills, either. He didn't copy any actions the way other children do. He was unable to play children's games like Simon Says. So again, I taught him how to imitate. Once he learned the physical imitation skills, I moved on to sound imitations. From sounds to syllables, syllables to words, words to phrases, words to sentences, it was all excruciatingly deliberate.

It sounds so easy when I write this, but it was onerous. Again, the method was to break any skill into very, very tiny steps so that he was able to learn. He should not get frustrated with learning. The feeling of success needed to be instantaneous. It should never be overwhelming for him. Success always breeds success.

Did I ever imagine back then that he would come this far? If this is not a miracle, then what is?

That evening, we talked about his career. Since we were talking about Malini's and Vish's careers and his cousins' careers, I didn't want Krish to feel that because he is disabled, he cannot have a career. I wanted him to know he can have a great career, too.

Nan asked on the computer, "Do you like writing as a career?"

Krish:	It is great, but I like math and physics. I require new topics to write.
Nan:	Why not write sequels to the first?
Krish:	I don't like autism again and again.
Nan:	You can write science books, too.
Krish:	Okay, but I love math and I want to teach math. Joke: teaching with no speech. Book on math, yes.

May 22, 1997

While driving to Newton, my husband and Krish had a conversation. Monkey stories are famous in India. There, monkeys are captured by monkey men, who train the animals to do tricks for the public so that they might earn a few pennies. The story he told Krish is as follows:

There is an iron box with a glass top, through which you can see what is inside the box. The glass top has a narrow opening through which you can insert a hand with fingers stretched straight, but not curled up, like in a fist. In the box, a banana can be seen through the glass lid. A curious monkey sees the box from a branch of a tree in the distance and decides to check it out. It sees a yellow, fresh-looking banana inside. It simply can't resist the temptation, so the monkey inserts its hand inside the opening and, to its immense delight, finds the banana. It is thrilled with the thought of finding the fruit with so very little effort. The monkey grabs the fruit tightly and tries to remove its hand, but to its amazement, cannot do so while grasping the banana. It tries very hard to remove its hand and the banana. But it has no luck. The only way it can get its hand out is by letting go of the banana. It has to decide whether to forgo the banana or be stuck there with its hand in the box. The monkey has to remember only one thing: If it decides not to forfeit the banana, the monkey man will soon come. . . . This is how we all live. We all have many bananas, but we all pay a very big price for them.

After hearing the story, Krish said, "Too far fetched." To that, my husband said, "No, it is not. Let me give you an example":

An alcoholic knows that drinking is bad. But he cannot resist the temptation to drink. He gets drunk one evening to feel better. He feels good with a few drinks, and it lifts up his mood and spirit, and so he drinks the second day, the third day, and slowly, he drinks regularly. With all kinds of hangovers, he cannot go to work regularly, and his performance on the job suffers. His boss notices and gives him several warnings. In the end, he is fired. Now he has no income, his confidence suffers a blow, his wife complains constantly for money to run the house and feed their kids. He sometimes loses it and physically abuses her and also the kids. One day, the wife decides to leave him, with the kids. Now, he loses everything; the job, the wife, the kids, the money, the self-esteem, the respect from society. If he doesn't notice and put a stop to it, the drinking will ultimately put him in the coffin. This man is choosing the drinking for the banana. Here, the banana is some good feeling after drinking, an instant gratification, not a long-term one.

Krishna listened to everything intensely, all this time. He became very reflective. My husband didn't leave it at that. He went on to say how Krish is also going for bananas:

You don't want to do the computer. You know in your heart that computer writing is very crucial for your survival in the area of communication. Again, you are taking the easy route by not working on the computer because it is hard for you to do that. Avoiding the stress of the computer keyboard punching is your banana. For that, you are willing to give up big gains in communication and in book writing, which is a possibility with your command of written language. One day you can be a writer. You are giving all that up for the banana of immediate gain, namely, relief from the stress of writing. Am I right in saying that?

To this, Krish answered, "Okay, I will try."

When Nan narrated his conversation with Krish to me that evening, and gloated about Krishna's change of mind, I couldn't help blurting out, "Well, I will believe it when I actually see it."

May 26, 1997

Krish's behavior has been steadily regressing. Yesterday, he jumped up and down with lots of loud and incoherent noise for no reason in the bathroom. Nan was giving him a massage before his shower. Ten minutes into the massage, Krish decided that he did not want it. He told Nan, and Nan stopped. Yet, he continued his jumping like a kangaroo.

Then, Krish asked for a shower. At that time, I was washing my hair in the other bathroom, which Krish usually uses for his shower. Nan wanted Krish to wait. Upon hearing this, Krish started jumping up and down, frustrated; he did not want to wait for me to get out. Although we have a second full bath upstairs, the other one did not have the shower curtain up that particular day. He didn't have the patience to hear any of this. He wanted to shower to reduce his mounting tension right then and there. He couldn't wait. I had no chance or choice. I had to get out of the tub right away. Every minute I delayed, his frustration mounted. I was angry, tensed up, and dejected.

Recently, at the least provocation, he gets irritated, frustrated, and angry. This is very frustrating to us in return.

It was a disastrous day. I had a lot of pressure on me, and I had to go and meet a person and sign a lease. I wanted to wash my hair before I went out. That's when Krishna got upset. People were out painting the exterior of the house. They must have heard him screaming and jumping. At that time, I almost wanted to die since I am extremely sensitive to his bizarre behavior.

Here is my son who can discuss Einstein's relativity theory, signal processing, and so on, but who looks so bizarre when his behavior is out of control. This hurts me immensely. If he is dumb and behaves in a dumb way, I can deal with that. But he is hardly dumb; he is brilliant. Regrettably his brilliance is visible only at home or in the company of the few people he knows very well. Otherwise, it is shrouded in the mystery of strange autistic behaviors.

Will anyone believe me when I say that Krish is smart and talented and, above all, a fine human being?

Right away, we gave him 1 mg of Haldol. In fifteen minutes, he was a pussycat, listening and very patient and reasonable. His irritability was totally gone. But why do I hate to give him drugs? I am positive that if I were to give him this medicine twice a day, there would be no scenes in this house. His listening, concentration, obedience, and calmness increase beyond belief. But we hate to give him this medicine, always thinking that it will hurt his brain in the long run. What's more, Haldol seems to make him sleepy, and after taking it for an extended period, he only wants to spend more time in bed. So it is obvious why I hate to give him Haldol daily. But I never refrain from giving him the medicine when he is unreasonable or unreachable with logic.

Haldol has some serious and debilitating side effects, such as tremors. So once his behavior changes for the better, we discontinue it. I am always worried about tremors in his fingers. I always have this picture in my mind that his nerves are stripped of myelin sheath, and this in turn causes his jitters, agitation, and nervous behavior. Either he has anxiety attacks without medication or I have anxiety attacks over his medication. What a choice!

Nowadays, I feel overworked and exhausted from all those years of working with Krish even though I have had more time to relax in the last six months since my husband quit his job to educate my son. Some days, I wonder why I feel so exhausted when Krish has come this far and Nan takes care of him. Right now, I should be celebrating my freedom and having fun doing what I always wanted to do. I very much want to know the reason for this feeling of exhaustion I am experiencing. Is there anyone who knows about this syndrome? Does it have a name? Is this called burnt-out syndrome? Will I ever get over this feeling of chronic tiredness?

May 30, 1997

The struggle against autism is a classic challenge of the unknown. In the annals of the human race, such challenges are often marked by considerable trials and errors. During such trying periods, three mental dispositions are essential for success: planning, patience, and perseverance.

One cannot rush when climbing Mount Everest. The whole climb has to be planned around the body getting used to high altitudes. The higher you climb, the tougher and more exhausting it is to walk. Modern tools cannot totally alleviate this exhaustion. So the trip is planned around exhaustion and physical weakness at high altitudes. Even people with enormous stamina and excellent rock-climbing ability limp like very old people on the last leg of the journey.

The most challenging and scariest climbing occurs during the last leg. It takes only one day of climbing to reach the peak, but it sometimes takes two or three weeks of planning to make it happen. One of the most chilling experiences on the climb is walking along a narrow strip of ladder, over a ravine some few hundred feet deep. It is done with extreme care and concentration. Similarly, climbing steep rocks is executed with meticulous care.

Patience, endurance, meticulous planning, discipline of mind, intensity of goal, unswerving concentration, supreme ability, incredible attention to details, and undying enthusiasm for reaching the goal are essential.

Just before the last climb, the climbers camp for a week to get the body adjusted to the altitude. But that is only a part of the waiting. The more significant waiting is for the right weather to arrive. An avalanche can be avoided only by carefully choosing the day. In this choice, one cannot hurry. Moreover, the wind at the peak can be deadly; the human body cannot endure it. Although the climbers are within striking distance of the peak, they have to wait for the perfect, flawless day, no matter how many weeks it takes.

Poorly planned expeditions have ended in tragic deaths. Perseverance is what is needed for fulfilling a goal such as climbing Mount Everest.

Similarly, the fight against autism involves planning, patience, and perseverance. This battle has to be executed with meticulous intensity. Without such single-minded dedication, success is not achievable; the dream will crumble, and the vision will be lost. In my opinion, the fight against autism is infinitely tougher than the most challenging and scariest climbing of Mount Everest. The former takes lifelong, intense, unrelenting, monumental effort with few or no rewards, no recognition, no fame or money. Whereas the latter requires preparation and execution of climbing for, say, two years, with a clear end in sight.

Like climbers of Mount Everest, Krishna has climbed many peaks in his development with our guidance. He has learned to crawl, to walk, to bite and chew foods, to go to the toilet. He has also achieved the imitation skills in speech and physical movements like jumping, throwing, and catching a ball; recognizing words; writing without assistance; and writing on a computer. He has achieved incredible, mind-boggling feats in academics. Right now, he is studying differential equations, advanced calculus, quantum physics, and other disciplines. But still there are a few more very essential peaks left to climb, such as appropriate behavior, better verbal communication, more social awareness, and finally, independent living. We as a family are working relentlessly and tirelessly toward these challenging goals.

The process has been mostly very difficult, often heart-wrenching, and at times, depressing. But when Krishna makes breakthroughs, there have been undeniable moments of elation and ecstasy beyond description, which have made the process itself very stimulating, invigorating, refreshing, and above all, challenging. I have to try to remember these glorious, rewarding moments of success whenever I am fearful of not realizing my dream for Krishna.

June 1997

June 5, 1997

Krish's attitude was one of pessimism and hopelessness; hence, he was dejected and depressed this evening. He came to me on his own, and said, "want to write." I got the pocket computer that is often used for writing, and immediately, he wrote, "Life stinks. It is unfair. No marriage."

I was caught off guard. For a minute, I stood there speechless. I knew that the ball was in my court. I had to handle this one very delicately. Many nights I myself have wondered about his future. Will he ever get married and have a family of his own? The obvious reality of the situation is that he cannot talk well.

The most important factor in any relationship, especially in marriage, is communication between a couple. Even though it seems as if only a very few partners are able to communicate well, in his case, he has to rely on the computers through which he communicates, and they have to be set up for him. He is in such a dependent state for many of his needs. Such dependency can add enormous stress to a marriage and even cause it to break up. On top of that, his insurmountable tension causes much of his unpredictable behavior.

I am looking for a guardian angel to be his wife. That, in my opinion, can happen only if and when he has demonstrated an unusual talent in some area that can be a common interest between them. Professor Hawkins, for example, who is unusually talented in astrophysics in spite of his extreme disability, got married to a woman who fell in love with him for who he was.

Despite my nagging doubts, I decided not to fan his depression any further by being honest and open. For his sake, I wanted to be more encouraging and hopeful; I wanted to boost his sagging confidence. I started with an inner prayer and a deep breath because I was not at all prepared to talk about this. I wish I could postpone talking about these matters, but I knew I couldn't. The situation demanded instant response. This is what I said to him:

Jalaja: Krish, don't be discouraged. This is not the time for it, especially since you are making phenomenal progress. You are going at the speed of a rocket. You cannot go any faster than this. Who knows, one day you might become almost normal or better than normal. Already in academics, you are better than many people. So please have faith in yourself, and also in God. With such faith, you are bound to create your own destiny. You become what you believe in. In your case, your tireless hard work and courage to persevere will make you a winner.

Krish: Quite easy to say. Actually, it is tough.

Jalaja: Yes, it is. But you can do it by having faith in yourself. When President Kennedy started the space program, we started from zero. He had a great vision, a vision to put a man on the moon, when not even a rocket had been sent into orbit. It is like a young woman, while pregnant for only three months, dreaming to have an astronaut as a son. It was that far fetched when President Kennedy dreamed of putting a man on the moon. Did it happen, or not?

Krish: True. But it took a lot of effort.

Jalaja: Agreed. But a change in attitude will give you boundless energy for the impossible. Similarly, if you want to marry and have a family of your own, you can. Nothing will stop you. But you have to work toward it. I want to tell you something. Listen very carefully. If I was not your mother and also a young woman, I certainly would fall in love with you, for the person you are, with all of your intelligence. You are a very deep, philosophical person, trapped in autism. But first and foremost, you are a person with warmth and sensitivity with or without autism. I am not a stupid person. If I can appreciate you, a lot of young women will appreciate you, too.

Krish: But I cannot talk, nor can I behave.

Jalaja: Your speech is not the real culprit here. Anyway, you are able to communicate through a keyboard. First, you have to be determined to overcome your behavior. Your behavior is your own enemy. But you make the decision to overcome it; nothing will stand in your way. You have to take a firm stand. You have to commit yourself to it. Once this commitment occurs in you, everything else will fall into place. Let me read to you the lines from Goethe. If you listen with one-pointed concentration, those lines will become your roadmap to recovery. They are lines of hope and help. So please listen with a purpose in mind. Are you ready?

Krish:	Yes.
Jalaja:	There is one elementary truth—
	The ignorance of which kills countless ideas
	And splendid plans.
	The moment one definitely commits oneself, then
	Providence moves too.
	All sorts of things occur to help on that never
	Otherwise would have occurred . . .
	Whatever you can do,
	Or dream you can do,
	Begin it.
	Boldness has genius, power and magic in it.
	Begin it now.

With a grin on his face, he walked away.

June 20, 1997

This morning, Krish did not want to get up from his bed. Nan tried everything in the book to entice him, but to no avail. He first tempted him with a hot cup of coffee. Next, he tried to inveigle him with a hot shower. Then he tried to lure him with breakfast at McDonald's. Nothing gave the desired result.

Then I decided to take over. I went and hugged him so hard that he couldn't breathe. I didn't care. I would rather have him dead with my smothering love than see him vegetate in his bed. In the last two or three weeks, whatever I say, he has listened with respect for me.

When he didn't get up when I asked him to, I looked at Nan and said in a serious tone, "Krish is not listening well for the last two days. He is stubborn, and I am concerned about his behavior. Wasn't his behavior extremely good for the last three weeks?"

Upon hearing my remarks, he jumped out of bed and said, "I want to take a shower."

Jalaja:	Krish doesn't want to regress in his behavior; he has high motivation to go forward and not backward.

48

Nan: Doesn't Dr. Rimland, who has an adult autistic son himself, and is also an authority on autism, say that children who make it in autism are the ones with motivation?

Today, Krish's actions clearly indicated that he is motivated to get better!

June 21, 1997

He was tired, and he wanted to eat in bed this evening. But I refused to serve him in bed even though he looked genuinely exhausted and sort of depressed. My heart was aching for him and his lot in life. I didn't know whether his tiredness was due to his sadness, to exhaustion, or to the Haldol I had given him for the past three weeks. Either way, I wanted to prop him up with love:

Krish, you know in your heart that Mom and Dad love you immensely and we will do anything humanly possible for you. Even if it is not humanly possible, we will try our hardest. I want you to remember that always, and never lose sight of it. Is there anybody who is loved more than you in this family?

Upon hearing me, he gave me a big smile and a hug, and later came down for his food when I asked him to. While he was eating, I read these following lines of Sai Baba of India to him:

Life is a song—sing it.
Life is a game—play it.
Life is a challenge—meet it.
Life is a dream—realize it.
Life is a sacrifice—offer it.
Life is love—enjoy it.

He wanted me to sing it with a tune. So I did. He was thrilled. When asked what he thought of it, he wrote, "Caring, hope giving new message, gives courage." After a minute or so, he started laughing. When I asked him why, he wrote, "One more line makes it complete. Life is a sucker—suck it up." We all laughed.

Later in the evening, I talked to Nan about my concern regarding Krishna's unusual tiredness and lethargy due to the Haldol. Though the dosage we give him never exceeds 1–2mg per day, this always happens after a few weeks on Haldol. This lack of energy will start interfering with his learning, also. So I feel we have to do something about it.

June 23, 1997

We had a wonderful session at Children's Hospital. Krish was tested by an expert in computer communication to find out how he can be helped, through such devices, to communicate more effectively.
In the morning, the whole family was nervous. Krish never does well on tests. He always regresses to puerility. There is nothing I can do to minimize it. His anxiety takes over, and he becomes involved in his own stereotypical behaviors. His senses totally shut down in a testing environment. This morning, he refused to type on his own at Children's Hospital. He wanted his Dad to touch him slightly on his thigh. He needed that emotional support.

In my opinion, three things stood out. Krish was willing to interact with people at an intellectual level in a new place. There were a total of six people in the room. He was candidly giving Cathy, the expert on computer devices, his opinions on the various devices. The machine had certain words in its library—verbs like "walk" and "see," and nouns like "book" and "man." When he was asked to type words that the machine can give suggestions for, even when he punches just the first two or three letters, Krish, with an impish smile, used the word *spectrograph,* a term used in speech processing. The computer library didn't have it. He started laughing mischievously. Cathy and the others joined in his laughter.

Cathy was able to judge his typing. She said that Krish typed and looked at the screen to check what he wrote. So he was definitely typing on his own. Actually, she felt that his father's touching him was slowing him down enormously.

"Krish," she told him, "you can type very well on your own, independently. Your Dad's touching you is slowing you down. It takes time for your Dad to know what you are writing. You don't need his approval."

Krish took this advice very seriously. When we came home, he started to type on his own, first slowly and tentatively, but faster and more confidently later on. He wrote, "Children's was great. Cinderella repeated again. I am charged about computer writing. It can make me communicate any time, anywhere. I like the portable one only."

June 25, 1997

In the last few weeks, Krish has gained the ability to lock and unlock the doors of public bathrooms. This is a big breakthrough since this had been a problem all of his life. His fingers are more agile and stronger. Nan had always held the door from the outside, which had caused untold embarrassment in the men's rooms at malls, restaurants, and elsewhere.

A few years ago, I was traveling with Krish from Boston to Atlanta by plane. At the airport, he needed to go to the toilet. I didn't want to send him in alone because he was unable to lock the door. I didn't want to accompany him into the men's room, either. Since no one was in the women's room, I took him in. When we were coming out of the place, a woman entered. On seeing us, she shrieked and shrieked, with all of her might. We just ran out, holding hands. I really didn't know what she thought we were doing in the ladies' room. Nor did I care. Anyway, I had to catch my plane. Later, I narrated this incident again, to Krish. He started giggling. We always have lots of fun reminiscing over such funny situations.

June 26, 1997

Jennifer Smith completed her Ph.D. at MIT and now works at MIT as a research associate in the field of speech processing. Early in her career, she worked with autistic children at Boston's Children's Hospital. Upon meeting Krishna, she took a keen interest in teaching him speech processing. The classes were held in the MIT speech processing laboratory.

Krishna has told me that speech processing deals with the theory of human speech characteristics and computer processing of speech for different applications. It covers areas such as acoustics and digital signal processing.

Jennifer had arranged a demo in the Media Lab at MIT with Deb, an AT&T fellow, for yesterday afternoon. Krish loves demos. They make his knowledge come alive.

In physics, as well as other branches of science, theory and experiments go together. Science is based on experiments, and experiments form the very basis of science. The theory has to agree with the experiments. In physics, it is the experiment that stimulates the theory. Any new prediction must be proved in the lab.

In Krish's case, he starts with the theory because it is easy to learn at home. But he needs to see the experiments to fully understand and appreciate theory. The demos give Krish a feel for the subject, so they are essential for his deeper understanding of the theory.

When Nan came home, he told me about the demo:

The first demo showed IPA alphabet on the screen, as someone spoke. The phonemes were shown. There was some overlap between different basic sounds. In scientific terms, these phonemes overlap to some extent, and the challenge is to really identify it. Here in the lab, there was a visual demonstration of the phonemes, which brought the overlap between adjacent vowels into sharp focus. It showed, in practical terms, how difficult it is to recognize speech.

Because there was quite a bit of confusion between adjacent vowels, Krish wrote, "The world of speech is complicated." Deb agreed with him. Again, Krish wrote, "Savvy program!" Deb responded with, "Thanks."

Deb showed another demo in which Toko, a bird created by the computer in living colors, is trained to recognize two objects named "Red" and "Green." When Deb called "Red," Toko turned toward "Red." When "Green" was called, Toko again showed recognition by turning toward "Green." Because Krish has speech difficulties, Deb was not sure whether Krish understood. So I asked Krish to write. Krish wrote, "Toko recognizes 'red' and 'green.'" Deb was really happy. I then asked Krish to give two different words. Krish wrote, "terrific" and "sad." Toko was trained to handle them, and it did.

At the end of the demo, Nan told me about this exchange between Krish and Deb:

Krish: These are simple words. Can it handle complicated sentences?

Deb:	It will take time.
Krish:	Can it handle feelings?
Jennifer:	Someone is trying.
Krish:	It will be useful for voiceless patients.
Jennifer:	Absolutely.
Krish:	Can you program taste?

They laughed because nobody knows how to do it. Here, his sense of humor is evident.

When my husband narrated the event, I was so elated with joy. He was able to relate with people like Deb, whom he hasn't seen before, yet was able to carry on an intellectual discussion with a group of three or four people. He asked questions boldly, with confidence. Nan didn't see any trace of fear in him regarding Deb. I am still reeling from the event.

He is showing more and more concern for people close to him. In the morning, Krish shut the bathroom door so quickly that my index finger got jammed. I was shrieking with pain. Nan gave me an ice pack and tried whatever he could do to help me, while Krish was praying, "Please God, help Mom." He was reciting the same thing, over and over, nonstop for at least ten or fifteen minutes. He really got worried. When I was lying down, he turned on the fan and sat next to me, waving his hands. On and off, he would say, "I love you. I will never do it again."

When my husband came into the room, he saw me crying. He thought that I was crying in pain. But that was not the reason for my tears. This is my son, who doesn't say much. I have to virtually scream at him to get any words out of him. This morning, he was praying out loud for my recovery, without being asked. On top of that, when I was hurt, he told me, "I love you. I will never do it again." I was so touched, the tears were rolling down my cheeks without my being aware of it. It was that instantaneous. My feelings gushed out so fast that I had no control over my crying. Krish got scared, and got up from the bed and stayed far away from me. He must have thought that he did something wrong again for me to cry so uncontrollably.

Once my emotions were under control, I told Krish that he did nothing wrong and that his love and sincerity touched me so much. I went to him and showered hugs and kisses on him, like the torrential rain in India during the monsoon season. "Leave me alone," Krish cried. "I can't," I protested. "You earned it. You came to me and showered me with love and concern. Now it is my payback time. It is time for you to receive in abundance." We both broke into laughter.

Later, I was telling my husband that there are two things for which I am proud of Krish. One is his love for me, and the other is his total responsibility, which came through in this event. He felt responsible for what had happened even though it was not his fault. It was only an accident. I never said that it was his fault, but he assumed responsibility. It didn't end there. He showed his commitment to this responsibility first by praying, seeking God's help, and later by telling me that he will never do it again. What he meant was that he will be more careful not to cause injury again.

What a sophisticated mind he has! This is the person I see from time to time, a gentle, caring, loving, responsible, sincere person. The first reaction in any so-called normal person, including me, is justification: "Why did you have your hand in the doorway?" "It was an accident." "I didn't mean it to happen." "I cannot take the total blame for it." We come up with a million excuses to escape any responsibility, even when we are responsible. Here, my autistic son is taking full responsibility, even when in actuality it was nothing but an accident.

Once, when we were visiting Malini and Vish in Chicago, I felt dizzy and tired, so I went to take a rest in the bedroom. Krish came after me and closed the bedroom door because the rest of the family was talking downstairs and making a lot of noise. He went up and down, several times, to make sure I was okay.

This concern and caring is not just for me alone. I have seen this sensitivity toward Vish also. For example, when Vish was dispirited, Krish went to his room and lovingly massaged his hands. Vish was so touched by this act of love. Krish didn't stop there; he also made sure that we all went out for a car ride. He wrote on the computer that no one is allowed to talk because all of us are tired and in a snappy mood. He took the leadership role for the family, and he made sure we all came back charged and with smiles. We actually did come back with our spirits restored.

This quality of taking charge is emerging in him, more and more. I am so very proud of my son for who he is: a sensitive, warm, and affectionate person. I think that we have done a super job with him, with God's help, of course.

June 27, 1997

This morning, I was still mesmerized from Krishna's behavior yesterday at the MIT Media Lab. The incident shows how much progress Krishna has made, especially in the area of his resistance to change, in contrast to how fast he crumbled under the stress of anything new or unknown when he was younger. Yesterday, he was totally comfortable in a new, crowded laboratory. He observed the demo with concentration and interacted with new people in a new environment. This event took my mind backwards to almost twenty years ago.

Resistance to change *was* the biggest hurdle on the road to recovery for him. Krish's insistence on sameness really stopped him from growing. He didn't like any change in his routine. Even the sheet on his bed had to be the same. A dark blue, striped sheet was the one he liked. If I changed the sheet, he screamed.

He needed order and organization. The house was kept very clean. If there were papers all over, he went berserk. If the beds were not made, he was anxious. Everything had to be methodical and in its place. A dirty house with things lying around created chaos in his mind. If family members fought with each other, it created a lot of stress in him. He wanted a Utopian family. His intense resistance to change created a lot of stress in the family. Every few hours, we had a crisis to cope with. No matter how much we tried, we never did anything right. Everything always ended up being wrong. He was anxious, and Nan and I often criticized each other for making him anxious: "You talked too loud. You laughed too loud. You flushed too much. Why did you pick up the phone and talk? Why did you answer the doorbell? You shouldn't have knocked on the door that long. You failed to beat the traffic light." We were feeling guilty for doing anything and everything and for not doing enough. In those days, nothing made sense in my life.

In retrospect, Krish was trying to introduce order into his otherwise chaotic world, with his malfunctioning senses. At that time, I was also very young, in my twenties. I did not understand a lot of things about him. I took him for an undisciplined, stubborn mule. I used to get frustrated. But for my spiritual inclination, I would have been a lost soul.

Before every change was introduced, I wanted to prepare him for it by talking about it. But he had no understanding of speech. He didn't begin to turn his head when his name was called until he was four. How could I have explained things to him? Whenever I spoke to him, I felt as though I were talking to a wall. At least a wall doesn't walk away from you. But Krish walked away from me.

I tried very hard not to change anything at home. Everything stayed the same. When we moved the TV to a different spot, he was unhappy and looked very anxious. So we put the TV back where it had been. When we bought a new TV, we stuck with the same size and didn't buy the one with a bigger screen for fear of upsetting him.

I had no freedom, not even in vacuuming my carpet. He hated the noise and became tense from it. He screamed louder than the vacuum cleaner. I always did the vacuuming, laundry, and other chores when he was out of the house, and I had to stop the washing machine and dishwasher when he entered the house.

His autism was the tyrant running my house. I was living from crisis to crisis, twenty-four hours a day, for years. When he was eight or nine, it got a little better. When he started school at the age of six, it also got better, for six hours a day. But many times, I took him out of school and kept him at home for months. Between the ages of seven and eight, he was home. We had no program for him. Again, around eleven or twelve, he stayed home for nearly a year without a program. When he was fourteen, we put him in a Japanese school in Tokyo.

I was trying to break his resistance to change. Every time I managed to change him in one routine, another unassailable routine would crop up. I was unable to attack the core of his rigidity. Nonetheless, once he realized that things could change around him without his world falling apart, he became more flexible.

It took months sometimes to wean him from a routine when he was adamant about holding on to it. His willpower was stronger than ours was. I often thought that growth in the brain function would give him the ability and maturity to learn new things more quickly. So I put my heart and soul in structuring him, teaching him a lot of new skills. My thought was to keep on giving him skills.

At some point, the brain should become disenchanted with autistic behaviors.

Whenever a new, repetitive behavior appeared or came to my attention, I tried to nip it in the bud. It is often hard to break a habit. It is easier to stop an inappropriate behavior when it first becomes apparent.

June 28, 1997

Nan had set up a meeting with Dr. Jennifer Smith at 10:00 in the morning. She had again arranged for a demo. Mark, a professional musician, played the trombone. He varied the length and the frequency of resonance. Krish enjoyed it thoroughly because he loves music. In the evening, Nan asked him some questions about the demo:

Nan:	Did you enjoy the session?
Krish:	Yes, very much. Love demos.
Nan:	What did you learn today?
Krish:	Longer the tube, lower is the frequency. Frequency proportionate to the inverse of length.

I had no idea what he was talking about—which actually made me feel as if I had gained the whole world.

Tonight, we talked about what is most important for Krish's growth. Sleep came to our minds. Without it, he is lost to questionable behavior and inefficacious learning. So how do we help him in this area instead of worrying? We decided on four strategies:

1. Nan will give him a massage before his shower, for half an hour.
2. Krish should have Nellikai water, a special ayurvedic medicine poured on his head for thirty minutes. The ayurvedic treatment will cool his brain.
3. We will not criticize him, and we will refrain from showing our anxiety over his sleeplessness.
4. We will talk to him in nonthreatening, low, soft voices. And we will keep the house noise free.

June 29, 1997

Krish hasn't been sleeping well. He is also eating like crazy. His excessive eating is making him so lethargic. He has gained two pounds in the last four or five days. This is not good, but I really don't know what to do about it.

His sleeplessness must be the product of some anxiety in his mind—or maybe the sleeplessness is causing his anxiety. What do most of us do when we are tossing and turning? We think of all the problems we are having or we are imagining. We are given so much time without any interruptions in the night, and what happens? We start believing the tricks played by our idle minds. As Mark Twain said, "My life is a series of tragedies that never happened." Our minds go crazy with some largely manufactured fears that in turn create anxiety. It is a vicious circle. It is a chicken-and-egg story.

Right now, his abilities are shrouded in the cloak of anxiety, and when the mercury of anxiety rises, his abilities and his behavior plummet. It is like a seesaw. Right now, his behavior is okay. But if his sleeplessness continues, his behavior will be affected. I am absolutely sure of it. But how do I eradicate this sleep problem? His autism has always included a component of sleeplessness and anxiety. Eradicating his anxiety might even awaken his dormant speech.

I have been having chest pains for the last two days in a row. I am feeling weak and dizzy. I haven't been frank with Nan because I don't want to worry him. And I don't want to scare Krish, either.

This morning, it dawned on me that the most important thing right now for this family is our health. The most precious gift I can give Krish is myself. Being alive with a healthy body and mind is what he needs from us now. But the stress caused by his behavior can cause worry and thus ill health in us. Suppose I don't fret over this? Then presumably my health won't suffer. I need a philosophy for living practically.

In the South of India, we draw a beautiful design on the floor every day, early in the morning, in the worship room, which is called a pooja room. The design from the previous day is removed, and the new day's design is added. Some are intricate, and others simple. Most of them symbolize the universe we live in, and also the planetary system, like a flag or a national anthem symbolize the whole nation. Each day also has a special prayer, celebrating each planet. The

58

designs are made with white rice powder, yellow turmeric powder, and different-colored flowers. The rice powder is for the insects and ants to eat. In Hinduism, we believe every action must be useful and benefit all creatures.

I once asked my grandmother, who lived with us until she died, about these daily designs. This is what she said:

> Creation of the design celebrates the birth of every day; removing it stands for the impermanence of everything in life. Birth and Death go hand in hand. Time is the Creator, Destroyer, and Sustainer. The design stands for the fact you cannot hold on to anything that is waiting to be destroyed by time. Time is a very powerful force, which annihilates everything. Every day, with its sunrise and sunset indicates birth and death, thus a new beginning and ending. Even the breath we inhale now cannot be held in for too long because it will suffocate us and kill us. A seed has to die to give birth to a plant. An eggshell has to break to give birth to a chicken. In both cases, the shape gets changed, but not the essence. Time cannot destroy the basic essence, the life force, but time annihilates the physical body of things.

When I was thinking about this incident, my body started relaxing. Everything comes to an end, and nothing in life is permanent, as long as decay and death are hovering over our existence. But my essence of being will be forever, and it is indestructible. My body became so relaxed that my chest pain vanished like a ghost. I am so happy that I was brought up with values. Without them, I couldn't survive autism.

Why worry about something that is going to change? Death is a change. Creation and destruction are both changes. Likewise, his sleeplessness will not be permanent. It, too, will change. It will die to give birth to sleepiness.

June 30, 1997

We see Krish improving in four areas:

1. Independent writing and independent typing
2. Locking bathroom doors, making his own toast, and opening the cheese

3. Showing warmth and concern for people
4. Interaction and conversation with people

Nan and Krish got ready without any incident this morning, and left for the Newton YMCA. Two days ago, Krish couldn't wait to get out of the car to hug Rich, whom he hadn't seen in five weeks. He was all smiles. He has such a warm, sensitive heart, and he never holds grudges against people, either.

He has been working with Jennifer, Rich, and Dave, very enthusiastically. When he came home in the late afternoon, he was a little upset. He was running wild in the family room, making incoherent noises. That means he had a lot of pent-up frustration in him. My job was to make him express those bothersome emotions and give positive direction to his negative feelings:

Jalaja:	How was Rich? Any problem with Rich?
Krish:	No. Everything is fine.
Jalaja:	Then what?
Krish:	Dad is going back to work. Is he?
Jalaja:	Yes, but it is only part time.
Krish:	How about my education? What is the plan for my education?
Jalaja:	Your education will not suffer. The work will be 8:00 a.m. to 12:00 noon. By 1:00 p.m., you will be home. From 8:00 to 12:00, you will do your jogging and other exercises. And also, you will go for a long walk. Being with other people is as important as education. So it is not a waste of time. From 2:00 p.m. to 8:00 p.m., you have time to learn your academics.
Krish:	I will be tired after four hours of working out.
Jalaja:	In that case, we will give you an hour of rest. You can start your education at 3:00 p.m. and go until 8:00.
Krish:	Can Dad be effective at work?
Jalaja:	That shouldn't be your concern. If he is not, he will quit. Believe me, Dad will not give a poor performance. If he thinks that he is not performing, we will decide that it is

not working out, and he will give his resignation. One thing is for sure, you will not suffer. I give you my promise that our loyalty is to you, and not to earning money. We have enough. Let's give it a try. What do you say?

Krish: Okay.

Then he went on to study probability theory.

July 1997

July 1, 1997

We have been doing everything we promised we would do on June 28 to help reduce his tension and help him sleep better. Krish's constant eating is normalized. His sleep is getting better. With it, his anxiety is also reduced. I am really happy and peaceful with what I have right now. I have no idea what is in store for me tomorrow, but I know I am not alone, either.

Is there anyone who knows for sure what's in store for him or her in the future? We humans are stupid to cling to our past and to feel certain about our future. The feeling of being alone can send chills through your spine. The moment you feel you are not alone, the moment you feel you have people on your side, you are given the confidence to face anything. Who doesn't worry about his or her future? The whole of humanity feels uncertain about the future. That fact gives me enormous strength to face life. So I am concerned but not worried terribly about tomorrow.

This sort of thinking always frees me from gripping fear and unleashes my inner power into spontaneous, creative energy. This doesn't mean I don't worry. I do worry, but not so much that I become immobilized.

July 2, 1997

Krish wrote this morning that being with Rich was great. He went for his usual long, brisk walk with Rich, and he also worked out on the treadmill.

Later, Krish and his Dad went to Fuddruckers. He said, "Want grilled cheese." The young man at the counter said that they have only *kid*'s grilled cheese. He also kiddingly and rather obnoxiously said, "You can pick your cookie like a kid, later on."

This remark bothered Krishna. On his pocket computer, he wrote, "That was a rude remark," and showed it to Nan. The pocket computer is really very helpful. He is able to use it anywhere and everywhere.

Again, he has been plagued by sleeplessness. This in turn is affecting his behavior. He is very edgy nowadays, so we are very careful in what we say to him.

July 3, 1997

Today, I am off to Chicago to visit my daughter. I need a few days off from my responsibilities with Krish. I need to recuperate my sagging energy and ailing health.

After I arrived in Chicago, Nan called, and during our conversation he told me that Krish is feeling lonely without me. He also said that he had a talk with Krish in the evening:

Nan:	How was the day?
Krish:	Very boring.
Nan:	Why? You went to Boston for an outing with Rich. You went to a restaurant. How can it be boring?
Krish:	Mom not here. Very sad. Miss her.
Nan:	What do you actually miss?
Krish:	Her cheer, her energy, her pep talk.
Nan:	How can I help?
Krish:	By talking more.

Upon hearing this, I told my husband that I would call home every morning and evening for half an hour to talk over the phone. Nan can put the phone on the speaker so that Krish can listen to me. (Krish doesn't like to hold the receiver near his ear for more than five minutes.) This way, he can hear my "pep talk," every day, morning and evening. Krish loved the idea.

July 7, 1997

Nan gave me an account of the recent demo at MIT. Janet is a musician by choice and training. She loves classical music. At some time in her life, she came to know that there is a connection between mathematics and music. So she studied math and was admitted to MIT graduate school. She did her Ph.D. work there.

There, she explored chaos theory and its application to music. One can take a piece from Mozart and change it ever so slightly to an incremental variation. These variations are basically generated by a set of mathematical equations.

Jennifer had arranged for a demo by Janet. First, she played the original Mozart piece; then she changed it. Krish heard the variations. Then she explained to Krish that the basic equations are called Lorenz equations. She showed the equations to Krish:

$$x' = a(y - x)$$
$$y' = rx - y - xz$$
$$z' = xy - bz$$

Then she went on to ask questions:

Janet:	How was the music?
Krish:	Serene.
Janet:	How many equations are there?
Krish:	Three.
Janet:	What's the nature of the equations?
Krish:	Coupled.
Janet:	Are they linear or nonlinear?
Krish:	Nonlinear.
Janet:	Why?
Krish:	xy.
Janet:	That is absolutely remarkable. Most of my students miss it completely. They do not see xy as nonlinear. Krish has an excellent grasp of differential equations. Who taught him?
Nan:	I did.
Janet:	Two things impressed me. Krish said the equations are coupled, and he said they are nonlinear due to xy. He did better than some MIT students I have taught.

Is there any other proof I need that he is smart?

When Krish came home from MIT that evening, he was "moon walking," though not the kind of moon walking he did when he was young and that was due to severe autism. This walking was done three feet above the ground; he was elated at being accepted by the external world.

July 8, 1997

The following is an account from Nan's diary:

> Krish got upset during his massage. We had a few minutes of fighting over the massage. He didn't want to study, and he lacked concentration for anything constructive. He got furious when I forced him to study.
>
> To relax him, we went for a long walk in the woods. I didn't miss my opportunity when he calmed down. I gave him a long lecture during our walk.
>
> Later at Jennifer's class, he was constantly saying, "tired," and was on edge throughout. It was one of those days, very difficult and frustrating. Lots of work with no satisfaction. Hyperactivity! Hyperactivity!

When I read this entry of Nan's, my mind wandered off to Krishna's early years when he was the epitome of bizarre, hyperactive behaviors that were caused by extreme tension and intense fear. His hyperactivity always robbed him of his senses, as well as his concentration. Compared to those early years, the restless hyperactive behavior that Nan had written about is quite mild. Krishna did put up a fight about the massage, but he went for a long walk and listened to his Dad's lectures, and he did go to his class for a couple of hours in spite of his anxiety. Two decades ago, the situation was quite hopeless and heart-wrenching.

Around the age of three, he exhibited many bizarre, unacceptable, *hyperactive* behaviors, like rocking, playing with his excretions, playing with his saliva, tapping his chin, looking at his hands, flapping and rubbing the surfaces of his hands, spinning, whining, making rhythmic sounds, grinding his teeth, shaking his head, and so on.

Until he was five, because of his lack of imitation skills and speech, the only way he could relate to the world was by screaming and throwing a tantrum. With constant practice, he became an expert at both. I believe the chaos created by the lack of understanding of the world around him contributed to his tantrums and fearful screaming.

Everything frightened him. He had so many fears interfering with his growth: the phone or doorbell ringing, the ice cream truck horn, loud TV, fireworks; new places and new people; a change in routine; shadows; trees swinging in the wind, lightning, heavy rain; crowds; fire engines and police sirens; and so on. Everything that we likely consider harmless terrified him. Fear dominated his entire existence.

He would scream for no apparent reason in the middle of the night. Twenty years later, he wrote on the computer that the jackets in the bedroom closets looked like ghosts. They were terrorizing him in the middle of the night when he was three or four.

At three or four, he was very withdrawn from the world. Since he displayed no interest in toys or games or people, all he wanted to do was self-stimulate. He never showed interest in exploring the world, and he lacked the skills to play with other kids. He also lacked imaginative play.

The very best way to stop his unacceptable behavior was to structure him with good behaviors, like learning. When he was learning, he had no time for bizarre activities. Just yelling at him, "Don't hit your head! Don't rock!" and then leaving him alone didn't work. Instead, I decided not to supply him with an opportunity to indulge in such activities. In order to do such unwanted rituals, he needed time to be alone. I refused to let him have it. In those days, I did not leave him alone for a minute, for fear of his unwanted behavior. Many days, I didn't use the bathroom—lest I give him an opportunity to misbehave—until my daughter came home from school at 3:45 in the afternoon.

The only way I was able to manage him was by ignoring him when he was throwing a tantrum. Once he was quiet, I rewarded him with something he liked. Sometimes I punished him, by putting him on the dining table. He hated that. Every time I did that, he stopped his tantrum and screams. The best method of controlling his outbursts was to structure him constantly and keep him occupied. When he started understanding speech, I would say, "Stop! No screaming!" and so on. He started responding to my voice around the age of five. Many normal children, at two or three, throw tantrums. But they outgrow it, whereas children like Krish take years and years before they learn to stop.

He has indeed come a long way from those days!

July 9, 1997

This afternoon, I came back to Boston. Nan and Krishna came to the airport to pick me up. I heard from Nan that Krish was all excited the night before my arrival and had trouble falling asleep. Nan had no idea what time he fell asleep. The next morning, the day of my arrival, Krishna was chirpy and ready to go to the airport at 5:00 a.m. But my plane was not supposed to land until 1:00 that afternoon. At the airport, when my plane had landed, Krish expected me to come out first. Instead, he was seeing lots of people coming to the gate but no sign of me. He waited and waited for me to emerge. Confused and frustrated, he started to hyperventilate. He wrote on the computer, "Where is Mom? Why is she taking so long?" When the long-awaited, thrilling moment came at last, he ran toward me like a discharged arrow.

Standing in front of me was this sweet, innocent son of mine who was full of love for me, and who couldn't tell me how much he had missed me. But he didn't have to. The look on his face spoke volumes. I was struggling to say something nice to him, but my overwhelming emotions choked me up. I pulled him close to me, and we held each other in a long, silent embrace. He was elated with joy and was smiling ear to ear.

I sat with him in the back seat of the car. He was massaging my arm and hands the whole time. He was very attentive to me and very cooperative.

Later, I cooked the most elaborate meal in the kitchen, spending three hours in preparation. I think I did this to try to alleviate the guilty feelings I had in Chicago, for leaving him with his Dad. Krish ate and ate and ate. He wanted to study only in the kitchen, where I was working. He didn't say much, but his actions spoke loudly. As Emerson once put it, "What you are, shouts so loudly in my ears, I cannot hear what you say." This is the same Krish who was unresponsive to love and hated being cuddled and kissed when he was three years old. It seems to me that Krish feels overwhelming love for his mother. That part of him is so fully manifested that I sometimes forget he is autistic.

This evening, he studied for two hours at a stretch. He had no difficulty concentrating. His motivation was in full swing. For the first time, I realized how motivation and love are intertwined. No wonder kids who don't communicate easily with their parents show so little motivation later in life.

When a baby is in the mother's womb, the baby's life totally depends on the environment of the womb. When the baby is born, the parents are crucial to connecting him or her to the external world.

This is so fundamental for human relationships, without which there can be no fulfillment in life.

It is like building a fifty-story building without a strong foundation. If an architect designs a building without a strong foundation, the building, however exquisite, will not withstand the severe storms. Only the ugly underground cement construction can give the building the strength to endure. Is it not the same for the human being?

I am so glad that we are able to give love and support to Krish. Above all, he knows that we love him unconditionally.

July 12, 1997

This morning, he started studying very early. By nine, he had finished an hour and thirty minutes of physics. He was concentrating very well. He studied angular momentum and magnetic moment. He wrote, "Great stuff. Terrific explanation." He was so elated that all of his equations were correct.

When it all came together for Krish in quantum physics, he was thrilled. This morning, I was full of curiosity for quantum physics because my son was studying it; otherwise, who cares! So I started asking Krish questions. The dumber I appeared, the happier I felt.

Jalaja:	What is momentum?
Krish:	Mass x velocity.
Jalaja:	What is angular momentum?
Krish:	Linear momentum x radius.
Jalaja:	Why do we need angular momentum?
Krish:	Motion needs angular momentum.
Jalaja:	Why do we worry about motion in physics?
Krish:	To describe circular motion, need angular momentum to do that. Example, need feet to measure length.
Jalaja:	Can you give an example of circular motion?
Krish:	Cup-and-saucer ride in the amusement park. Earth rotates around the Sun.
Jalaja:	With the tools from technology, it must be easy to do that. Am I correct?

Krish:	Very wrong. Measuring angular momentum inside an atom is very tough.
Jalaja:	Why is that?
Krish:	Because it is too small, too invisible for measurement.
Jalaja:	Then how do you do that?
Krish:	Magnetic field helps.
Jalaja:	How?
Krish:	Angular momentum is proportionate to magnetic momentum.
Jalaja:	What does that show?
Krish:	Angular momentum is quantized.
Jalaja:	What do you mean by "quantized"?
Krish:	Fixed discrete values only. Can't have in-between values.
Jalaja:	Do you have equations to show that? If so, can you show me?
Krish:	Yes to equations. You need to read quantum physics. Can't help you any more.
Jalaja:	Come on Krish! You can't do this to me. I helped you with a lot of your learning. Please, pretty please, tell me about quantum physics.
Krish:	Mom in her mood for teasing me.

And he left with a smile.

My son, whose understanding of commonplace things in life is so deficient, has an extraordinary understanding of arcane subjects like quantum physics. Will the world ever recognize him to be very bright in spite of his autism? Will I ever get a chance to know that my dear son is understood for who he truly is, by at least a handful of outsiders, before I die? Or is this too much to ask from the world? I know expectation of any kind will cause me heartache. Yet, how I long for some recognition of him from the world!

William Wordsworth's "The World Is Too Much With Us" reflects my mental state, my heartache today:

The world is too much with us; late and soon,
Getting and spending, we lay waste our powers;
Little we see in nature that is ours;
We have given our hearts away, a sordid boon!

July 15, 1997

This morning, he was very jittery from the moment he woke up. While having a massage, he grabbed Nan's shirt and tried to provoke him. Nan did well by not reciprocating.

But when he went to the MIT library, he behaved extremely well. He listened to Oppenheim's tape. Listening to videotapes opens up a whole new way of learning.

Today, Rich said, "Krish is using the weights properly by fully extending his hand. He is much more responsive to me, nowadays."

In the evening, he fought twice about eating. He is eating too much. His hunger hormones must be on very high production. Whenever his inner tension escalates, his pangs of hunger increase proportionately. Every time he wanted to eat, I said that he should concentrate on something else. By doing something interesting, he can divert his restless mind from boredom. But he wouldn't or couldn't listen. He was adamant about opening the refrigerator. I scolded him for not listening and not going to bed. He got angry and threw bread pieces on the floor, and started to hyperventilate. I decided to be out of sight. Time to back off.

After fifteen minutes, he was calm. So I decided to talk to him about what he did:

Jalaja:	Why did you do it?
Krish:	Very tired.
Jalaja:	If you are tired, where is the energy coming from for such stupidity?
Krish:	Enormous energy comes from fury.
Jalaja:	Can't fury generate energy for constructive activities?
Krish:	No! Fury is a negative emotion. Generate energy for negative, debilitating actions.

He is very good in analyzing his own emotions and thoughts. He has a keen psychological insight into his own behavior. But this terrible demon called autism won't let him shine. What a waste of talent!

Once he calmed down, he studied probability and signals for an hour before going to bed.

July 16, 1997

Krish hasn't been himself since this morning. He has been the epitome of hyperactivity all day, with an unusual amount of restless movements in his hands. He is walking in circles. His breathing has been so heavy, as if he just finished playing a three-set, tie-breaking singles match in tennis. If he doesn't stop hyperventilating soon, he might have a massive heart attack from the stress.

Right now, he doesn't look like a person who can write an equation for electromagnetic field theory or comprehend Einstein's relativity theory. A person in the street would call me a liar for saying that Krish is very bright. At this moment, Krish looks strange and brainless. This always hurts me because I know who he is: a very intelligent, sensitive, kind human being.

Why? What is happening in his brain? Has something like a short-circuit happened? I know for sure that he is not himself. He is more restless, aimless, and hyper, and he is having difficulty concentrating. These bizarre, aimless, repetitive behaviors, like flexing his fingers and hyperventilating, are thieves that rob him of his senses.

Today, we are frantically structuring him, not leaving him alone for a minute. His restless body movements are reduced when his mind is distracted with other constructive activities. But they are looming in the background, waiting to return the minute he is alone. His senses are under siege, and they seem hopelessly overwhelmed with external stimuli. They lack focus.

Dr. Delacato talks about blindism in blind people and deafism in deaf people in his book. According to him, blindism consists of head rocking, hand moving in front of the eyes, and spinning objects without a break. All these bizarre activities are caused by vision impairment. The deafisms found in deaf children are rhythmic noises, rhythmic tapping on surfaces, and so on. These strange behaviors are caused by deafness. He says that a child's behavior problems stem from his or her sensory problems.

In that case, Krish's repetitive behaviors must be produced by his sensory integration difficulties. Autistic children are known to have this problem extensively. When he was young, Krish displayed more than twenty such repetitive behaviors. Now he has only three or four of them. Still, these few bizarre, strange, unacceptable behaviors make him look weird and brainless.

I often pour some cold water under my shirt, in front and in back, to keep me cool whenever I am having hot flashes. Often, my shirt is soaking wet. I like it that way when I am hot. For an on-looker who doesn't know about my hot flashes, I look weird, maybe even crazy. Pouring water under my shirt looks meaningless and downright insane. But to me, it is a meaningful, useful activity. Who knows why autistic people do what they do? To them, those repetitive, bizarre behaviors may be very meaningful though to us they look like meaningless, purposeless, useless, stupid, aimless, deranged activities.

Dr. Fay has written that convulsive seizure is a necessity for all water-living animals that are removed from the water. A fish caught in a fishing net always jumps up and down violently in order to escape because it cannot live outside water. It has to get back in the water. It cannot survive in air. The seemingly purposeless thrashing of the fish is a very meaningful and extremely important lifesaving act.

We don't know in what way these children are saved by their meaningless, strange activities since they don't always know how to occupy themselves with meaningful activity. Maybe these bizarre activities are giving necessary stimulation to their impaired senses, especially when they are not structured by others. I have seen this in Krish; whenever he is structured and stimulated, his strange behaviors are in abeyance.

Life is full of hidden messages. The messages are not always blatant. We have to look beneath the surface. Where is the precious pearl? Where do you find gold? Where are the priceless diamonds? Where is the crude oil that runs our industries? We, too, must excavate the hidden messages from these children.

It is said that animals in captivity develop repetitive behaviors, whereas in their natural habitats, they exhibit no such behaviors. I can see why. In the wild, they roam freely all over. They get a lot of stimulation from roaming. Whereas in the zoo, they are confined in cages and have very little room to roam about. Maybe animals in captivity have a lot of stress and boredom! That may be the reason they exhibit repetitive behaviors.

If that is so, is our son also held in captivity by autism? Are autistic children bored and stressed out? Are they trying to alleviate their boredom and stress by repetitive behaviors? Maybe they are actually smarter than we are. Maybe their instincts guide them with such activities for survival. Research should be done on those so-called bizarre behaviors in order to understand autism.

Right before going to bed, Krish wrote: "Today my bizarre behavior went out of control. The behavior degenerates frequently. The behavior permeates everything. It wrecks education since the latter needs concentration."

July 17, 1997

Krish had a restless night. He was continually making trips to the bathroom and leaving the lights on. Because I was so much aware of what was going on, I didn't sleep well either. This is the habit I have been trying to break, but with scant success. It started when he was young. In those years, I had to keep a record of his sleep hours in order to understand the correlation between his next day's behavior and his previous night's sleep. So I always went to sleep only after I made sure that he had slept. Even now, rarely am I able to fall asleep when I know he is awake in bed.

The next morning, Krish got up late, and he didn't look very happy. But that was okay, as long as he was not sad or mad.

Today, we have a meeting with the DMR (Department of Mental Retardation) people. Before the meeting, I wanted to know his mind:

Jalaja:	Do you know we have a meeting with DMR?
Krish:	Yes. Very nervous.
Jalaja	Was it the reason you couldn't sleep?
Krishna:	Of course, very worried.
Jalaja:	What do you think of ASA or Class? [Both provide programs for the autistic and other people with disabilities.]
Krish:	They are babysitting places, as far as education is concerned. No mental challenge.
Jalaja:	What do you think of our program?
Krish:	Excellent. Learning is fantastic.
Jalaja:	What do you think of both Rich and Richard?
Krish:	Useful in the gym, having lots of fun.

| Jalaja: | How about Jennifer Smith at MIT? |
| Krish: | Great for building my sagging confidence. |

In the meeting, the DMR people felt that Krish should attend a day program. It will give us, the parents, some relief during the day, they said. Nan told them about Krish's progress in his studies. The top man attending the meeting said that he could not understand Krish fully, and that he wanted an independent evaluation. Another person from DMR asked, "How can he study physics, math, and engineering with such a restless mind? My brother is an engineer. He studied a lot."

They were concerned about our long-term plan, to which Nan said:

> I believe in taking care of today. By doing so, a tomorrow will shape up. I don't want to give him a future based on what he is today. He is making so many breakthroughs; there is no way I will settle for less now. Let me wait and see how far he goes. He has grown a lot in the last four years. Who knows, he may be better than many of us. Already he is better than I am in physics and math, and also in his written English.

Mark, the psychologist, felt that we needed a lot of help. He was advocating more help for us at a time when DMR didn't feel like giving us as much as they had previously. I didn't realize how tough the year was going to be because of DMR's lack of understanding of our situation. They have never met anyone like Krish or, even, us, his parents. To them, we are troublemakers.

Dag Hammarskjold, the former secretary general of the United Nations, once said, "It is more noble to give yourself completely to one individual than to labor diligently for the salvation of the masses." This profound statement has given me enormous hope in times of stress and doubt about whether I am doing the right thing.

We are not working with Krish day and night just so that we can feel noble. It is our karma. We are his parents. If he had been normal, we would have given him every available resource to develop him. That's exactly what we have done for our daughter. Just because he is autistic, I can't discard him like "damaged goods" in the factory line. He is our child, with or without autism. Nan and I are committed to him, no matter what, until our deaths. I wish DMR could really understand who we are.

Krish wasn't happy about the meeting. We promised Krish that we would write a letter to DMR, emphasizing our point of view. And as promised, we did write that letter to DMR. When Krishna read the letter, he came over to me and hugged me, and said, "I love you dearly."

July 18, 1997

Lately, we have been groping in the dark regarding his behavior. Every day, we are spinning out new ideas that we feel would change it for the better, but with little luck. Today's menu for better behavior, according to Nan, is prayer. This morning, he came to the conclusion that only God, not human beings, could help Krish. So we decided that Krishna should spend more time on prayer, scripture reading, and chanting to win God over. This could take three or four hours a day and indicates how baseless some of our ideas are in regard to curing his autistic behavior.

There is not enough time in a day for Krish to be engaged in spiritual prayer as well as take lessons at MIT. What's more, he goes to the YMCA to work out, which he requires largely to help ease his tension. He also needs an hour or more of walking every day to relax him. Then there are his treatments, oil massage and Nellikai water, followed by a bath, which takes another two hours. He also needs speech work from me to help him get out of his mood swings and to become motivated to study, read, and write well.

I told Nan that Krish cannot abandon his education as well as other activities for religion. Learning at MIT gives him a moral boost. When Dr. Smith or other people in the lab praise him, Krish feels more confident. His confidence is being built up by his education. The purpose of his education is not so that he can earn money but to build up his confidence. He can do forty-five minutes of daily prayer. That should be enough for now.

A few years ago, I did the same thing my husband is talking about. I made Krish pray for two hours and read religious and self-improvement books for hours. But this did not help him with his tension and behavior.

To spend the majority of your time in prayer and reading spiritual books requires a very special mind, the kind of mind that would not get depressed by doing that all day. But Krishna is too young for a serious spiritual discipline; his mind is not at that level of maturity. If he were to pray for hours a day, he would likely jump off a cliff. My husband agreed with me.

Along with prayer, he needs his ayurvedic treatment to stabilize his moods. We talked about how the Nellikai water helped him a good deal over a nine-month period in 1994. One night, Krish went to the symphony. His behavior was impeccable, and nobody regarded him as different. I can recount many occasions like that. Once he was standing in line in the IRS office. A lady approached him and asked, "Sir, do you need any help?" I was elated because that meant he must have looked normal, not autistic. Once it happened in the bank, also.

All he needs is calmness, and we can bring that out with Nellikai water, to some degree. Though he is resisting it, we have to make sure that he continues to take it. We should not care about how upset he gets. He has to accept this treatment. Without the calmness, no matter how much he learns, he is not going to be treated with dignity and respect. He may be treated with pity, but I don't want that in place of respect.

July 19, 1997

This morning, Krish got up late because he had a rough night. I gave him the ayurvedic medicine that I prepared for him. He was not in a good mood all morning. He gave me a lot of trouble about going to MIT, such as aggressively pulling on my shirt because I was hurrying him to get ready. He did the opposite of everything we asked for. He was Mr. Hyde again this morning. This is what happens whenever he suffers from lack of sleep.

In the evening, he wrote, "I need constant pep talk."

Jalaja:	Why?
Krish:	Fear of my unknown future can be broken only by your pep talk.
Jalaja:	How?
Krish:	Elevate my mind beyond the ordinary.
Jalaja:	Then what happens?
Krish:	Disappearance of fear.

Jalaja: Do you want to hear what Nelson Mandella once said?

Krish: Yes, please.

I read Krish the following lines by Nelson Mandella while he was eating dinner:

Our deepest fear is not that we are inadequate,
Our deepest fear is that we are powerful beyond measure.
It is our Light, not our Darkness, that frightens us.
We ask ourselves, who am I to be brilliant,
Gorgeous, talented, fabulous?
Actually, who are you not to be?
You are a child of God; your playing small does not serve the world.
There is nothing enlightened about shrinking so that
Other people won't feel insecure around you.
We were born to make manifest the glory of God
That is within us.
It is not just in some of us; it is in everyone.
And as we let our Light shine, we unconsciously
Give other people permission to do the same.
As we are liberated from our own fear, our
Presence automatically liberates others.

I did not understand the first two lines. How can our fear be due to our being powerful beyond measure? How can our fear not be due to our inadequacy?

I had the following conversation with Krish:

Jalaja: Any comments?

Krish: True, true statement.

Jalaja: What do you think of the first two lines, "Our deepest fear is not that we are inadequate; Our deepest fear is that we are powerful beyond measure"?

Krish: Rather we avoid glory. Great people are able to be themselves. Enemy is ourself.

Jalaja: Do you really think so?

Krish: The statement is a twist on reality, to make a point. Truly, mediocrity suits us.

Krish, my autistic son, is telling me how to interpret the statement by Mandella. He is giving new dimensions to my thinking. How is it possible for him to dive deep to get the precious pearls, while I am swimming on the surface, entangled in moss? Right! That's what I was doing with the first few lines, not knowing the wisdom of the statement. He emitted Light to my Darkness of ignorance. Again, how much I wish the world would see him the way he truly is—an intelligent, incredibly smart, gentle, wise person!

July 20, 1997

The things we crave require hard work and sacrifice. To have a baby, the mother has to carry it for nine months and endure the pain of labor. Looking good doesn't come easy either. Diet and exercise are an integral part of looking good. Everything worth having is a mixed blessing. My desire, that is, my commitment to my vision of normalcy for Krishna, also carries with it a very heavy price, namely, social isolation and intense work. Although it seems that the tedious, frustrating, hard work is disproportionate to the tiny improvements we see in him, to me personally it is well worth it. This kind of intense life of penance does leave footprints on the sand of character.

Two decades of living with an autistic child under the same roof has made me understand what life is all about. Because of this incredibly complicated life, I am bestowed with a poignant appreciation for small things. There are no more little things for me. To understand and appreciate the shady tree, one needs to walk in the scorching sun for a long time without the hope of finding one. What wisdom does is let you face the pairs of opposites like pain and pleasure, good and bad, wrong and right, and believe they are mixed blessings from God and should be accepted with equanimity. The result of this is peace of mind and contentment.

Today, something special happened. Krish watched a movie in Tamil (my mother tongue). I wasn't watching the movie because I was busy watching my own hero, Krish, watching the movie. I was happy whenever he was engrossed in the movie, and I was sad whenever he was making trips to the bathroom. He understood most of it, and he loved it though he refused to see the end because it was a tragedy. It is always good to know different languages and cultures. Such knowledge enhances one's character, with flexibility, acceptance, and understanding.

August 1997

August 6, 1997

On July 28, Krish had a wonderful morning. He studied hard and long. Nan wanted to take him to MIT for his audiotape lessons since he so much enjoys them. Right after his shave, he ran, as if in flight, toward the family room, reminding us all how much he loathes shaving. On his way, he fell down and somehow got his index finger on his left hand stuck in the wall radiator. Nan managed to extricate him, but Krish was bleeding profusely with a deep cut. Krish was out of control with intense fear caused by the trauma. He was running throughout the house with blood dripping all over the floor and carpet. Because he was in a state of shock, he became unreachable with reason.

When he calmed down, I got a clean, wet cloth and wrapped the wound with great difficulty, putting pressure on the cut with my thumb in order to stop the bleeding. I also wrapped some ice in a cloth and applied it over the wound. After quite some time, the bleeding stopped.

Nan took him to the emergency room, where Krish refused stitches, in spite of his being given 8 mg of Haldol by the emergency room doctor. The cut was very deep, so they gave him a tetanus shot. Still, he protested furiously about letting anybody go near him to dress the wound. When Nan and Krish came back, almost half a day had been spent in the emergency room. Again, it shows how a simple event that would not terribly affect others cripples Krish. He was put on some heavy antibiotic.

Since we started Krish on the antibiotic, his behavior has been steadily deteriorating. There is nothing anybody can do about it. I am tempted to stop the antibiotic, but he could get his finger infected, and that could lead to amputation. That scares me. His downslide also scares me. His behavior is getting worse, with diarrhea, indigestion, insomnia, restlessness, lack of appetite, lack of concentration, and exhaustion; on top of all this, he is very impatient and peevish. He tells me that he is tired all the time.

August 7, 1997

I woke up at 5:45 a.m. and helped Nan get Krish ready. I cleaned his cut with the solution, applied antibiotic, and dressed the cut. Krish was very patient and cooperative. He took his vitamins and penicillin and went with Nan to Newton. He spent a lot of time walking with Rich. When he came home, he did not want to do anything. He wanted to listen to some audiotapes, so I put on the tape about the Vietnam war. After listening for a while, he wanted to take a shower. He took at least three or four showers, one right after the other. This seemed to relax him.

Agitation in Krish means breathing hard; making verbal noises, sometimes meaningful, sometimes incoherent; moving his hands and fingers in front of his face; and so on. At such times, he cannot listen or obey commands. He didn't talk much about his wound, but neither did he have to because we knew how he felt from his whining, moaning, and irritable behavior. He must also have worried about amputation since the nurse mentioned it.

Whenever he is agitated or nervous, he takes long showers. It makes him relax. It is like giving him a tranquilizer. When he is in such a mood, instead of drugging him with antidepressants and tranquilizers, we let him take as many showers as he feels he needs. We prefer showers. There is no harm, and he has to get relief from somewhere.

Later in the day, he became edgy and demanding, frequently saying give me this, give me that. He was getting upset every time he saw us. Nan and I, exhausted from his restless, disagreeable, unreasonable moods, decided not to cater to him anymore. It was already 9:30 p.m. So we went to our bedroom, locked the door, and started watching a movie. After all, it was a Friday night, and we deserved some peace, some happiness. We decided that not showing our faces would be the best thing to do in order to stop his unreasonableness. We watched a movie, and when we came out to check on him a couple of hours later, he was sleeping.

August 8, 1997

Sometimes what we see and what really exists are two different things. These are called illusions, the mistaken identities of things around us. Illusions are entirely different from what they actually are. The magician creates illusions before our eyes, and we call it magic.

For example, if I am walking in a very faintly lighted area in the middle of the night, I could falsely mistake a piece of rope on the floor for a poisonous snake. Right now, I can see myself screaming breathlessly out of fear at the sight of it. The dim light plays tricks on my vision and on my imagination.

When a short, fat woman wears a dress with long, thin lines, she looks taller and thinner. The same short, fat woman wearing a dress with dark, bold horizontal lines looks shorter and fatter. That is illusion. We see the same thing in a movie, which is a series of still pictures that are run so fast that we see motion.

In the same way, autistic children also create wrong and distorted illusions of themselves with their bizarre, stereotypical behaviors. The illusion they create may not be true. What illusion do they create?

They are mentally deranged and emotionally in an embryonic state. Furthermore, they are insane, bizarre, antisocial, retarded, incapable of expressing love and affection, and schizophrenic. This is the quilt of illusions we have spun on autism based on what we see as behavior.

For the professionals, as well as for others, it is very difficult to see beyond this fabricated fortress of illusions. To see the autistic beyond these behavioral walls, one needs first to reject whatever he or she sees visually. Once this step is taken, the mystery will reveal itself, little by little, and even though this may not be enough to see the whole, it is clearer than before.

Just like the "snake" in the dimly lighted room is true to the beholder, this wrong perception of ours about autism seems true. Only when a bright light is brought in and the lifeless rope is held in the hand of a person whom we trust very much does the illusion disappear.

Only when a number of autistic people grow up to be intelligent, not passively, but actively, will our myth about autism disappear. Those who are close to the autistic person can see him or her as a warm, loving, very intelligent individual. They understand the autistic person, but others don't. The world judges them by their outward behavior, so behavior is important.

Now you can understand why I dwell on Krish's behavior, its social repercussions and its effects on the family. We have been working so hard, ever since Krish was a baby, to alter his outward behavior in order to give him quality of life. Quality of life is very much connected to who we are in society and how we are perceived. We can never exist alone in body, mind, or soul. Along with other treatments, behavior management has always been indispensable. Behavior modification through reward and punishment has yielded good results in the past.

Krish has to be given boundaries, rules, and limits for his behavior. His brain cannot deal with freedom without boundaries. If given total freedom, he starts to degenerate. He goes to a level where a change in situation or a denial of what he wants makes him frustrated. When the outside world doesn't understand him, he becomes remorseful and depressed. Thus, it is a vicious cycle.

To him, routines and structure are undoubtedly important. Routine jobs make him active; an active mind gives stability, and thus, happiness. Through involvement in activities, he becomes structured. The more he becomes structured, the more concentrated he becomes. The concentration gives him control of his mind and increases his learning capabilities.

I cannot stress enough the role of discipline. It is his oxygen. Ann Sullivan didn't give potent drugs to Helen Keller to tame her unruly behavior; rather, she gave her strict discipline. It took a few months to get any results. Discipline reduces Krish's level of frustration and anxiety. But it is very hard sometimes. The bottom line is, Krish is living in a society, and it is he who has to change, not the society.

Today, he didn't want to help me put away the groceries. When I insisted, he started getting upset, making angry noises and jumping up and down. If I had persisted, he would have grabbed me. I didn't put anything away. I went to my room and locked the door. I wanted to give him time to cool off. When I went to the kitchen after fifteen minutes, he was calm. I asked him, "Are you ready to help me?" He said, "Yes." He put all the groceries away by himself.

I asked him again, "What do you think of your tantrums?"

Krish:	Bad.
Jalaja:	Do you think it is beneficial or negative for your future?
Krish:	Negative.
Jalaja:	If you want to go to Maine, you cannot take the route to New York. If you want a positive, constructive life in the future, you cannot take the routes of tantrums and disobedience. They are the routes to self-destruction. Do you get it?

Krish: Agreed.

Now he was calm enough to take my advice. If I had given the same advice when he was in a bad mood, we would have had a very discouraging day.

August 9, 1997

This morning, he was not himself. He was altogether querulous. I had just had it with him. I told him in a very stern voice:

> Your mind is in your hands. Don't try to find an excuse to be mad. You can decide right now whether to be happy or unhappy. The choice is yours. In life, attitude is everything. Nothing is more important than attitude. Without the right frame of mind, life is miserable. Try to be cheerful. Life isn't that bad. There are people who suffer more than you do. Count your blessings.

Thank God, he cheered up right away. He was happy while he was drinking his coffee.

I talked about humor and how it could actually lessen the stress of the body and mind. The chemistry of the brain and the body as well are altered by laughter. I cracked a few jokes, and he smiled and looked relaxed.

A few minutes later, he became tense, went to his room, and listened to the Vietnam tape. Then he took his second shower. I made a dosa, a thin crepe made out of lentils and rice stuffed with spiced potatoes and onions, to cheer him up, which he enjoyed. He then got ready for our trip to Boston. Nan and I were going to an Indian celebration while Krish worked out at the YMCA with Rich.

On the way, we were talking about the penicillin's effect on his system. He has been on that medicine for more than ten days, and he is going crazy—as am I. How long do I have to live with this anxiety, this anguish? Suffering, at the moment, fully as much as Krish, I said to Nan, "Let Krishna be with Rich for four hours since he is not doing much at home." At this, Krish became furious and grabbed my shirt. He has long nails, which he refuses to let me cut out of fear. I got a few scratches from his nails and became upset myself.

His behavior is steadily worsening. I am extremely concerned. I started feeling self-pity. Here I am, going out with my husband after a month of virtual confinement, and Krish made sure that I am angry and upset. "It's unfair of you to make my day with Dad so miserable," I complained. "Dad and I have so little time together as it is."

I am like a crystal prism that has no color of its own. It assumes the color of the object next to it. If a red rose is near by, the prism will look red. In the same way, my moods, my feelings, my emotions, my actions are very much influenced by Krish's state of mind. I am his Siamese twin. I don't know how to uncouple myself from him, any more than I know how to couple myself with Nan. I have imbibed so much of Krish and his autism that I myself seem autistic. I call myself "the autistic Mom."

After half an hour, he quieted down. He got me all worked up with his mood swings. He is angry, and his cut is hurting. The antibiotic is making him miserable. He is an erupting volcano. Neither Nan nor I know what to do or how to arrest the slide in his behavior.

At such times, the only virtue I need is patience, patience to get through this painful period. I don't feel as though I have it in me anymore to struggle to realize my dream. Today, I am in such a bad mood that my present attitude is corrupting my inner wisdom. The alpha and omega of any accomplishment is this wisdom, which owing to my impatience, I am in danger of jeopardizing.

To try to reclaim myself, I often think of people who have shown enormous courage in the face of unthinkable adversities. Today, my great-grandmother is my inspiration.

My great-grandmother married into a wealthy family, but her father-in-law squandered his wealth. Then her husband, the youngest judge in the state, died at the age of thirty-two. At that time, she had three children under seven, including a six-month-old baby. To raise three children with no income was an immense challenge.

She decided not to wallow in self-pity but to work hard to raise her children; they, she determined, must be well educated. All of her time and energy was devoted to her children, and even though she was a widow at the age of twenty-four, she never cried in front of them. She strove for a glorious future by taking care of the glamourless present. Doesn't the present become the past and the future become the present? By taking care of herself and her children now, she also took care of the past and the future. Her mantra for rightful living was "Be patient; nothing will stay permanent, neither joy nor sorrow. Everything is subject to change."

The words of a widow in an Indian hamlet are echoed in Tennyson's "Nothing will die":

> *The stream flows,*
> *The wind blows,*
> *The cloud fleets,*
> *The heart beats,*
> *Nothing will die.*
>
> *The world was never made;*
> *It will change; but it will not fade.*
>
> *Nothing was born;*
> *Nothing will die;*
> *All things will change.*

She put both of her sons through college. One became a successful engineer, and the other became a barrister. When this frail, poor woman died, she had achieved what she dreamed of. And if my great-grandmother can do it with patience and determination, so, too, can I.

August 10, 1997

Today, I awoke at 5:30 a.m. and found Krish in my room. He had to have awoken at least an hour earlier. On seeing me stir, he said he wanted the water adjusted for his shower. Since he doesn't have the fine motor skills to correctly position the shower knob, the water is often too hot or too cold. So while my husband went to turn the shower on for him, I made breakfast. Nan and Krish were leaving for Newton at 7:00 a.m. Krish will be with Rich for three hours, going to the YMCA for his workout, and then for a long walk. In the meantime, Nan works at KSA. And later that day, Krishna has a demo at MIT.

Krish came downstairs for his breakfast at 6:15. Right after breakfast, I gave him his B complex, vitamin E, and vitamin C, as well as his antibiotic. After endlessly searching for Krish's jogging shoes, Nan and Krish left to begin their day, and I sat down to have my first cup of coffee.

This simple cup of coffee is always so pleasurable. Drinking it, I feel very little pressure concerning Krish. I let myself tune in to the birds chirping or the leaves gently swaying in the mild morning breeze. The pressures of living with my autistic son have done something quite incredible for me. Through him—being with him, caring for him, suffering with him—I have come to realize that I am never lonely when I am alone. I do not need to be entertained; television and movies hold no charms for me. I am happy being alone and doing nothing.

My mind is my ally, my thoughts my companions, my inner prayer my silent guide, and nature, forever revealing the vital lessons of life, my teacher. In a raging storm, which will survive: a humble, wispy blade of grass or a proud, mighty oak tree? Of course, the grass because it has the flexibility and suppleness to bend with the wind and not resist it. Krishna's autism has given me such a contemplating mind; I have come to understand that nature is constantly giving out messages. All we have to do is to tune to our nature channel and we will receive understanding in abundance.

After my coffee break, I took a shower, cleaned the house, folded the clothes, and then wrote in my journal for a couple of hours. I also had a chance to sing before Krish and Nan returned at 1:00 p.m.

Nan said that at MIT Krish didn't want to study in the library, but wanted to rest. So Nan let him lie down in the audio room because no one else was using it. I became very upset about this:

> If you let him lie down one day in the library audio room, he might demand it on other days when he feels tired. I don't want him to get this idea in his head. Right now, he is well behaved at MIT. Before you know it, he might want to take a nap in Jennifer's class whenever he is tired.

In my opinion, Krish has the capacity to do Ph.D. work, but his behavior is very immature despite his intelligence. There is a big gap between his intellectual capacity and his actions. This has always hurt me. Only rarely, very rarely, does someone see him for who he is: a sensitive, bright, witty, and loving human being. There are people in this world who, though they have scant education, know how to behave reasonably well in public, so they are understood. When will his behavior come closer to his logical, analytical, keen mind?

I called my daughter, Malini, and talked to her about my frustration. She was very soothing. She tried her best to be supportive by saying:

> You are fighting fate with your effort. You are always fighting the odds. But he is doing great at MIT. There is no setback here. Now he is irritable because he is on an antibiotic. It is only a minor roadblock. He will be okay when he is off the antibiotic.

Later, I saw the *Maury Povich Show*. I rarely watch TV, but I am glad I saw it. The show was about people with disabilities. A seven-year-old girl, named Carmen, who has neither legs nor hands, was one of the guests. The doctors advised the parents to put her away right after her birth. But the parents decided otherwise. She has artificial legs, but refused the artificial hands because they were too heavy. She looked very confident and cheerful. She wrote her name by holding the pen in her mouth and said, "I can do anything." That is courage. I have no disability, and my son, who has no physical disability, is growing beautifully in spite of autism, yet I so often complain and feel miserable. What an ungrateful mother I am.

The second guest, Joe, was involved in a car accident when he was a baby. More than 80 percent of his body was badly burned. He has had forty-five operations since that accident. He said, with no bitterness, that God had a message for him, "Never to give up, no matter how bad it gets." He has a total of three fingers and one toe. He has not let anything slow him down. He is in college, and he doesn't want anybody to treat him differently. Undaunted by his looks or his disability, he lives his life with such strength of mind and courage. He is my hero of inspiration today. No more negative thoughts.

August 11, 1997

The day started with Krish's behavior at its worst yesterday. Sunday was also a bad day. Ever since he started taking the antibiotic for the cut on his hand, his behavior has been getting worse. My desperation in watching Krish unravel is profound.

We were also concerned about his diarrhea, which occurs three or four times a day now. Owing to this, he could be losing all the important nutrients from his body, which could be altering the behavior. We decided to call our son-in-law, Vish, a cardiology fellow and an internist at a hospital. This is what he said:

> When you have diarrhea, you are losing sodium and potassium. They are not replaced. Krish has been on the antibiotic for eleven days now. The cut is healing without infection. So stop the antibiotic, but apply the antibiotic cream every day, over the cut, after washing it with the solution. Change the bandage every day. Give him a lot of bananas, since they have potassium, and mix some salt in the lemonade, for sodium. Go to the doctor every few days to make sure the finger is healing well. His behavior is likely caused by the extreme fatigue he is feeling, due to depletion of potassium and sodium that's caused by the diarrhea.

So we stopped the antibiotic on Sunday evening. He was very restless and complained about his tiredness, but he could not sleep. That night, he did fall asleep. But in the morning following, Monday, he was miserable and furious. He was irritable, restless, frustrated. So we left him alone.

I am so distressed about my faith, my God, my charity, about everything else in my life. I give a good deal to charity, believing if I please God with good deeds, like helping others with my money, God will help me with Krish. Since Nan and I spend all of our time with Krish, we have very little time for volunteer work. Though Nan left a job with a six-figure salary to help Krish get educated, we, as husband and wife, are unable to spend much time together. We live an impossibly stressful life.

God cannot find fault with me on that. There is no way anybody can say we could give more time to Krish because we share every minute of our waking life with him. From the minute he gets up, his time is structured throughout the day until the time he goes to sleep. Nan sends out the bills and takes care of the stock portfolio only after 9:00 p.m. When I am doing the cleaning, cooking, washing and folding of the clothes, or when I am taking my shower, I am also praying. I have no other time to pray. My meditation is in the shower or right before going to sleep. Every minute of my day is accounted for, and the same holds for Nan.

He wakes up very early in the morning to meditate and pray. When he walks with Krish in the woods, he also prays. He prays when he brushes his teeth, takes his bath, and drives the car. We cannot live a more disciplined life. My husband takes him to MIT two or three times a week, for two hours each time. So God cannot be annoyed at us for not praying and not taking care of Krish to the best of our abilities.

He knows that we spend so much time and money on Krish and his education. We give him an expensive three-month ayurvedic treatment in India every year, which costs several thousands of dollars plus the airfare. His medicines cost no less than a few thousand a year, and not a penny is reimbursed by the government or by the insurance company. The offshore treatment is not covered by any agency. What more can we do for Krishna?

We nearly killed ourselves to save when we were young. We created a Sharada Trust for ourselves. "Without a rich heart, wealth is an ugly beggar." Every year, we contribute, thinking that God will be pleased with us for doing so. We will not fly business class, which has more space and is thus more comfortable when traveling with Krish, but economy class. But we will give a check for a few thousand dollars for a school building or to help feed the poor, thinking God would appreciate this.

Today, I feel as though God never appreciated our efforts to be good. He doesn't care. We are killing ourselves in every way, but God does not care. If he really cared, he wouldn't stop Krishna's growth by putting obstacles in his way every month. Krishna was doing so well before taking the antibiotic. Why should he get a deep cut? Why didn't God make Krishna more able to tolerate the antibiotic? Why did he allow Krishna to become aggressive during those times? Couldn't Krishna be docile as easily?

I am not asking God to cure him and make him totally normal. I can accept him for who he is, with his speech difficulties and other problems. But why must he be aggressive whenever he is sick? Why can't God let him be sick but not aggressive? For the last twenty years, I have been trying to live well, doing only what is right. I am denying many things to myself so that Krish can grow and reach his potential. My husband and I are intensive care nurses, 365 days a year. Why can't God give us a break? Maybe I am trying too hard. God is telling me, "Live for yourself, have fun, and forget charity. Only those people who help themselves, I help. Not people like you."

Later in the day, I realized what I was doing. This negativism, if left unchecked, will eat away my goal little by little like termites feeding on a building. Who am I to question the Creator? I am here to take orders from Him, not sit in judgment of Him. The words of Lord Tennyson's "The Charge of the Light Brigade" flashed across my troubled mind:

I

Half a league, half a league,
Half a league onward,
All in the valley of Death
Rode the six hundred.
'Forward, the Light Brigade!
Charge for the guns!' he said:
Into the valley of Death
Rode the six hundred.

II

'Forward, the Light Brigade!'
Was there a man dismay'd?
Not tho' the soldier knew
Some one had blunder'd:
Their's not to make reply,
Their's not to reason why,
Their's but to do and die:
Into the valley of Death
Rode the six hundred.

III

Cannon to the right of them,
Cannon to the left of them,
Cannon in front of them
Volley'd and thunder'd;
Storm'd at with shot and shell,
Boldly they rode and well,
Into the jaws of Death,
Into the mouth of Hell
Rode the six hundred.

August 12, 1997

We went for a four-hour ride. Krish wanted to do nothing else, and we couldn't persuade him to do anything else. He looked sullen and miserable. He wanted to go in the car, so we went. Nan and I talked about how Krish lacked control in spite of his brilliant mind. He understands everything when it is explained to him logically, but his actions do not match his understanding. There is little correlation between his intellect and his behavior.

After a couple of hours of talk in the car, I came to know the root cause of his behavior. He understands, intellectually, but the mind control needed to carry out his understanding is lacking because of fear. The gap between his logic and his action is due to this unreasonable fear. He will grow faster if his fear can be eliminated.

The other day, he said, "I agree with the doctor. I have to have stitches. I'll show my hand." Then, when the time came, he hid his hand from the doctor.

Fear was gripping him. That's why the healing took such a long time despite the antibiotic. He can learn physics, math, and engineering, but he cannot suffer stitches. Every small thing is hugely difficult for him. When it comes to basic things in life, he appears dull-witted. Fear is destroying him. His mind is being ravaged by fear. Hereafter, he will make it in life only if he is able to eliminate this unreasonable, pervasive fear. We should seek the help of an orthomolecular psychiatrist. But how do we find a doctor who is both knowledgeable and compassionate? Krish was listening, all ears, to our conversation.

When we were quiet, he, very politely, asked for french fries. Nan agreed to look for a McDonald's, so we stopped at a gas station for directions. Krish became a little peevish. I reassured him about our plans, but that didn't appease him. Krish doesn't like to travel in a car with all the windows rolled up because he feels as though he is choking. So I have to keep at least one window rolled down even though the air conditioning may be turned on.

Because we were moving slowly in heavy traffic on a hot day, he got angry. If I had put the window up and kept the air conditioning on, the car would have been comfortable, but he didn't want that. If I kept the window down on a hot day, the car should move fast enough to generate a breeze, but with the traffic jam that did not happen. Or the McDonald's could have been closer, but it was a few miles away. Clearly, we did not have God's grace. Krish was getting angrier and angrier. Because he has been on the antibiotic for twelve days and has had diarrhea, his self-control was lacking. Normally, when he is healthy, he can put up with such situations quietly. But not yesterday. Yesterday, he lost his mind.

He started coming at me, in the front, trying to fight with me. Nan was at the wheel, and tried to stop him. This turmoil went on for a few seconds. The fear of getting into an accident made me lose control and scream, "You lay one finger on me, that will break this camel's back, and I will not hesitate to look for a residential program. You understand?" A couple of minutes later, I noticed a heavy silence in the car. I even dreaded to look back. It all stopped the way it started. Then Krish broke the ice of silence with an apology. "I love you. I am sorry," he said. His voice quivered, and the words came out in a tide of emotions. I was still fuming, so I said:

> If you really love me, you should stop attacking me. You knew that the situation got out of control. You also knew that you are the sole cause of the mood I am in now. So you want to contain the situation with your "sorry." I am not even sure you really are sorry. You know damn well that once I am worked up, it is impossible for me to bounce back to my cheerful self. You have already let go of your steam with your outburst. Now it is my turn. You better take my angry words.

My husband also vented out his anger:

> He doesn't know enough to control himself because there is no punishment for bad behavior in our house. We don't believe in punishment. Not once did we ground Malini for misbehaving. Look at society. If you fail to stop at a red light, you may be ticketed. If you shoplift, you may find yourself in jail. If you don't work hard for your employer, you may be fired. Violation of rules is punishable.

Nan and I decided that we should deprive him of something he likes as a punishment. We praise him a lot, but we don't punish him enough. So yesterday I decided not to cook for him. I let him eat sandwiches or plain rice and plain yogurt. For the first time, there would be no spicy Indian curry. Krish was disappointed, but I did not relent. Later, he was laughing, and for the first time in many days. When Nan asked what happened, Krish answered, "Wrong attitude," and implied in his limited vocabulary that his mother's speech in the car made him change his attitude. I was glad.

I couldn't fall asleep that night. Too much had happened. The whole event of the day unraveled like reels of a movie. Suddenly, I was looking at the scene with a different perspective. It occurred to me how Krishna might have felt helpless about his fear. Also he may have felt mad at himself, mad at the world, mad at everything around him. Being smart, he knows that he cannot live in fear. There is no quality of life. It will destroy him, little by little, like a termite.

Unfortunately, Nan and I talked only about the negative side, and didn't talk about how to rectify the situation. If he had heard us talk about a specific, practicable, logical plan that would reduce, if not eliminate, his fear, he would not have erupted. He also did not have the speech to let us know how he felt. If only he had the ability to point out, "Hey, you guys, you talked about my fear, with all its gory details, but never once attempted to come up with some workable solutions for it," then we would have known his mind. Instead, he was bottled up, his temper was rising to a boiling point, and his emotions erupted like a volcano, without warning.

Further, if we had talked about this subject in an open, parklike setting, he could have managed without an outburst. But we didn't. Knowing him to be claustrophobic, we talked about a very serious issue inside a closed space, the car. Had it been only for a few minutes, he would have survived it without an incident. We didn't do that either. For more than an hour, we discussed about his gripping fear, how he is mangled, twisted, and victimized by it, without coming up with a workable plan to reduce it. Even his asking for McDonald's is his way of handling stress by putting an end to the hopelessly demoralizing discussion. Maybe we were so carried away by the serious issue that we didn't notice or react to his frustrations.

After this tantrum, he calmed down and apologized. Again, the communication seemed to be a bigger problem than the fear. The question is, how do we make him talk more?

Now, sorrow and guilt overwhelmed me. I felt irrevocably bad for not accepting his apology and reciprocating his love. Instead, I rejected his love and, on top of that, punished him. Tears welled up in my eyes. I felt a huge lump stuck in my throat. I was feeling very sad.

I had to apologize to my son, so I went to his room. It was 11:30 p.m. I saw him tossing and turning when I entered the room. I was glad he was awake. I sat next to him, and whispered to him, "Krish, I am terribly sorry about not accepting your apology. I know you love me very much. I love you very much, too." Then, I put my arms around him and held him in a long, silent embrace, trying to ease my pain of guilt and sadness, as well as his pain of loneliness and fear.

August 13, 1997

This afternoon, I explained to Krish how important it is to learn new concepts and think new ideas:

> They are like road maps. You want to go to Florida. The road map tells you how to get there. Reading the road maps alone will not suffice. You also need to drive. Without the map, you don't know where you are going. Learning will give you new ideas with which you can navigate your life.

I also talked about how he could learn to live without his fear. If he decides to get rid of his fear, he will be able to. Simply deciding to live free of fear will allow him to do so. Thinking affects the body. Body and mind are very much related; they are not separate entities. Many ailments, like hypertension, are direct products of mental tension produced by chemical changes in the brain. If he develops courage and fearlessness, his body and brain chemistry will undergo chemical changes, just as his fearfulness now creates changes like sweating, hyperventilation, and shaking. The reactions to his courageous thoughts will be the opposite: no sweating, no muscle tension, no sour disposition.

This talk seemed to work wonders. Before talking to him, he said he didn't want to learn, but afterward, he started working on the computer. My role always is to mold him and motivate him.

On Sunday, we stopped the antibiotic, and today he is a pussycat. He traded two minutes of stitching time for two weeks of disruption and destruction. He could have avoided this agony for the whole family by having had the stitches earlier. I told him, "Please think about this fear. This fear doesn't help. It actually hurts you. Don't destroy your life with fear." He promised to think about it. Then, fifteen minutes later, I went into his room to see whether he was thinking, and willing to put his thoughts down on a piece of paper. I found him snoring. That's Krish!

August 14, 1997

Krish was sipping coffee when I found him this morning. I said, "Good morning, Krish." No answer. I said good morning again. He began to whine. I wanted to set him right, so I told him, "Krish, don't give in to negative feelings early in the morning. That will set the tone for the day. Be cheerful." But he became increasingly upset. He wanted to take a shower. For much of the morning, he was moody. I decided not to lecture him anymore, and started singing devotional songs while I cooked our lunch.

This afternoon, I asked my husband what affluence is. He said, "the feeling of plenty; abundance is affluence." I thought about it. If the feeling of plenty is abundance, we do live an affluent life, for we need not worry about how much we spend on basic necessities. I understand what affluence is in terms of money. It simply is an attitude of contentment. But how, I wondered, do we achieve that affluence, that feeling of plenty, in the case of Krish? I voiced this thought to Nan:

> You accept Krish as he is and have no expectations for his future. When you have no expectations, there is no worry and anxiety, and you are not setting yourself up for any disappointment. You don't care who says what about him. He has enough basic skills to enjoy life. He loves good food. He enjoys good music, good talking tapes, good outings, and so on. Above all, he loves learning.
>
> If we lessen our expectations of Krish, we can have a great life. He is bright, but his behavior is sometimes intolerable. We often feel stressed by his behavior because of our expectations of him. You might reduce your expectations and accept that, though he is smart, his behavior is uncontrollable sometimes. I will not worry about it. I will do what I can and leave the rest to God. When you accept the good of him as well as the bad, you feel a relief. You don't worry about him. That is affluence in terms of Krish.

This evening, Krish wrote a line or two about his anger, and then he had an outburst. He wants to say so much, but he is unable to. That's why he is having these angry outbursts. It is not that he is angry at us; he is angry at himself. He has to speak more. He went into one of the bedrooms and closed the door. My husband and I talked further about Krish's behavior.

We felt that it is not all that bad that he is getting frustrated. Maybe his frustration stems from the awareness that, for all of his intelligence, he is unable to speak, unable to communicate and be normal. He wants to say so much, but he can't. His outbursts are his way of raging against his condition, his dependency, his inability to speak, and so on. He does not accept it in a docile manner. This is good.

Why do revolutions take place? What is the nature of revolution? Does it have a purpose? If so, what is the purpose? What is rebellion all about?

Revolutions took place because people rebelled against the existing conditions in the society. Consider the French Revolution, the Russian Revolution, the American Revolutionary War against the British, Gandhi's ahimsa war (nonviolence war) against the English. Look at Mandella, the president of South Africa, now. What was his fate a few years back? He was condemned to a life in prison by the ruling white class. Now, he is ruling them. His rebellion brought about this change. No revolution is peaceful and relaxing to the participants. Similarly, Krish's rebellion is good. Although it is tough on us now, without it, the desired change will not likely occur. He has to go through this excruciating pain in order to grow emotionally and change effectively for the better. And we have to prepare ourselves for a tough ride ahead.

Any and every dream has a price tag attached. Like everything else in life, a fantasy is never free. The bigger the fantasy, the higher the price. A dream by itself will not come true. Efforts and sacrifices must be made. Our goal to make our son almost normal is not excluded from this universal truth. Henry David Thoreau wrote, "The cost of a thing is the amount of what I will call life which is required to be exchanged for it immediately or in the long run."

August 15, 1997

Today, Krish had an oil massage for the first time in six weeks. Right after his shower, he came to me, and he didn't want to do anything. I told him that he cannot go on doing nothing. That is very dangerous to his mind. His mind cannot exist in a vacuum. It will get filled with wrong, negative thoughts. He listened and then he went back to write on the computer. He wrote only two lines before getting upset and angry. He started to jump up and down with incoherent, absurd noises. He went downstairs to go on an eating binge. After a few minutes, I followed him to the kitchen.

Upon seeing me, he approached me with an angry look on his face, and asked for juice in a rude, demanding voice. I had just about had it. Before I knew what was happening, I exploded. I showed him a glass and said angrily:

> This is an empty glass. Either you fill the glass with nutritious, delicious, rich-looking, fresh orange juice or you fill the glass with ka-ka water and urine. It is your choice. Nobody, not even God, can make that choice for you. It is up to you. Which one do you want?

"Juice," he said. Then he started laughing, and looked at me, surprised that I would go that far. I reassured him that I will match his behavior with my words because I cannot match his behavior with my behavior. I also told him that he is contaminating his brain with ugly, angry thoughts. He is what he thinks. Actions always follow thoughts. You think angry, you act angry. You want to fill your brain with the orange juice of peaceful, loving thoughts, not the ka-ka water and urine of ugly thoughts. He got my message and, despite his tiredness, studied physics for twenty minutes before going to bed.

Why does he behave so immaturely? I have to lecture him almost every day. On good days, I don't have to lecture him at all, but I wish there were more good days. Because we don't want to give him medication, the bad days occur with more frequency than we would like. It is tough on us, but we believe that trying to reason with him is better for him in the long run than medicating him. We may be totally wrong.

August 16, 1997

This morning, after ten days of grouchiness, he woke up with a grin. He smiled at me and said good morning. When I asked him what juice he wanted this morning, he said, "Love you." I was glad to see him relaxed and happy. He came to me after his shower and said, "Talk more." So I asked him whether he wanted another discussion because his mind is getting weaker. He said, yes. So I set up the computer for him to write.

Jalaja:	We are doing so much to make sure your cut finger is not infected. We gave you an antibiotic. We wash it every day and put on antibiotic cream. We change your bandage. We take you to the doctor every few days to make sure it is not infected. All this is for infection. Don't you think we have to prevent infection of the brain, too?
Krishna:	Yes, we should.
Jalaja:	Compared to a finger, the brain is everything. If a finger gets infected and is then amputated, you don't lose much. You can still live a productive life. But if the brain gets infected with negative thoughts, what happens to you?
Krish:	Behavior goes whacko, and I go wild.
Jalaja:	Behavior makes or breaks a person, right? Look at Andrew Cunnanan. He killed five people. So the brain is the most precious organ of the body. You can poison it with negative thoughts, but when it gets infected, . . . why don't you complete the sentence?
Krishna:	Can't amputate it.
Jalaja:	So you see why you cannot infect your brain with negative thoughts. It is difficult to correct it and dangerous to live with them.
Krishna:	Good point, thanks.

A few minutes later, Krishna said very clearly, "Hitler, Hitler." I wanted to probe, so I asked, "What do you mean?" After a long pause, he said, "Killed people." Again, I asked him, "What do you think the reason was for his killing people?" He again took some time. I didn't let him leave me without an answer. When he started walking away from me, I repeated the question a couple of times. He stopped walking, consulted his hands, and said with a certain tone, "No control of mind." And then walked over to me with a smile and gave me a hug.

August 17, 1997

I got up early, around 6:00 this morning. I went to see whether Krish was awake or not. I had heard him get up a few times between 4:30 and 5:30, making trips to the bathroom. That was the reason I woke up early. I never want Krishna lying in bed thinking negative thoughts and fuming. So I woke up at 6:00 and went to see him. He was sleeping. I decided not to wake him. Without sleep, he turns into a monster. My husband joined me for coffee, and we started talking about ayurvedic treatment and its effects on him. Because the western treatments offer so little hope in curing autism, we wanted to try an ancient treatment called ayurvedam.

Ayur in Sanskrit means "life," and *vedam* means "knowledge." Thus, the word *ayurvedam* means "knowledge of life." It looks at the totality of a human being. It treats the root cause of affliction, not simply the symptoms.

Ayurvedam is a 6,000- or 7,000-year-old treatment. More than 100,000 plants are used for treating different ailments. For instance, the massage therapy used now in Greece came from ayurvedam. Insanity, hyperactivity, infertility, and so on have prescribed treatments in ayurvedam. Acupuncture, which is mentioned in ayurvedam, is now used throughout the world. It deals with how the different nerve centers of the body regulate the body's electrical current simply by applying pressure. This particular treatment in ayurvedam is called chavuti uzhichel. The pressure on nerve centers is applied by foot.

Krishna has improved immensely since we started him on this treatment. His writing blossomed, which opened up his education. We were able to test him on how much he knew. The majority of his unwanted behaviors have been eliminated. The improvement is slow, but whatever we gain, we do not then lose. Every time we give him the treatment, we never fail to see improvement. And we don't see any unwanted side effects either.

The treatments given to Krishna in India are thakra dhara, oil dhara, khizhi, and chavuti uzhichel. They last approximately one hour. Treatments are given one at a time, not simultaneously.

1. Thakra dhara is a white medicated liquid that is poured over the head, especially in the frontal lobe area. It is for controlling aggression and for inducing sleep. It is done daily for an hour for three weeks.
2. Oil dhara is a medicated oil poured in slow flow over the head for an hour. This is for lubrication and for improving the brain function, especially memory. It is given daily for an hour for three weeks.

3. Khizhi is a medicated fomentation applied over the body. Before the fomentation, a medicated oil is applied. Bones become supple and can bend. One cannot bend a palm leaf in the middle, but by applying oil on the leaf, one can bend it. The same principle applies to human bones. They become less brittle, hence bone fracture in old age is minimized. Khizhi is also a nerve tonic.

4. Chavuti uzhichel is the hardest treatment to give. The person who administers it must be knowledgeable in martial art, yoga, and other disciplines. It is done very deliberately with the foot. The practitioner looks very meditative during the treatment and usually doesn't talk much the entire day. He knows all the nerve junctions and centers, and he knows where to apply pressure and where not to. By turning on a "switch," the electricity is made to flow, in much the same way the energy flow is restored by foot massage. Neurological problems can be helped by this treatment. The oil used for this treatment is extremely expensive. This specific treatment has helped Krish to write independently and to type faster on the computer.

Since August 14, we have been giving him Nellikai water and oil massage. Just before his shower, Nan gives him a half-hour massage all over his body, especially his arms and hands. In the evening, he gets his Nellikai water. I have Krishna help me make this special medicinal water in the afternoon.

I mix the herbal powder in a huge pot of water, and then boil it for nearly two hours. The amount has to reduce to one third, or one quarter. Then it has to cool for a few hours. By the time the water is sufficiently cool, it is evening. We have to pour this water on Krish's head for half an hour. This seems to cool him down. In as little as a few days or as long as a few weeks, his anger melts away and his demeanor is affable. The Nellikai water treatment also helps reduce his tension and makes him sleep well in the evening.

When I write this, it looks very simple. But it is not. Krishna abhors this treatment. Yesterday, I told him all the good points, but still he did not want to take it. He is a stubborn mule. Every day, he will take it only reluctantly, with lots of fussing and whining. Nan and I know how good it is, but to make a well-built, grown-up man take it is next to impossible. Making Nellikai water is not easy either. You cannot make it for the whole week in one day. It has to be freshly made, every day. If he is cooperative, I don't mind doing it, but he resists me.

Yesterday, as I tried to persuade him to take the treatment, he got into a fighting mood. After some heated words, Krish stalked off to his room. Feeling miserable, we also retreated to our bedroom and locked the door. In there, we decided that he is not dictating whether he will have the Nellikai treatment. He is going to have it. I went to his room and told him as much:

> If you don't take the treatment, you cannot stay home, enjoy the good food, get our affection, or go to MIT for your academics. And we will put you in a residential program, and they will not put up with your aggressive behavior. They will drug you with Haldol or Melleril in order to handle you. We pay as high a price as you do for your not taking the treatment. If you get upset, you make our lives miserable. We don't want to live with you when you are in this mood. Here, we will not drug you; we will not make you drowsy and lethargic because we want your intellect to be sharp so that you can learn.

When I asked him what his choice is, he said he wanted to stay and take the treatment. But I wasn't sure of this because he has agreed to such things before only to not take the treatment. Then he asked me to get a fan for him. He was sweating profusely. My heart wanted to give him the fan, but I said no.

I told him, whenever he wants something, I am always ready to make his life comfortable and happy, but when I want something, he doesn't care. Even if he doesn't want this Nellikai water, why can't he do it for his mother's sake? How can he be so selfish when he knows that I, every evening, cook his favorite Indian meals for him and prepare his medicines? I can't even talk to his Dad until late in the evening because he is busy working or educating Krish or taking him to MIT. So now I am going to let him sweat. I will not get the fan for him. He heard me silently. I wanted him to know that I expect something in return. It cannot always be Nan and I, giving relentlessly. He has to give to us, too. Then I left the room.

Later, Krish went down to the basement and took the Nellikai water for half an hour, though with much protesting and whining. I do not care how he takes it. All I care about is that he does take it so that he can sleep at night and behave decently during the day. Without good behavior, there is no way he can learn anything.

August 18, 1997

My love has been so unconditional that he has no motivation to take responsibility for his behavior. He thinks, for good reason, that I'll endure any behavior from him and still love him. When he was young, he was very unresponsive to love and affection, so I gave him a lot of love. But now, he gloats over my love for him, and I can no longer give love this freely. From now on, I am going to make sure that he earns my love and respect. He is very bright. He can behave better. I have just about had it with him. Why would he want to do anything differently if he knows that I will love him no matter what he does or how he behaves? There is no incentive for him to earn it. I told my husband about my idea, and he agreed.

I also told Nan that he should not scold or scream at Krishna downstairs in the basement because that part of the house is closer to the neighbor's family room. They might hear angry loud noises and misunderstand. Although I agree that Krish cannot push us around and that we should fight back and show him that we are also tough, we have to be politic also.

Nan did not agree with me.

Nan:	How does it matter what they think? We are all going to be gone, dead, in some years.
Jalaja:	But death is not the problem. We have to live. People's perception could really hurt or help us. Remember when we rented out the place from Bob a few years back when we returned from Tokyo? In the beginning, when I was in India giving treatment to Krish, and you moved into the house alone, Bob thought the world of you until Krish came back from India. Then he changed his perception about you, and wanted us out because, at that time, Krish had a behavior problem. Bob couldn't deal with that. That is reality. You have to be realistic about life, and you have to take steps to assure yourself a peaceful life. We don't want any misunderstanding from our neighbors. They might inform the social services that we are mistreating a disabled person. A floodgate of insurmountable problems will open up. Instead of planning and working toward his improvement, we would be working day and night to ward off the agency. So why

> don't you roughhouse in our front room, which is far away from them? We have to be smart, too.

I showed him the cup of coffee and continued:

> If this coffee is cold, you can't talk philosophy and make it hot. You have to heat it in the microwave to make it hot. In the same way, we have to make sure that people don't misunderstand us.

> Otherwise, their attitudes could make us unhappy or angry, which will only hurt Krish.

Nan: I see your point, and I do agree with you.

August 19, 1997

We talked about instant gratification versus postponed gratification. I told him about a show in which a man said that he stole a car. He went to prison for that. When he was asked why he did not earn and save and buy a car, he replied that would take years and he wanted it right away. So he stole. He did not think about prison. It is the same thing with Krish. He doesn't believe in long-term benefits. He himself wrote, "The short term is immediately painful. The long term is so far away and so it goes away." He said this in regard to taking a shot in order to numb his finger for stitches. He refused the shot. Intellectually, he understood it, but emotionally he couldn't come to grips with the pain of a shot.

Even though the doctor gave him 8 mg of Haldol, Krish did not let him go near his finger. I did not see any weakness in Krish; he was alert and aware. He was single-mindedly bent on the goal of protecting his cut finger from stitches. The medication did not knock him out. He willed it so that the medication became powerless. This is mind over matter. If he could similarly concentrate with his intense mind on his behavior, he would be all right.

Within five minutes of arriving home from the hospital, he was sound asleep. The danger of getting stitches was gone. Maybe therein lies a lesson for us. We can modify his tantrums and aggressive behavior with immediate punishment instead of long lectures. He himself says that he is more concerned about avoiding immediate pain than any long-term gain.

That's what I did a couple of days ago. He knew no fan would be available to him unless he took the treatment. He wanted the fan so badly that he decided to take the treatment. If I hadn't deprived him of the comfort of the fan, I am sure he wouldn't have taken the treatment.

August 20, 1997

Black hole.

Why do I feel Krishna is my black hole today? Anything that goes near the black hole is immediately consumed by it. Nor is there any escape from it.

The universal law says that masses attract each other. Our earth is so big that it attracts everything toward it. The sun is much bigger than our earth, so the sun's pull is much stronger. That's why the earth is rotating around the sun. A black hole in the galaxy attracts everything that goes near it. It even attracts the light. The light cannot escape from its pull. It is a tremendous force, and a lot more powerful than the gravity of the earth. But when the black hole and autism are pitted against each other, I don't know which will emerge the winner.

Autism has tremendous pull. It absorbs the lives of people around it. Anyone coming in contact with it is completely metamorphosed. No matter how hard one tries, there is no escape from it. It is tremendously powerful and incredibly magnetic. I am a small nail near a big block of magnet. I cannot escape the powerful, crushing, gargantuan grip of autism.

When I am away from Krish, I am funny, frivolous, stupid, and very light-hearted. No sooner am I in his presence than I become serious, soul searching, philosophical, prayerful, intense.

August 21, 1997

How could I have written what I wrote over the last couple of days? I must have been very selfish to think that I am suffering when I see Krish struggle day and night to do simple tasks that I and so many others take for granted.

Anyone with this horrendous syndrome is in a concentration camp. How can they survive such a setting? Their minds are not their own. Their thoughts are not their own. Their feelings are not their own. Everything is twisted, distorted, disguised. I have seen it in Krishna. A gentle, kind, caring Krish becomes a frustrated and angry creature. When we ask him why does he behave badly, why is he frustrated or irritable, all he can reply is, "Tension and fear. Please help me."

It simply amazes me that he can be such a nice person in spite of being a lifelong slave to autism. That, I will say, is the grace of God. Autistics not only have to wage war with the disease they are afflicted with, they have to deal with the perceptions and demeaning attitudes of the world around them.

Here I am, complaining about being consumed by a black hole. This behavior of mine is very immature and inappropriate because what I am going through is nothing compared to what he is going through! I had a life *until* he was born. At least I got to know what it is to be married and be a mother. Whereas, he is never free of autism. It is a shadow that has followed him since birth. My pain pales compared to his. He will always feel pangs of loneliness that I will never understand. My silent, lonely son works tirelessly for rewards so disproportionate to his monumental efforts. Now anyone can understand why I feel guilty about what I wrote yesterday. Life has been unfair to him; now I, his mother, am being unfair to him. In his case, he can't even hate autism because it is inseparable from who he is. It would be almost like hating yourself.

August 22, 1997

Yesterday, Krish and Nan went to Jennifer's house. We wanted to find out if Krish could learn from her alone, without Dad by his side. Because Rich was on vacation, Monday was the best day to explore this. Krish was with her for two and a half hours, all by himself. Unlike a few years ago, we feel as though he could have a fun time with anyone now. The major breakthrough came when he learned speech processing from Jennifer. This could also make Nan's life easier. He could go to work for longer hours. Right now, he is consulting for only ten hours a week because Krish needs his Dad for going to Jennifer and MIT. Let us wait and see.

After the lesson with Jennifer, Nan took Krish to the MIT library to watch videotapes. The MIT video room is very small and crowded with five or six TV sets and chairs. It also contains shelves of videotapes on the walls. In the summer, it is hardly ever crowded since very few students are using it. Most of them are on vacation. At such times, Krish loves to sit and watch the video on laser technology with energy and enthusiasm.

This particular day, Krish was watching a digital signal processing tape for more than thirty minutes. There were no other people in the room besides Krish and his Dad. He was enjoying the tape and having fun. But suddenly, a group of three young men entered the room and surrounded him. Later, he wrote that he felt as if someone was pushing his head under water and he was drowning. He could hardly breathe. He was gripped with intense fear and overwhelmed with acute anxiety. It was a time to flee. But at that time, Nan didn't understand fully the agitation or the stress in Krish. Nan asked Krish to stay for ten more minutes since he was enjoying the video. Krish tried to stay for his Dad's sake. But his restlessness and tension would not let him relax; they were escalating to a point when he needed to get out and get some fresh air. Nan saw the mood that Krish was in and he realized that the tape had to be rewound and put back before they could leave. That would take a few minutes. But Krish was desperate. So Nan put the tape back without rewinding it.

Krish was obviously agitated as he stood up to flee the room. I have taught him over the years to take a deep breath to steady his nerves. But this time, I guess it didn't work. He took a quick, desperate, jerky dive toward the door. In the process, he sprained his ankle. I have a feeling the three men must have been amused at the way Krish exited the room. I guess they would tell this story about a dozen times and have a hearty laugh at our family's expense. At least there is a bright side to the humiliation.

Krish started to get angry for having been put in such a position. He got angry and started to lose his control. Later he wrote, "What was the big deal about rewinding and putting it back when I was panic-stricken with anxiety? I was feeling claustrophobic and out of control at that very moment. I wanted to leave, but Daddy was delaying."

When they left this tiny video room, they had to walk through a big library hall where a lot of people were studying and go to the front desk to hand over the earphones and sign out. The front desk area is also a very small room. As soon as Krish got out of the tiny video room into the bigger room, he was a little bit better. He wasn't that claustrophobic, but he was still in a foul mood. The place where Nan had to return the earphones was also crowded. When Krish saw that the place was mobbed, his feeling of desperation came back. So Nan gave the earphones back but he didn't sign out. He told the lady in charge that he would be back in a minute. She looked at him, puzzled, and started to say something. But Nan knew the urgency of the situation with Krish demanded the utmost attention right then and there, lest Krish make a big fool of himself in the library. Nan didn't want that to happen. So he didn't stay long enough to respond to the lady. He must have looked very rude, in her eyes. He took Krish outside the library and asked him to sit on a bench near the elevator while he went back in to sign out.

When Nan came out, Krish was still steaming mad and ready to explode. Krish very much wanted to be out in the open, with the fresh air blowing in his face. They couldn't even get in the elevator because every time it came, it was full of people. Nan was looking for a staircase to get out. But there were no stairs available. At last, the long awaited moment of an empty elevator arrived. They got in, but unfortunately, it didn't last long. Two floors down, four people squeezed into the elevator. Krish was ready to tear Nan apart.

When they got out of the elevator again, they needed to go through a long corridor crowded with students before they would be out in the open. Nan didn't think that Krish could last that long. Nan was looking desperately for an exit to the outside. To his amazement, he saw one. Nan dashed out. Krishna, even with his hurt foot, ran after him into the open. All this took nearly twenty minutes, from the time those three people entered the video room to the time Krish came out to the open area. It seems now that he tried with all his might to keep his stress and anxiety-induced anger from exploding in public. In spite of his desperation to be out in the open, he succeeded in minimizing his claustrophobic feeling before it got out of control. He did not make a scene. Except for his Dad, no one was aware of what was going on.

Once they came out into the open area, Krish started grabbing his Dad. He was very much ready for a fight. He was fuming, "Why did you make me stay in the tiny video room? Why did you do everything wrong to escalate my tension and anxiety? Why didn't you get out fast?" He didn't say all this orally. But his facial expressions of anger and his stiff body posture of tension spoke much more effectively than mere words.

Nan walked away very briskly and crossed over to the Charles River side. By that time, Krish had calmed down, so they had a long walk along the river and then returned to the car. As soon as he got in, though, Krish said, "I am sorry. Please don't shout at me," he still looked angry and unhappy. Nan decided to put on some good music, and he started to drive.

Krish listened for twenty-five minutes; then suddenly, he got very stressed out and was getting angry and frustrated for no apparent reason.

When they reached North Andover, Nan next took Krish to the public park so that they could walk in the woods. Since being in nature always relaxes him, after he cooled off, Nan asked him questions about his behavior at MIT on the pocket computer that they sometimes use to communicate with. Krish said that he did not want to go to the MIT library because at this time of the year parents of students are visiting. So it is always crowded, which makes him feel tense. He was going along with his Dad only to please him. Hereafter, he wants to go to MIT only for his lessons, and then return home. Nan learned a good deal about Krish's behavior on their walk.

That evening, I told Krish that no matter what bothered him, he cannot become so frustrated that he loses self-control to the extent that he is ready to start a fight with his Dad. If his Dad hadn't been sensitive to his needs and hadn't taken the right steps, Krishna would have had an outburst. That wouldn't be good. Krish agreed. I also told him that he is very bright and that he can make it in life provided that he changes his behavior. His behavior makes him look like a fool or a bad person, which he is not. People outside the family don't know that he can do relativity theory or statistics, but they can see how he behaves, and they will judge him on that. Their negative perception, in turn, may worsen his behavior and thus erode his confidence. It is a vicious cycle. He has to stop this behavior. He has to let people know how he is feeling so that he does not become so tense that he goes out of control. He should have communicated to his Dad that he doesn't like to stay in the crowded video room long before his eruption.

He agreed. He is a very gentle person when he is not tensed up. But all of his life, this tension has been his constant companion. We never know when it will creep up.

In the evening, when I was writing this incident, the truth dawned on me. There is a positive side to this episode. How desperately he tried to contain the uncontrollable tension-induced outburst! How well he succeeded in not creating an unforgettable scene in public! That says a lot about his motivation in wanting to be accepted by others.

Moreover, autism in Krishna has been teaching us a very good lesson, by giving us incessant therapy in getting over ceaseless public humiliations. As parents, we have learned how to survive and overcome the feelings of hurt and move on with life. Autism has taught us that the past is history, and we should ignore it as such. Our future is a mystery and we should try not to worry. By this attitude, the present has become a lot more precious, without any hindrance from the past or the future.

August 23, 1997

Jennifer is going away for Labor Day, so there will be no lessons next week. This week, Rich is on vacation, so there will be no YMCA either. Today he has been calm and well behaved. Listening. We are doing Nellikai water every evening, along with massage. This was started on the fourteenth. Krish doesn't give any resistance to his treatment.

In the afternoon, Krish was a little peevish. I averted his mood slide by telling him a couple of jokes. He loves jokes. I said, "Krish, just as the sun gets eclipsed, when your intelligence is eclipsed by your negative moods, your behavior changes. In your case, you are eclipsed several times a day, whereas the sun is not." Upon hearing this, he started laughing loudly for several seconds. Another time, I asked him:

Jalaja:	Krish, you are an American by birth, so you can run for president as your career. Would you like that?
Krish:	Yes, I want to be the president.

111

Jalaja: What will you do as president?

Krish: Do no work, play golf, and have fun.

We both laughed.

He wanted the water adjusted for his shower in the evening. I asked him to wait for fifteen minutes because I was in the middle of something. Usually, he will not wait for two minutes, never mind fifteen, once he wants to shower. Yesterday, he patiently waited. I think the Nellikai water is helping to reduce his tension. He is talking more willingly. Sudden outbursts of anger due to tension have been reduced. I think if we do it for a month, he will be much better. I have to wait and see.

August 24, 1997

Nan called Beth Israel Hospital and made an appointment for Krish to see a behavioral neurologist on September 5. The doctor will decide whether Krish should have an MRI. I want Krish to have one. Perhaps he has a blood clot or structural abnormality in his brain that could be corrected. That might ameliorate some of his behavioral problems. How I wish that might be the case with him! Can anyone on the earth understand a mother entertaining such an unlikely, such a bizarre wish?

The Department of Mental Retardation is giving us trouble; they have frozen the funding for Krishna until this evaluation is done. Because they don't think keeping Krish at home and having him educated at a higher level is the right thing to do, they want him placed in some special autistic programs, which we resist with all intensity. In our opinion, he is smart, and so he should be educated at his level. I made my husband give up his job to educate Krish at home. That means the loss of a six-figure salary. We didn't do that for nothing. We believe that much in education. How can they expect us to put him in a classroom for the low-functioning autistic? That's absurd.

Last night, while he was eating supper, he started behaving badly. I left the table right away and asked my husband to do so also. We left without our food and went into our bedroom. Twenty minutes later, I went to see how he was doing. He was smiling and cheerful.

The best thing to do when he is upset or frustrated and making unreasonable demands is to leave him alone and make sure that we are not visible to him. This makes him cool down fast. On the other hand, if I lecture him and ask him to behave well, he becomes more frustrated. Avoidance is the best way to handle him when he is unreasonable.

He was tired by 8:00 p.m., after the Nellikai water. He did not want to study, but when Nan insisted on his studying physics for half an hour, I was amazed when he simply went into the study room to study. Usually, when we insist on his doing something like this, when he is tired, he gets upset. But last night, he followed his Dad into the room and studied. That means the treatment is putting a lid on his frustrations. His tolerance is getting better. He can handle pressures better.

During his lessons, he looked in his Dad's eyes and smiled at him whenever Nan made an interesting point. Krish is fascinated with the subject of physics. He went to the computer and answered questions and wrote the equations. He is very smart in physics and math. I hope one day the world will think of him as smart.

He also studied this morning for a stretch of one hour and forty-five minutes. That shows his concentration is improving. He was cheerful, and when I greeted him with "Good morning," he, smilingly, extended the courtesy.

Krish took his shower this morning. When I walked by the bathroom door, I heard him say, "I have no pants." This was on his own. I had forgotten to return his pants after laundering them. When he came for breakfast, I gave him a surprise, by saying, "You are going to McDonald's for your breakfast." That made him happy, and he said, "I want pancakes."

His eye contact is very good, and he listens well. He talks more than usual. His anger is under control. He is communicating without any prodding or prompting. I know it is the treatment. The last four days have been great without any incidents.

August 25, 1997

Yesterday afternoon I was talking to him about Nellikai water and how good it is:

> Let me tell you a story about a great ship named the *Titanic*—a ship that was considered unsinkable. When, some eighty-five years ago, the *Titanic* went under the sea, the news shocked the entire world. Thousands of lives were lost.

An iceberg sitting like a glistening white rock in the middle of the ocean was the culprit. It did not move to attack the ship, of course. It was immobile. But the ship was moving fast, and it hit the iceberg. Why do you think that happened?

The carelessness caused by the arrogance of the human mind created a terrible situation where there was no available alternative course except to hit the iceberg. If the captain and the crew had watched carefully and ran the ship slowly, the tragedy could have been avoided. But the owner of the ship wanted to reach New York in record time, so the captain's orders were to move the ship speedily.

Here, your anger is like an iceberg. You are the captain of your own mind. All you have to do is navigate your mind through the iceberg of anger slowly and carefully. Don't get into a situation where anger takes over your intellect and reasoning so that you have no control over who you are. Don't let anger attack your reason and judgment and scatter it into many pieces. The outcome of such an attack is the loss of your mind's stability. Then you are not the master anymore but a timid, helpless overworked lackey just like the captain on the *Titanic*. Though he worked hard to save the ship, he did so to no avail. The ship sank. People died.

Let's suppose the *Titanic* had the ability to fire torpedoes into the iceberg. The torpedoes would have blasted the iceberg to bits, and tragedy would have been averted. For you, the Nellikai water is your torpedo. It will disperse your iceberg of anger. It cools your heated brain and restores your mind's stability.

He gave me a big grin upon hearing this.

Later in the day when we were talking, I asked him on the portable computer:

Jalaja:	How do I look?
Krishna:	Ugly. Kidding.

We both laughed.

Jalaja:	What do you think of Nellekai water?
Krishna:	Terrific.
Nan:	Jal, why don't you take some vitamins for your tiredness and for sore muscles?
Jalaja:	I don't like to take vitamins.

Nan:	But you always tell us how important it is to take B complex and vitamin C for good health.
Krish:	Advice is for others.

We all just broke into laughter. His communication is really blossoming since February.

In the evening, Krish was feeling restless and, after his supper, repeatedly asked for some bread to eat. But even last night, his behavior was under control. He did not take the bread and make a mess out of it. He did not jump up and down. He did not make demands or querulously ask for things. He asked in a nice voice. He did not get mad when I said politely that he had had a very good supper just an hour ago. He can divert his mind from food with good music or a good audiotape. The stressed-out mind is asking for food, not his hungry stomach. He was quiet for a moment and, then again, asked for more food. I gave him half a cheese sandwich and went into my room and locked the door.

Once I went into my room, he kept quiet, listening to some tapes. I have to believe in the treatment. Otherwise, I lose hope about his behavior. Krish's major problem now is behavior, behavior, behavior. It will either make him or break him.

August 26, 1997

This morning, he was Mr. Groucho. He had his bath, and later he was protesting. His Dad wanted him to study, but Krish refused, and on top of that he was whining. I gave him a lecture:

Ultimately, your responsible behavior will help appease your autism. You have enough education and enough speech and other skills to lead a good life. But your behavior is interfering. You have to finally decide how you want to behave. I can't decide for you. It is solely your decision. That's what is called motivation. I can give you skills, but not motivation. It has to come from within. In *For the Love of Anne*, Anne had it. That is how she made it in life, by shattering the walls of autism. Krish, you have to make up your mind to control your peevishness and cultivate a positive attitude in life. I can give you pointers like a road map, but you have to do the traveling. In real estate, they proclaim,

"Location, location, location." To you, I proclaim, "Behavior, behavior, behavior." It is up to you to make it in life.

I left the room. He was eating his sandwich, but I didn't hear any whining. That means my lecture was having some effect on his mind. A half hour later, he went to his study room, with no whining and no protesting, and started studying with Dad. My lectures seem to work much of the time, but I have to spend a lot of time lecturing him every day. Why can't he retain my advice?

August 27, 1997

Yesterday, while we were watching *60 Minutes,* Krish became tense and very frustrated. He already had supper, but he wanted more. Whenever he says, "I am hungry!" in an urgent, demanding voice, I know that he is having one of those episodes. I was eating some cereal when he tried to grab it. He was on the verge of going berserk. I left the room, went in to my bedroom, and closed the door.

He wanted to take his shower. For some reason, when he is in this mood, taking a twenty-minute shower helps him to calm down. So we let him take showers three or four times a day. It is harmless; it is not like drugging him with potent medications. After a few minutes, Nan turned the water on for his shower. Adjusting the water so that it is neither too hot nor too cold is a problem for Krish despite his physics and math skills. Right now, we don't worry about that. A time will come when his fine-motor skills will develop to a point where his hands can fine-tune the shower knob. We don't want to pressure him to learn every skill when he is not physically ready.

After the shower, Krish felt relaxed. He studied physics for an hour. In the meantime, I called my son-in-law, Vish, to find out more about seizures. Nan and I suspect that Krish might be having occasional seizures. His frustration seems to come out of the blue. His behavior changes drastically, he doesn't listen to reason, and he behaves wildly. Can this be the result of a seizure? Vishwa, who is doing a cardiology fellowship, said that it could be:

Krishna should have an EEG right away. There are different kinds of seizures. We have medications made for all of them. If it is that, you need not go through this alone. It can be handled. Maybe he is having a temporal one. The EEG is very effective in detecting this problem. The MRI shows the structural abnormalities of the brain. It detects tumors and things like that. You can do that also for Krish.

This was good news, for I actually wanted Krish to be having seizures. At least then, I thought, there would be an explanation for his unruly behavior and sudden emotional swings.

That night, as usual, my husband and I talked about Krish. This dialogue between us has been going on for years. Always, we are planning what to do next. Suddenly, I am having doubts about Nellikai water. Nothing seems to work now. Haldol doesn't work, nor, now, does Nellikai seem to. But I am not altogether correct in saying that Nellikai doesn't help. Since we started the treatment, we have had to endure only two or three episodes of Krish's unruly mood swings in the past two weeks. Their intensity was also much less.

These mood swings come and go, especially in the evening. During those times, we are paralyzed. Even though I try to reason with him, it doesn't always help. When we leave him alone listening to classical music, it does help sometimes. A hot shower also seems to help him. But why must such an intelligent, gentle human being have these attacks? Is this hysteria? I have to go to a neurologist to find out. But when he was young, we visited a few neurologists. They did not help him in the least, so I gave up on their being able to help Krish and this family.

After Krish's diagnosis at Children's Hospital, we went to see a neurologist who gave him Haldol. This medication did more harm than good. He was asleep more hours than he was awake. Already, the little awareness he had, the few sparks that I had been fanning feverishly into flame, was slowly dying out. He also started drooling, something he had never done before taking this awful medication. Now one more bizarre behavior had been added to his repertoire.

We soon stopped the Haldol and tried another doctor, a psychiatrist in New York who believed in megavitamin therapy. We decided to try this treatment for Krish, who at the time was six years old. Dr. Cott gave us hope by telling us that Krish would grow up to be near normal. He also believed that Krish was intelligent, so finding this man was like finding a shady tree in the desert after a long walk in the scorching sun. For eight years, until he went to Tokyo for schooling, I gave him twenty-two vitamin pills a day. Over all those years, there was no obvious improvement in Krish's abilities or behavior. Still, I believe they must have done some good to his nervous system.

We also consulted an allergy specialist, Dr. O'Shea, who asked us to stay away from artificial coloring, flavors, and sweets. To this day, we are careful about these things.

When Krish was nine years old, we took him to the Philadelphia Brain Institute, run by Drs. Doman and Delacato. I was impressed with Dr. Delacato when I met him the first time. He spent a lot of time with Krish and us. He sincerely wanted to help.

For the first time since Krish was diagnosed as autistic, I heard phrases like sensory problem, sensory integration, and so on. According to Dr. Delacato, in the autistic, it is either hyper or hypo. Either way, autistics are impaired in their reception of stimuli through the senses. He attributed all Krish's bizarre behaviors to malfunctioning senses.

Krish was diagnosed as hyper in hearing. We were told that he heard every minute sound in the environment, whether it be a neighbor's telephone ringing or a crow cawing in the yard. In his vision and tactility, he was hypo, meaning he wasn't able to see or feel as well as others. I found Dr. Delacato's theory logical and fascinating.

We were advised to do nearly three hours of exercises with him every day. Though we spent all those hours with him for a year, we did not see much improvement in Krish's behavior, so we eventually stopped Delacato's exercise regimen. In retrospect, I feel that we did not do enough justice to the program by stopping it prematurely.

When he was having trouble in school, around the age of twelve or thirteen, I went to see a local neurologist. He prescribed Melleril. The medicine also proved to have side effects, like masturbation, which he started to engage in irrespective of the setting. We soon stopped giving him Melleril, and his public displays disappeared within a week.

When he was sixteen, we went to see a neurologist from a Boston hospital who was very much involved in bringing the Tokyo School to Massachusetts. The medication he prescribed for Krish didn't help either. He was spending more time in bed. So, that too, we stopped giving him. The doctor was very honest with us. He never said the medicine would help Krish; he said a few autistic children get some relief from the medicine and that he had no idea whether Krish would be helped.

Another neurologist that we went to said, "the autistic cannot be helped by medications because we don't even know what causes it, whether it is chemical or not, organic or not, genetic or not." He was so pessimistic. After two decades of searching for professional help, we gave it up.

From then on, Nan and I were opposed to medications for calming Krish down. The side effects of all those that we had tried were more demoralizing than they were uplifting.

Right now, we are worried about his behavior. Instead, we should be celebrating his major breakthroughs. He is so bright, so humorous, so talented, so gentle. Yet his behavior is killing his spirit as well as ours. This is going to be our number-one priority—improving his behavior. Once we conquer this, he should be all right with the skills he has. He can always have someone to do simple things for him, and he can write books. He writes such beautiful English.

August 28, 1997

There is a saying that the body and mind are one and that if the mind is weak, the body, too, will be weak. Similarly, if the body is weak, the mind will be weak.

Dr. Inosa, the founder of the Japanese School, believed that autistic children are very weak in mind and body. They lack the power of endurance. By building up the physical body, the mind also can be strengthened. So in the Japanese School, physical education plays a major role in teaching the autistic child. The physical education is given in groups because the school doesn't believe in one-on-one teaching.

According to Dr. Inosa, since autistic children live a truly solitary existence, there is no point in teaching them individually. It is like performing heart surgery to remove cataracts from the eyes. She believed that by gathering these children in a group, they would start relying on one another and thus engage in group dynamics. The support from the group is extremely important for each child's growth. The ability to participate in and adapt to a group through physical education is believed to spread to other spheres of life and study.

Restless, bizarre movements and the inability to play with peers can be overcome through this group physical education. This is the basis of Dr. Inosa's daily life therapy in her school. Her theory sounded interesting and authentic to us.

Academics are given less importance. The daily living skills are given paramount importance in the Japanese School, both in Boston and Tokyo. Krish spent more than seven years of his life in these schools. But, unfortunately, Krishna didn't gain much. Even though the school's philosophy appeals to my logical mind, I cannot comprehend why so many autistic children who attend the Japanese School seem unable to break through the walls of autism. What is lacking in Dr. Inosa's philosophy? Maybe she did not lack anything. Maybe it simply means that the solution to autism is beyond the reach of us frail, imperfect human beings. We need God's intervention for solving the mysteries of autism. I have to say in all honesty that many parents were, and still are, happy with the program.

Since the school doesn't believe in individuality, it cannot recognize each child's individual strengths. Krishna has an aptitude for math. But because the school believes in group learning, it cannot easily teach him high math. The school had him doing simple arithmetic in a group, and he was bored; many of his outbursts were due, it seems to me, to his being bored.

I still believe that the Japanese School teachers are extremely committed and sincere in what they do. They work twelve to fifteen hours a day. Every one of them is an Anne Sullivan in their dedication. I also feel enormous respect for the late Dr. Inosa. She was wholly dedicated to autistic children, and she showed unwavering kindness and understanding toward them.

When he came home in 1993, after seven years in the Japanese school, Krish was wetting the bed every day. He was aggressive, and he was depressed. He had so many bizarre behaviors: running in the parking lot the minute we stopped the car, taking bites out of the soap cake, grimacing, looking at his hands, flapping his hands, spitting on one hand and then rubbing it with his other hand, drooling deliberately and then rubbing it on his chin, moon walking with squint eyes, running aimlessly from one room to the other, looking angrily at his tensed-up fingers (this we call "consulting his hands"), moving his fingers (this is when he is not mad), grinding his teeth, unnecessary teasing, and laughing uncontrollably to the point of choking. Now, all these behaviors have abated except looking angrily at his hands, as if he were consulting them, and the occasional angry outburst.

He returned home from the residential program with no computer skills, no reading skills, no writing skills, no vocabulary, no effective means of communication. In retrospect, I taught him more than this school, or any other school, ever did. Maybe it was not the school's problem; instead, it was his problem. We didn't rely on conventional methods, but on whatever worked for him. We ignored his output deficiency and concentrated on his strengths, whereas the school put all the emphasis on his output. In my opinion, his nervous system was not ready for this, and he was failing miserably. This in turn discouraged him, hence the anger.

We had to be very innovative to teach him academics. The school did not believe in one on one, and Krishna was unable to learn in a group. He simply did not have the necessary concentration to survive in a group. The distraction was too much to handle. So he came home with fewer skills and enormous anger.

The school thought that I gave him too much love and that I spoiled him. Once, I had an argument with Dr. Inosa in Tokyo. She said, "You should not say that he is handsome. Praise in turn makes him disobedient and unruly." I said, "Already he is disabled in many ways. He is aware of that. This awareness is enough to shatter anybody's self-esteem. I want to make him feel good. So I praise him like that." She did not agree with me. In later years, I began to see her point and tried to implement what she said. Her advice was beneficial when he was in a manipulating mood.

I started my role as his teacher when he was a baby. I never gave up that role until he went to Japan at the age of fourteen. Again, when he came home to stay for good, at age twenty-two, Nan and I resumed the teaching. I can never forgive myself for not having had faith in our own teaching ability and for relinquishing it to other people, and thus relinquishing his growth.

Now, after four years, he is doing signals and systems, differential equations, and quantum mechanics at home. He is also writing eloquently on the computer. Right now, he is writing about autism. His written English is very good, and he has a phenomenal vocabulary. You can ask him the meaning of any word, and he will give it to you. He is our dictionary. Another skill he has developed since he has been home is using the computer. While I write this, I feel my confidence is building up. Nan and I talked about all this last night.

Prior to last night's talk, we were saying that we made a stupid decision in keeping Krish at home. How dumb we were to think we could spend every minute of our lives with him. Maybe we should have put him in a residential program when he was young. We ignored everybody's advice. Now it is too late because we have invested too much time in him.

We talked about Joe Kennedy, Sr. He was smart to put his daughter Rosemary in an institution. He and his wife, Rose, didn't spoil their lives. Compared to us, they were extremely wealthy. They could have kept the retarded girl at home and had people attend to her around the clock. They had the money to do that. Here, when we worked with Krishna when he was young, we didn't have that financial freedom. Every penny counted. We had to do everything ourselves. We were middle-class people. We had no inheritance or financial support from our relatives. Yet later in his life, when we had achieved financial security, Nan gave up high-paying jobs to take care of Krish. Are we crazy?

Something must be wrong. We are not normal. That is why Krish is not. We were going downhill in our confidence. After all of our conscientious work, we felt we were stupid and unrealistic and crazy. And we felt sad about that. Then we started talking about what we have achieved in doing all this intense work. What is the effect of this cause? That's when we realized that we had, in our sorrow and pain, forgotten the past Krish and the improvements he has made over these four years and the first fourteen years of his life at home. That's unfair to Krish. He has been working so hard and improving tremendously. As we talked more and more, we started feeling better and better.

The ayurvedic treatment has got a lot to do with his improvements. His education is also reducing his aimlessness. If he had been doing the same basic simple arithmetic, his mind would not be challenged. If we challenge Krish's mind, we can reduce his restlessness. Structuring alone is not enough. His mind has to be challenged and involved in order to be sharp and alert. That is where the schools went wrong in his case. I know my son, and I know this is the right method for him.

August 29, 1997

As a Hindu, I believe in reincarnation. The individual soul doesn't die with one's physical death. The soul enters another body, just as energy is not destroyed but converted from one to another form like kinetic to electric.

I also believe in cause and effect. We have Krish for a reason, whereas my sisters and brothers and my in-laws have normal children. I must have done something terrible in my previous births to deserve this. There must be a definite cause for this effect called autism. How can a result exist without a cause? Even though we don't see electricity or gravity with our naked eye, can we say they don't exist? Just because I don't see the cause of autism doesn't mean there is no cause.

For instance, Andrew Cunnanan committed suicide after murdering five people. He really did not suffer enough for his crimes. In one minute, he ended his life. Suppose he is born again, he might be apprehended for a crime he did not commit, and he might suffer lifetime imprisonment or the death penalty. We have seen that happen.

Nobody goes free in nature. Nature is fair and just. There are no favors in nature. No matter how much you repent, you have to suffer the consequences. Even though you may be a brilliant scientist or a very nice man, if you cross the road without looking both ways, you may be hit by a car. That's nature. Your scientific or humanistic talents will not save you at that moment of crossing. There is a natural rule that you have to look both ways before crossing.

If you plant a rose garden and take care of it, you get roses. You cannot envy the neighbor who is getting apples because she planted an apple tree. You reap what you sow. So I am reaping autism for what I did in my previous birth. Maybe I neglected my child for my other interests, or maybe I was careless when I was taking care of my neighbor's or my relative's child. How do I know what I did to deserve this?

Maybe the effects of some causes are produced not right away, but a long time afterward. A plantain tree gives bananas in a year or two, whereas a coconut tree gives coconuts after fifteen or twenty years of care. The result is not immediate. Just because a man and woman make love for a few minutes does not mean the baby is born that very day. Their action takes nine months to make a baby, whereas cooking produces results right away. In one birth, you can get all of your action's results. Some results take a few births before they bear fruit. God is never unjust. He rewards and punishes according to one's actions. This is the Hindu Karma theory.

I was feeling unhappy. I very much wanted to know what I did wrong. In nature, we cannot know everything. We don't always remember what we did when we were three or four years old. Even in this life, memory is a problem for many of us. Can we know why so many seeds look alike but produce entirely different plants?

August 30, 1997

When my husband came to bed, I was depressed about Krishna. What good is it if he does great math and physics but can't adjust the water for his shower or tie his shoes? Nan did not agree with me. He reminded me of Dr. Steven Hawkins, who is afflicted with motor neuron disease:

> When he was a young man, he was diagnosed with this disease. He was not that great a student during his undergraduate program. This diagnosis motivated him to go into graduate studies. He wanted to get his Ph.D. He was not even sure that he would be alive to finish. That inspired him to work very hard. He wanted to achieve because of the disease. He was slowly losing the use of the legs, hands, and so on. At last, he lost his speech also. He was devastated when that happened. He got a divorce. He is now totally paralyzed with no speech.
>
> A nurse is always with him, to take care of his bathroom needs, his eating, dressing, and bathing. Everything is done for him by a nurse. He cannot take care of himself in the most basic areas. Yet, he occupies the most prestigious chair in Cambridge University—a chair once occupied by Newton. He communicates through the computer. He is living an extremely productive life in spite of his disability.
>
> Compared to him, Krishna can walk, use the bathroom, take his own shower (though the water temperature needs to be adjusted), brush his teeth, feed himself, go to the YMCA. He can do a lot of things with his hands, except tie his shoes. He talks in a limited way, but he definitely communicates. He is also very bright in mathematics and physics. In four years, he has covered fifteen years of math and physics and electrical engineering with only two to three hours of learning a day.

What do you call that? Is it brilliance or what? Let us not get discouraged now when he is doing so well. The bad behavior lasts for only fifteen or twenty minutes a day. In that, too, if you leave him alone for half an hour, he comes back with energy and enthusiasm. You are really making a mountain out of a molehill. Don't compare him with normal people of his age. Look at him with his autism, and see how far he has come in spite of the disease. If you compare Professor Hawkins with people who have motor abilities, he is worse than a newborn baby. You have to consider his abilities. You cannot say he is a cipher because he is not using the toilet, any more than you can say Krish is a cipher because he throws a tantrum for ten minutes or he cannot adjust his own bath water. Look at his intelligence in solving mathematical problems.

I felt a lot better about Krish after hearing about Professor Hawkins.

August 31, 1997

I spent all of today visualizing my dream for a nearly normal son and what it would take to achieve this. I came up with three rules for myself: (1) faithfully believe in your beliefs, (2) relentlessly pursue your dreams, and (3) know that recognition will come sooner or later. We should not give up. I have three stories to illustrate these rules.

People who achieve are people who persevere. Without perseverance, results are not forthcoming. For perseverance, you need conviction in your beliefs and in your ability. Thomas Edison did 2,000 experiments before producing the light bulb. He had enormous conviction in his belief that it would work out in spite of so many failed experiments. To him, the 2,000 failed experiments were 2,000 successful steps to an invention. That is perseverance.

The story about the founder of Sony Corporation, Akio Morita, is very inspiring. After the Second World War, Akio Morita went ahead to develop a machine called a tape recorder. When he tried to sell it, he had little success. Even though he saw some usefulness in the gadget, especially in the courts, the Japanese didn't think it had much use.

Then one day, when he was strolling through the shopping centers, out of curiosity, he went inside an antique shop to look around. While he was looking at the pieces, he saw a lady buying an antique chair at an exorbitant price. He wondered why anybody would buy a chair at such a high price. It occurred to him then that it is not for lack of funds that people do not buy. People come up with the money if they really desire something.

Similarly, people would buy a tape recorder if they found some usefulness in it. He had to convince the public of the usefulness of his product. This would spur sales. He appointed a team of people to think of different uses of the machine. This idea helped him to sell the tape recorder. Instead of designing a product and selling it, he watched the people and what they would like to have and then designed it.

That is how he came up with the idea of a Walkman. He saw the Japanese spending three or fours hours on a subway and doing a lot of walking, since few Japanese drive their cars to work. He felt that they could use a gadget during those hours of walking. The Walkman was an instantaneous success. What does this story show? It shows that Akio Morita relentlessly pursued what he believed in. So great was his conviction that he had to succeed.

The Indian astrophysicist Chandrasekar received the Nobel Prize for work he did when he was a young man. He did that work in his mind, while on a boat from India to London. Once in England, his boss did not appreciate his work; he thought it was far fetched. This discouraged Chandrasekar, so he went into another area. Over the next few decades, people did a good deal of work, and came closer and closer to the theory Chandrasekar had thought of years earlier. He was awarded the Nobel Prize decades after having done his work. What is the lesson that we derive from this? If at one time, the world does not recognize something, that does not mean the world will never recognize it.

We also, in Krish's case, pursue his growth relentlessly and without any doubt. The local school system always made us feel as though what we were doing was not academically appropriate for Krish. Now the DMR militates against us for teaching him physics and math. The whole world might laugh at us now for our conviction. It might even think that we are in our own world. But at some point, the world will recognize what we have been doing is good for Krish. Right now, our energy should be on Krish, not on worrying about the world. We as parents have to be doing whatever we think is right for Krish, irrespective of the world's opinion.

KRISHNA IN HIS FIRST YEAR

With mom

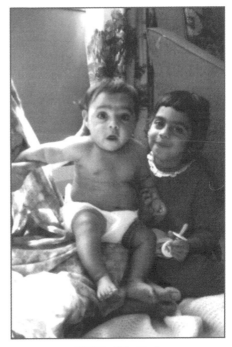

With Malini

With Dad

Krishna as a child

Krishna at two

Stressful Canobie Lake Park
trip—Krishna & his sister
tired out

Krishna at five

Krishna at seven

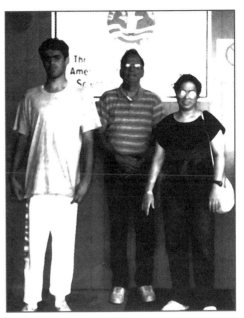
Krishna, Dad & Mom — 1992

As our life was extremely hectic around Krishna,
we took very few pictures after his third year.

Krishna taking Ayurvedic treatment — Dhara

Septemeber 1997

September 1, 1997

This morning, Krishna wanted me to put the water on for his shower. I said in a nice voice, "Krish, without coffee, I can't do it. I am going to have my coffee first. If you want coffee, you can join me in the kitchen." For the first time in a year, he joined me for coffee. I was still drinking while he finished his coffee and asked for breakfast. I said, "I have to finish my coffee; will you please wait until I finish?" He waited very patiently and did not demand anything; in fact, he then spontaneously said:

Krish:	I love you.
Jalaja:	I love you, too. Do you think action has to speak louder than words?
Krishna:	Yes, I do.
Jalaja:	Can you show your love for me in actions, also, like writing your essay? That will please me immensely.
Krish:	Okay.

Over my coffee, I also told him:

Once a great scientist said, "genius is 1 percent inspiration, and 99 percent perspiration." Einstein worked very hard. From a deep and subtle concept, he discovered epoch-making laws in physics. He let logic take him wherever it could. He did not let his work be thwarted by doubts or negativism. Thirty or forty years later, his work was proved. He is the father of the theory of relativity. We are not bigger than he is, so if he worked hard, we all have to work hard. Krish, you have to work even harder with more discipline in order to break the shell of autism.

He was listening attentively, with a serious look on his face.

All morning, he was very polite and kind. For the first time, he went, without being prodded, to the computer to work on his essay. He waited for lunch, set the table, and ate without being demanding. Above all, he listened well. He did not constantly challenge me.

Discipline is the only thing that can make him behave well. He is bright, but his behavior is ruining him. If we really love him, we have to be tough with him. If the mind is disciplined, he won't go berserk over small things. For the mind to be strong, we have to work the emotional muscles, just as we do the physical muscles for the body to be strong. We don't stay in bed all day long and read *National Enquirer* to develop our muscles. Hard work in the gym develops the muscles. The same hard work strengthens our mind. Nothing is possible without discipline. When we do as we please, the mind becomes flabby and undisciplined.

Recently, I saw a program on CBS called *Ordinary and Extraordinary*. The program talked about a couple of brain-damaged people and how they almost recovered to normalcy because they did not give up. The first case was about Brian, a young man who wanted to become a pilot. He was working on a plane when an accident left him severely brain damaged.

After surgery, he was unable to move the right part of his body, including his fingers. Eventually, when he got a little bit of movement back in his fingers, he was given some clay to play with. Since he had very little to do, he played with the clay almost every day. In time, he started adding a nose or a mouth to the figures he was trying to mold. Slowly, he became interested in sculpture.

Today, he is able to sell his creations for as much as $6,000. According to him, by becoming a sculptor instead of a pilot, he has made a mark on history. This, he feels, is better than his original dream of becoming a pilot.

I was very much touched by the story. It was inspirational to see the progress in Brian. To me, it meant that Krish, too, has a lot of hope. With lots of hard work, he can make it in life. With intensity, growth is not just proportional to time, it is exponential. Krish also can make a mark in history if he chooses to. In my opinion, he can reach more people by being autistic than he could by being normal.

Then a doubt occurred to me: perhaps Krish is not as motivated as people like Brian. He can work for a maximum of a couple of hours with lots of breaks, but not for more than that at a time. His brain doesn't have enough energy. Because of that, I feel Krish may be hurt in the part of the brain that is the seat of motivation. It must be the frontal lobe, which controls the emotions as well as the motivation. Is his frontal lobe hurt? Right now, he has enough skills. All he needs is behavior. But that seems to be an unattainable goal.

Today, Malini has arrived from Chicago. She says Krish's face doesn't look as sharp as it was in May, the last time she was home.

She also is concerned about his weight gain. She feels Krish's disruptive behavior is due to our having run out of an ayurvedic medicine that he had taken. She also thinks that so long as the ayurvedic treatment is kept up, he behaves well. He doesn't need to be disciplined so much if he is consistently on the ayurvedic treatment. The medicines do the job, she feels. So her suggestion is to go to India and get the treatment right away.

When a tennis player has an injury, he can't play much. When his injury has healed, he may go to a tennis camp to revitalize his game. In the same way, Krish's behavior has worsened. The best thing to do is to give him the treatment as early as we can so that his behavior problem is arrested and he doesn't get any worse.

We went for a long drive and ate pizza. Krish was well behaved. Then, in the night, he came to our bedroom. We were all talking and having a good time. Krish did not want to leave me. He was trying to be nice and loving. He started massaging my left arm when I talked about the shooting pain in my arm. Krish is a very loving, sensitive, warm person. Without the autism, he would be a wonderful gentleman. But this enigma called autism makes him look stupid, wild, and uncaring. How I wish it would leave him alone.

September 2, 1997

Krishna woke up very early this morning. Malini said that he came to her room four or five times in the night. For the last few weeks, his sleeping has not been normal. His behavior always plummets along with inadequate sleep.

He was good with me this morning. I was very firm with him, and I did not budge an inch. But it was not the same with Nan. Nan was too nice. Usually, it is very hard for Nan to discipline Krish, and he manipulates his father much too much. If Krish says he wants a break, Nan thinks that is what Krish needs. He always tries to understand his motives. So, of course, do I, but I see Krish as largely manipulating.

This morning, I was very upset with Nan. I had not been yielding to Krish, and he was doing just fine. But then Krishna became demanding; his behavior, uncontrollable. I got very depressed. All the good behavior, the listening, the obedience, his worrying about my approval, all have been squandered. I became hysterical. What's more, whenever Nan and I fight with each other over the methods of discipline, Krishna gets worse. It is a vicious cycle. We are fueling each other's frustration. We get frustrated with his behavior, then he gets upset because we are frustrated. Then we become more frustrated because he is upset. This leads to still more misbehavior. Once this cycle starts, it is hard to stop it.

I have reached my peak of insanity. My clear thinking is totally gone. We are trying to save an autistic with his severe behavior problems. In the process, I am losing myself. I am becoming hysterical and out of control. I wanted Krishna to stay home with us. But now, it looks as if I will end up in a mental hospital. The stress of coping with his behavior is too much. I am being destroyed in the process of improving him. I believe it is okay to sacrifice myself though I do not want to sacrifice him. What have I gained by sacrificing my life all these years? Nothing, it seems. If I can't make him a functioning human being, I have lost.

Today, I feel I am a failure. My work with him has not paid off. All that I have ended up with in my life is enormous hard work, and all for nothing. I lost out on my youth. Now, I am losing my middle years. I am not too far away from death. Before I know it, I'll be old. To tell the truth, I don't know how the last twenty years of my life were spent. Before I know it, another twenty years will pass the same way. When I get to be old, I will be thinking how did I get here? Where did the years go?

September 3, 1997

Last night, I felt totally lost regarding how to handle Krishna with his tantrums. I had a lot of nagging doubt. Is Krishna crumbling under my strict discipline? Should I be less stern? I wish his mind were a little stronger and could cope with life's everyday inconveniences and displeasures. If anything goes wrong, he is off his rocker. It is becoming clearer, as years pass, that his behavior is the biggest obstacle to his having a normal, livable life and even, perhaps, to his recovery. He has enough skills to have a good life if he has a good, positive attitude about life. Although he has several reasons to be negative about himself and his future, he has reason enough to be positive also.

He is bright and good looking; he has dedicated parents and enough money for a very comfortable life; he receives good treatment in India; he has a loving sister and other family members. All he needs now is faith in himself. I have read many positive-thinking writers to him—American authors like Norman Vincent Peal and Dr. Schuller, and Indian philosophers like Swami Chinmayananda and Adi Shankara. I don't know why he should feel so hopeless and frustrated at times. I hate to drug him with Haldol or Melleril in order to reduce his anxiety.

I was talking to my daughter about sending Krish to a neuropsychiatrist and telling her about my concern regarding a psychiatrist. Once a psychiatrist sees Krish, a report will be written about him, and that report will find its way to other professionals. It will become a permanent record. Every move of his will be judged in the light of his psychiatric evaluation.

On the other hand, a neurologist strikes me as being far more scientific. He is more concerned about the lesions in the brain. A neurologist knows which part of the brain controls speech, which part controls behavior, and so on. He takes an MRI or an EEG and tries to find out the abnormalities of the brain; then he prescribes treatment. A psychiatrist, on the other hand, would watch Krish's behavior and diagnose him based on it. Then Krish's every move is explained according to his diagnosis. That is scary.

The other day, I slipped and fell. My neck was hurting, so I was wearing a collar. A psychiatrist from DMR came to our house to see me. I wasn't feeling well, so I canceled our meeting, but not before he saw me with the collar. When my husband later went to a meeting at DMR, a person from the state agency implied that my neck pain had something to do with Krish and that we are under a lot of stress. If I had a normal son, they wouldn't have implied that my neck pain was caused by him. In reality, I fell down and hurt my neck.

My main concern is that DMR not dictate to us whether Krish should stay home or not. People are scrutinizing us because of Krish's autism. He is a little frustrated, but that certainly doesn't mean he is mentally ill. If we go to a psychiatrist, Krish will be labeled, and that label will stay on his records permanently. I do not want that. On top of it, I don't even know whether they could cure him of his behavior that is due to anxiety about his future and his speech problem. If that was the case, why then are there so many residential placements for the autistic?

I decided to cancel our appointment with the neuropsychiatrist. I decided to go with the neurologist. I want to know whether anything is structurally wrong with Krish's brain. I want scientific facts, not suspect opinions.*

September 4, 1997

Last night, I couldn't fall asleep. I was thinking about Krish. Yesterday evening, Krish's father became so upset with Krish's behavior that he decided not to give in to his demands. He also wanted Krish to help clean the house. Krish did not want to help, and he was whining and screaming. "I don't want to! I don't want to!" Nan wouldn't let him get away with this behavior. He said in a no-nonsense voice that he had better help around the house or he is in big trouble.

Krish started wrestling with his Dad. The fight went on for only a few minutes. Krish respects and loves his father very dearly, but when he is fighting or angry, he looks and acts like a demon. After the fighting, Krish became calmer and started doing the work. He vacuumed the whole house and cleaned up his room with no resistance. Maybe he needs to fight occasionally to release his stress, his tension, his anger, and his frustration. The fights never last long. After a fight, he always feels sorry, and he always looks calmer. On the other hand, I always look agitated. Why can't I let go of this fight? Why do I feel so hopeless and victimized?

For the past few weeks, he has been altogether out of sync. He looks like a ship without an anchor, tossing to and fro. Yesterday, he looked like a computer with a virus. He went berserk. His stubbornness made no sense. To whatever we said, he said no:

Jalaja:	Do you want to be a good person?
Krish:	No, I don't.
Jalaja:	Do you want to be a bad person?
Krish:	No, I don't.

---

*In June 1999, however, I reversed my position and sought out the help of a psychiatrist for Krish.

Jalaja:	Do you want to be Krishna?
Krish:	No, I don't.
Jalaja:	Do you at least want to be a human being?
Krish:	No, I don't.
Jalaja:	Do you then want to be God?
Krish:	Yes.
Jalaja:	Why?
Krish:	Freedom.
Jalaja:	Freedom from what?
Krish:	Autism. I can cure myself.

The other day, he took a quart of orange juice and started drinking it so fast that he was gasping for breath. I did not want him to choke on orange juice, so I grabbed the carton from him and asked him to slow down. He could have drunk a whole bottle of Clorox before he realized that it was not juice. He was drinking so fast that his brain would not have had enough time to process the information of what he was drinking and stop the action. He is so hyper that I feel short of breath in his presence.

Before he got that cut on his finger, he was like a smooth-running Lexus. But now, he is like a car that has an engine problem and won't start. I am coaxing, cajoling, begging, threatening, and kicking the car. Nothing seems to work. The car goes puff, puff, puff, puff, and then stops. After a lot of work, it does start and run, but it stops at the green lights with lots of cars behind it. It will stall on a hill and start rolling backward. That's what Krish is like now. I wish I could turn Krish in for a new model.

A boxer has to be physically fit, mentally tough, and emotionally secure before entering the ring. I have to be the same way in order to wage this war on autism. This war cannot be won by a weakling. Right now, I am not energetic enough—physically, mentally, or emotionally—to fight this war. I need some time to recuperate. I need to go away, or I will die of pain all over my body. Ayurvedic treatment will definitely help me.

Nan feels that I should go away for a month, and he will manage Krish with Richard. My mental strength and physical energy are so important for Krishna that I myself should undergo ayurvedic treatment for my aches and pains. I agree with Nan on that point. I feel exhausted, but I don't feel good about leaving them alone. I feel downright guilty about putting the entire burden directly on Nan. Will I ever live to do anything I want without a conflict? I stay here with the physical pain, or I go away with the guilt—either way I am damned. This is what autism does to a parent.

September 5, 1997

Today, Krish is sick. I am glad that we can leave him alone without structuring his time. That gives us time off from him. I don't need to feel guilty about that. What a great feeling! But my feeling of happiness doesn't last long because Nan is also sick. That means my workload increases with serving two sick people.

I saw a program in which a woman was gored by an angry bull. She was thrashed repeatedly for a few minutes, and then the bull walked away from her. She was barely alive. When she was taken to the hospital, it took more than two years for her to recover. A few minutes of being attacked by a bull took two years of recovery time.

In Krish's case, for more than two decades, he has been viciously attacked by the relentless raging bull called autism. It is mind-boggling for me to think that Krish survives these attacks and makes improvements on top of that. If this is not grace, what then is?

September 6, 1997

Krish is sick today, but quite cheerful in spite of it. This morning, Krish and his Dad went to drop off Malini at Brigham Hospital for her subinternship in neurosurgery.

I have been watching the TV coverage of Princess Diana's death. It is very sad that at so young an age her life was plucked away by such violence. This shouldn't happen to any human being. But it does happen around the world. At least she did not suffer in poverty or shame. She did not have a disabled husband or disabled children. She wasn't ugly or fat; nor was she in great pain owing to cancer or another illness. She was not beaten to death by a drunken husband. In my opinion, though she died young, she had a wonderful life, with beauty, money, fame, good children, good health, and the true love she found in Dodi. I have seen people suffer a great deal more than she did.

We have to count our blessings in order to know happiness. Without doing so, I never could have survived my son's autism.

When the world is so occupied with beauty, youth, and glamour, where is the room for a disabled person? Usually, a celebrity has to be afflicted with a serious illness before it gets any attention.

I was told that there are fifty million disabled people in the United States. In the first sixty years of this century, some 50,000 mentally retarded people were forcibly sterilized in order to stop them from procreating children with not so good genes.

Many people will find me angry or bitter. I am speaking from my experience. How many times has Krish been mistreated, stared at, and not given respect because he is autistic. The world is so cruel at times. We have lost our compassion and tolerance. We have tolerance for the young and beautiful, but not for the disabled. Very rarely, I do see a TV show about a disabled person, about how courageously the family fights for their child, and what immense stresses the family endures in raising him or her.

September 7, 1997

Even though Krish writes intelligently, his behavior has no connection whatsoever to his ability to intellectualize. When Nan asked why, Krish wrote:

Krish:	The reason is rigidity. The more rigid one's mind is, the more disparity one finds between attitude and behavior.
Nan:	What's attitude?
Krish:	Attitude is a result of two things. One is brainwashing, and another is thinking. Thinking is the right way to develop attitude.
Nan:	Why?
Krish:	Thinking connects cause and effect. By analyzing cause and its effect, one can develop the right attitude.

This morning, Krish wanted to take a shower, and Nan told him no since Krish had a very bad cold and a severe, lung-collapsing cough. So Nan gave him the choice:

Do you want to be a bull-headed, rigid, idiotic autistic, or do you want to be an intelligent person who understands the relationship between cause and effect? You have a choice. The cause of taking a shower will lead to the effect of developing fever and pneumonia, and more coughing, and prolonging the sickness.

The water was already running. Krish, who normally showers three times a day, took the responsibility on himself to get well, and chose not to take the shower.

Krish was reading one of Richard Feynman's books. He is a well-known physicist. He said that once Newton's laws were considered God given. Einstein proved Newton's laws to be wrong. Hence, we now know everything can be wrong. Krish read that and started hyperventilating. Whenever he does that, it means that he has something to say. When Nan asked him what he wanted to say, Krish wrote on the computer: "Daring humility—far too humble. Newton was not totally wrong but only at high velocities close to that of light." Krish is a born writer and a philosopher as well. Why won't he write every day? He writes his essay on autism on the computer only very rarely. But now we cannot push him because he is very sick. Let him get better first.

September 8, 1997

Good news! Our tickets to India were confirmed. We are leaving on October 23 and returning on January 26. Krish will have three months of treatment.

My million-dollar question for today is, why doesn't he do anything on his own—why not even a simple task, like making a sandwich or coffee? If I direct him, step by step, he will do it, but he doesn't do the entire thing on his own. Why is that? He needs to be pushed or encouraged or tutored. He needs constant cueing. But he has no problem in deriving an equation step by step on his own. There he doesn't require any help. Why is this?

Is it a short-term memory problem or a coordination problem, an eye problem or a motivation problem? He seems to have problems across the board. The brain is hurt all over. The speech part is hurt, the fine-motor skills part is hurt, and the behavior part of the brain is hurt. That's why, despite all the work we do with him, day and night, he is improving so very slowly. But it is not the case with academics. There, his brain is shining like the lustrous sun, not covered with the dark cloak of autism. How is it possible that the intellectual part of his brain is unscathed by his brain damage?

This evening, right after supper, he was in a bad mood for no apparent reason. We left him alone for half an hour to calm down. Right now, he is okay. He is hearing the tape on General Patton. He loves to hear these tapes. He said the other day, "*War as I Knew It,* by George S. Patton, is very interesting." I am glad we have a huge library with lots of inspiring tapes.

September 9, 1997

A saint named Adi Shankara said, "We are only a banker. The wealth is in our custody only. It is not ours."

Similarly, Krishna is in our custody only, but I find it very difficult to think in those terms. The thought that he is our son is always with me. That is why I worry. I don't worry very much about other autistic children. When a newscast shows someone's house burning, it doesn't affect us; we simply watch, uninvolved. But when our own house is on fire, we scream and cry and become very sad because it is ours. Bill Gates doesn't worry when AT&T is running at a loss. Our view is very narrow. Always, we say, *my* house, *my* kids, *my* book, *my* furniture, *my* clothes, *my* flight, *my* train, *my* friends. It is this attachment that causes the pain in us about Krish. Krish's teachers don't have anxiety attacks because of Krish. Only we do.

I have been blaming God left and right for not making Krish all right in spite of my prayers. What is God? Man gave God a human body. Think of all the gods of the different religions. They are all given human forms. But is God in one body? Of course not. He permeates everything. He is everything.

Nature is God. Only cause and effect of Nature governs this universe. There are three aspects in Nature: creation, sustenance, and destruction. If there is birth, there is death. A seed gives rise to a tree. A tree gives rise to a seed. We have to live by the laws of Nature created by God. Then we are in harmony with Nature. Acceptance is also an important rule of Nature. We cannot wish for summer during winter, and cry for not having it. That is insane. Summer is summer; winter is winter. You cannot cry about it. Similarly, I cannot cry over Krish's condition. I have to accept it with detachment. Otherwise, there is no peace of mind for me.

My attachment to Krish is what is causing my problem. Ben, our friend's son, is autistic, but his autism doesn't cause anxiety in me. Why then does Krish's? If I wear red glasses, naturally I see everything red. I blame God for making me see everything red. But it is not God's fault; it is my own. God is showing me a way. He is telling me, "Remove your red glasses, and you can see everything naturally." For me to be happy, I have to doff my ego. The minute I start thinking that my child is autistic, I worry. I thought about how I have to do everything in my power to make him better, but I cannot worry on account of attachment. This attachment has to go.

We are all like waves in the ocean. The oceans' waves break on the shore every minute and die every minute to be born again. It goes on forever. A wave worrying about being dashed against the shore—how ridiculous is this? All waves are made of the same substance. They are not different in nature. Can they envy each other because one wave is bigger than another?

It is that ridiculous when we human beings compare and contrast and get jealous and sad because we are all made of the same stuff. All of us have souls. Just like the ocean beneath the waves is calm and serene, we have serenity deep inside us. I cannot let Krish's behavior drag me into chaos and confusion. I have to rise above those trials and tribulations of autism to enjoy the peace residing in my bosom.

When we are looking at the east, we cannot see the west. If I want to see what's happening behind me, I have to divert my gaze from the front to the back by turning my body. In the same way, if I want to live an anxiety-free life with Krishna, I have to divert my attention from him and concentrate on other things, like my writing. My writing this journal has great therapeutic value because it reduces my anxiety over Krish and gives me an outlet for expressing my frustrations.

September 10, 1997

Krishna has been going to the YMCA with Rich. But this week, Krish got so sick that he stayed home. During our phone conversation, I told Rich that he should treat Krish as an intelligent person even though Krish's actions—his lack of coordination and inability to speak well—sometimes belie his innate intelligence.

I told him that he should explain everything to Krish beforehand so that he doesn't wonder. This relieves quite a bit of his anxiety. Rich agreed to do that. He promised that he would slow down instead of going from activity to activity, and explain every exercise before they start the workout.

I felt he was sincere because he called me and asked me about Krish. He asked me a lot of questions regarding Krish's academics. He was curious why an autistic should learn high-level academics, and what is the purpose? I said the following:

Krish may have problems in a lot of areas. He is autistic. But there is one area he is fascinated by and interested in, and that is his academics. He loves physics, he loves math. Conceptwise, his brain is better than normal. But in physical action or speech, it is not normal. Why constantly make him feel like a failure by dealing with those areas in which he is deficient? Why not make him feel like a success by encouraging him to learn something he loves? Why should we deny him physics and math because he is autistic? If he can learn and enjoy, that's what matters. He should not be denied that enjoyment.

We used to read the classics to him—Dickens, Thomas Hardy, and others—when he was ten or eleven. We didn't know how much he understood, then. But one day in 1994, when he was twenty-three, he wrote about David and Agnes of *David Copperfield*. Then we knew he had been taking in a lot from the environment although his output was damaged. This happened twelve years after he heard us read *David Copperfield* to him. He is taking in everything. Don't judge him from his output, which is really bad. There is a discrepancy between his intellectual capacity and his actions. We also have the same discrepancy.

People who take drugs know that it is harmful. Alcoholics know that drinking is really destroying them. And still they do it. We all are compelled to do what we should not. My mother-in-law died of diabetes. She never wanted to avoid eating sweets even though she knew that staying away from sweets was the right thing to do. We all do it. I know intellectually that I have to exercise, but I don't. We all choose not to listen to our inner voice, our intuition, and we all get in to trouble.

Krishna's gap between his understanding and his action is a lot wider and deeper than ours because of his autism.

Today, Rich spent much time in trying to understand Krish. He said that he always knew intuitively that Krish was smart. When I heard him say that, I jumped on that idea right away. I said that we should always listen to our intuition, our inner voices. They are always right. Intuition is not so readily accepted in western society. In the United States, we want everything to be reasonable and proved; here, we so often ignore our inner feelings and intuition. Intuition is the greatest gift from God.

I always went by my intuition, which told me when he was a toddler that because his eyes are sparkling, he must be smart. On that theory, we educated him, read classics to him, and he has come this far. The school system and the professionals ridiculed me for what I was doing, namely, educating him. In school meetings, I invariably had to defend myself. Even now, with DMR, we have to defend our position. But it doesn't deter us from educating Krish.

Don't deny or discount your intuition. If your intuition says that he is smart, then that is what Krish is to you. Intuition is a lot more powerful than mere logic will ever be. We curse intuition even though it is right, and worship logic even at times when the assumptions are wrong.

Today, all day, Krish refused to study, so we didn't push him. He is also very sick and has been for the last few days. The last several weeks have been oppressive. First, there was the deep cut in his finger, and now he has a severe cold, sinus trouble, and a bad cough. We simply have to wait it out.

September 11, 1997

Nan and I talked about the time we were vacationing in Tennessee. Krish was home for the summer from his residential school. One day, we went to see a cave. Krish had been asking for a bathroom when we were deep inside the cave. There were a lot of people, and the guide was busy explaining things. Krish and I were way behind everybody else. I didn't know how to get out of the cave, so I ignored Krish's concerns. Suddenly, I heard a peeing sound. I turned to Krish in the dim light and saw him peeing. I said in a whisper, "Krishna."

He pulled up his pants in a flash of a second. Nan and I recounted that incident and were laughing our heads off for a few seconds. We shared a lot of laughter last night when we were reminiscing about such incidents.

For the past few days, Krish has been having tantrums. It takes at least half an hour for him to calm down. Then he is all smiles and back to normal. The day before yesterday, my husband asked Krish whether he was having seizures. Krish wrote that it is not seizures; it is the disease of autism that makes him scared and worried. Who wouldn't be? I thought. With his communication problems and his lack of coordination, anybody would be upset.

Yesterday was one of those very bad days. When he came home from being with Rich at the YMCA, he was okay. But later in the afternoon, he started going downhill when Nan asked him to work on his essay on autism on the computer. When Nan insisted that he work on his essay, Krish got upset and lost control. He was screaming and jumping up and down like a two-year-old. Because he is still doing this, even though he is twenty-five years old, I become quite despondent. He didn't study for the rest of the day. He is willing to answer questions, but not to write his essay. This frustrates me. I am becoming more educated about his feelings, his mind, his ideas, his intentions from his essay. When we ask him questions, it is not the same.

I told my husband that maybe we are indirectly rewarding this negative behavior. Perhaps that's why he is doing this, to get what he wants. Our backing off is what he wants us to do at that time. That is exactly what we are doing every time. He did not agree. He said:

> You are dealing with an autistic adult on whom we are putting a lot of demands to study, communicate, write on the computer, and behave as normally as he can, at home and in the community. We don't let up on that. Certainly, our expectations push him to new levels of growth. But you are forgetting one thing here. He is autistic. For an autistic, he's doing well. He is not docile; he is asserting himself; he is putting his foot down; that means he is developing his own mind, his own opinions. That's great. He is a full-blast person now. I agree, he has outbursts at least once a day. But the whole day goes smoothly except for those ten or fifteen minutes. For the mind-boggling problems he has, for the amount of pressure we put on him to learn and improve in so many different areas, and for not drugging him with potent medications, he is

doing just fine. We should not worry about these fifteen minutes a day as long as we can teach him and as long as he can learn.

I agreed with him. But still I was depressed.

September 12, 1997

This morning I was cheerful. Over coffee, Nan and I again talked about Krish. This is the way he is going to be: up and down. We have to remember that, in spite of everything, he is learning and moving forward. That's all that matters. Knowledge, in any form, cannot harm the person who possesses it. Ignorance, on the other hand, is harmful. How can one say that knowledge of physics or math is not beneficial to an autistic, especially when Krish is interested in learning? How does it matter what he learns? Learning has to happen, and it is happening in him. He is not vegetating; his intellect is stimulated; his curiosity aroused. This learning will help him in the future. We should not always judge him solely on his behavior.

Yesterday was a disastrous day. In the evening, when Krish was having his Nellikai water treatment, he became upset because a couple of songs did not sound good enough in the tape recorder. He got up and jumped up and down to show us that he was frustrated. During his oil massage, he was whining. Here, Nan was doing the tough work of giving massage, and Krish was showing his displeasure. Later that evening, when I was eating something, he came up to me and demanded some food. I said, "I'll fix something after I finish what I am eating." Then he tried to grab my bowl. I was angry, but I let him have it, for the fear of things getting out of control. Also I was too exhausted for a fight.

The next thing that night, he wanted lemon juice. Nan told him, "You wait in the study room. I'll get some lemonade." But Krish didn't listen and followed him, demanding lemon juice in his impolite voice. Nan got the juice in a glass and asked Krish to go up to his study room and have the juice. Krish did not like the order he was getting. Nan had just had it with Krish.

All day, we had been his doormat. He was demanding things from us left and right. We did not want any flare-ups, but Krish was pushing us over the cliff. Nan said in an equally demanding voice, "Go up.

I'll bring the juice." He wouldn't. So Nan said angrily, "I'll dump the juice if you don't listen. I don't have to yield to you constantly." Instead, Krish tried to wrest the glass away from his Dad. Nan had no choice. He went ahead and dumped the juice. Right away, Krish showed his power by throwing a cup on the floor and breaking it. That was all that was needed for all hell to break loose.

Nan became very upset. He went to Krish and grabbed him. The stress of putting up with Krish's behavior for the last few weeks was too much. He told him, "This behavior is unacceptable. Who do you think you are? I am going to put you away. I don't have to put up with you." Nan never wanted to fight with him, but today, he wanted to give Krish the message that he cannot push him around and show his defiance toward him.

I was petrified because I did not want Nan to have a stroke or a heart attack. He is in his mid-fifties, and he has high blood pressure. But he was not going to let Krish off the hook; he was intent on teaching him a lesson. But I did not want any lesson to be taught at that moment. Who cares about a lesson? All I wanted was a living, breathing human being in my husband, not a dead man. After a few minutes, Krishna did back off. When we asked him to stand in the corner quietly for a few minutes, he did so. I was still trembling with fear and anger from the incident. I started lashing out against Krishna:

> You cannot be a control freak like this. We are giving our lives to educate you. Dad has given up his career just for you. Is this the way to treat him? To fight with the person who is dedicated to you? Is this the way to say thank you?
>
> If this is the way you are going to behave, we don't need to keep you home. Because we think we can make you get better, we are keeping you home. If you don't want to improve, and if you maintain this negative attitude, you can go to a residential program where the people taking care of you will not bother to teach you academics; they will drug you in order to control your behavior. You will become very lethargic and drowsy most of the time. That is the way those places work. Do you want to go to such a place and learn nothing? Or do you want to stay home and learn? It is your choice.
>
> But we will not drug you to control you. It has to come from within you. You have to decide. We have decided that we would like to help you, but we will not tolerate this unruliness, this anger, this misbehavior. You

can stay if you are willing to control your behavior. We will not be your doormat. That's as of this minute.

He heard every bit, and he was quiet. He looked sorry. I also told him that he has to do a few things from today onward. He has to help me around the home. He has to write his essay on the computer. He has to study for *two* hours. If he misbehaves, if I am not happy with his behavior, I will not give him Indian curry rice. We have always catered to his every whim, but not any more. He has to give something back to us.

Two days ago, I was singing in the kitchen while he was walking in the family room. He wanted me to stop singing. I stopped. Hereafter, if he doesn't like my singing, I am not going to stop. Instead, he has to go to some other room, where he won't hear me sing. In the morning, before I make my coffee, I give him his coffee in bed; then I have my coffee peacefully. That's unfair. I like to have my coffee first, too. I am going to have it that way. We are catering to him too much, and thus, we are spoiling him. The other day, when we laughed, he wanted us to stop. I thought the loud noise bothered him since he is sensitive to noise. We stopped. He is controlling us too much.

Because we don't want any fights, we are always accommodating to his wishes. He is like a bully pushing us around. Always, his terms are heard, not ours. He is so self-centered, domineering, and stubborn because of his autism. We don't want to live like this. If he wants to stay at home, he has to obey certain rules. I told him all this.

Later that night, Krish worked well. He put a load of laundry in and put the trash outside for pickup. He cleaned up his room and wrote on the computer. So he has enough control to work for two hours diligently. The same work, without our shouting and ultimatums, would have taken him half a day with lots of resistance. By the time it usually takes him to do one hour of work, I am tired from reasoning and pleading with him.

When I had time later that night, I was wondering, where is this resistance coming from? He is not always stubborn. He often displays good intentions, but they are at times thwarted by his stupid mood swings. Is this also part of his brain injury? If that is the case, am I right in being this hard on him?

When all the best minds of the world in neurology, in psychology, and in psychiatry cannot decipher the problem of autism, then how can I expect Krish to solve it all by himself, especially when his brain is hurt? Maybe it is absurd to compare him and his behavior with people who are not brain injured. I am not being fair to him. Hereafter, I should use a different yardstick to measure his behavior. That way, I will not get disappointed or discouraged with him.

September 13, 1997

We all went to Andover Phillips Academy for a walk. Krishna is familiar with the grounds since Malini studied there. For the first ten minutes, he looked fine. Then all of a sudden, he started hyperventilating. Nan asked him on the pocket calculator, "How are you?"

Krishna:	Very sad. Depressed.
Nan:	Why? The weather is good, the grounds are beautiful.
Krishna:	No degree, no degree. No good.
Nan:	So what, no degree? The students you see may not know calculus. They definitely don't study differential equations, electricity and magnetism with Maxwell's equations, nor quantum physics with Schroedinger's partial differential equation, nor Einstein's relativity theory. You have gained so much knowledge in math and physics and electrical engineering. If knowledge is what gives a person a degree, you have a degree, in my opinion. Also Krishna, if you write four or five books, the university will bestow an honorary doctorate on you. So what do you say now?
Krishna:	Thanks, Dad. True.

Right away, Krishna's sadness vanished and his face lightened up. He started walking with a bounce and a beaming smile.

September 15, 1997

Dr. Jekyl and Mr. Hyde, that's who Krish is. Two people in one body. Some days, he is gentle, listening, cute, eager to learn, energetic for positive things, and communicative. Whereas other days, he is frustrated, noncommunicative, angry, tense, upset, stubborn, and depressed. The second personality always puts stress on the family. He has been Mr. Hyde for more than a month. Usually, this negative personality will vanish in a few days and will be replaced by his true gentle nature. But since he got a cut in his finger and was put on high doses of antibiotics, it has been prolonged.

This morning, we compared Krish's growth to the stock market. He has lots of ups and downs, much like the Dow Jones. In the last five years, Krish's growth has been phenomenal despite his behavior. In the last ten years, the Dow has gained nearly 5,000 points, from around 3,000 to 8,000. These were bear as well as bull markets. In the last five years alone, stocks like Intel and Microsoft have doubled or tripled. But there are days when they have plummeted. For instance, a few months back, Intel fell almost 30 points in one day. But we were not worried because we know it will bounce back in a few weeks or months. It did and has gone beyond our expectations, as has our son.

This year, Warren Buffet is the second richest man in the United States, next to Bill Gates. He made billions with the same fluctuating stock market. What is his secret? Patience. He bought stocks in a few companies like American Express, Washington Post, Coca Cola, Walt Disney, and held those stocks long term and made money. He had confidence in those stocks even when they fell. Because of the knowledge of those companies, he had confidence in them. He gives time for the stocks to go up. He has confidence in the companies he bought stock in, and he has the patience to hold on to them.

That is what we have to do with Krish. Armed with the knowledge that Krish is intelligent, we should not lose our confidence in him. We should be patient whenever Krish's behavior worsens. Overall, Krish is doing well. He is improving steadily. There are weeks when he learns nothing and his behavior is dreadful, but if we consider the last four years, his improvement is nothing short of miraculous.

In the past few weeks, he has been behaving like Intel stock in 1995-constantly sliding. But the people who didn't sell it at that time have made a lot of money now. I have to be patient, like Warren Buffet, with Krish. I should not get panicky, but be patient and confident in Krish's potential. Krish will come back to his positive state and start learning and behaving.

Over the short term, he looks like a loser, but over the long run, he is a winner. In the last four years, Krish has gone from basic math to calculus, differential equations, probability theory, and statistics. In physics, he now studies quantum physics and relativity theory. In electrical engineering, he now studies signals and systems, speech processing, computer science, and acoustics.

We should not become discouraged with his on-and-off behavior problems. They are not going to go away in one day. As he grows and matures, his emotional side will improve and thus stabilize his behavior. I have to believe that and be patient.

Today, he wanted to take his third shower. I did not allow him to do so because he has a very bad cough. I put my foot down. I simply refused to put the water on for his bath. He, in turn, became upset and started to jump up and down. Later, he felt badly. He came to my room, sat down on my bed, and he held my hand and said, "I will not fight. I love you." These words from him always have a very powerful effect on me because they remind me of his early years when he was unreciprocative to human love. I put my arms around him and kissed his head. But I also wanted to give him some advice, which comes naturally to me when I see him:

Jalaja: Don't you think you are wasting your precious time and energy in fighting? You are smart in math and physics. Why can't you put that smartness in learning to control your temper? You have to change your negative attitude. You are fighting with people who love you.

Krish: The life is tough for me, too.

Jalaja: Do you think self-pity will help you?

Krish: I think you have to accept my disease. You are too idealistic.

Jalaja: I will not accept your disease, and I will not let you surrender to autism as long as I live.

Krish: I love you.

Jalaja: Do you mean to say you agree with me?

Krish: Absolutely, for your sake.

September 16, 1997

Today was a great day. Krish was coming back to his normal sweetness after his couple of outbursts over the last few days. Nan was resting his head on Malini's lap, and I was sitting next to them. We were talking about neurosurgery.

Krish was walking in the family room, which is 26 feet by 26 feet. It is a very big room. We were talking in a corner while Krish was walking around the sitting area. He was listening to our talk the whole time. When Malini commented, "Mom, you and Dad are working much harder than people do in neurosurgery. In my neurosurgery internship, I was working 120 hours a week. After my work, I at least had my time off. But you are living with unpredictability. That's hard," Krishna started whining.

I knew immediately what was wrong. My job is to watch constantly for his expressions, to detect any disapproval or unhappiness; I am always trying to read his mind. He is going through a very difficult period. He easily gets hurt because he is so aware of his condition. Just like the skin, which is there to protect the body from infections, we parents are always there to protect him from any sneers or ridicule from the outside world.

I started praising him right away by saying that we are creating a beautiful, gentle, fine human being. Nothing can ever match this creation. Then we all went on to say how smart he is in math and other subjects.

Upon hearing this, he became a lark again, smiling and cooing. He is such an innocent, sweet person. He is unable to sustain anger at any one person, nor is he able to sustain any jealousy toward his sister or his cousins, all of whom are very accomplished. He doesn't hold a grudge against anyone. He is an open book. Very simple, very gentle, very kind when he is his true self. Anybody who comes to know him always says that Krish is a fine, gentle man. Dr. Inosa always said that. Many of his teachers also remarked that he is a good kid.

Krish came to us and rested his head on his Dad's chest and hugged him. Nan and Malini both were stroking him, and Krish was immersed in bliss. It was a great sight to see. And we were talking about our coming trip to India. Krish was listening and enjoying his sister's love. This went on for forty minutes. I have a feeling that our worst period of three or four weeks is over; hereafter, it is only going to get better. He is beyond his wretched negative mood!

Overall, it was a wonderful day. We went out for a car ride. We ate pizza and had a good time. Last week, Mal was very busy applying for neurosurgery, and Krish was in his melancholy mood, with a terrible cough and cold. This weekend, he is feeling much better physically, and that reflects in his emotional health.

September 17, 1997

Last night, Krish had trouble falling asleep. This is the unpredictability I am talking about. Why can't he fall asleep like normal people when he is tired? I don't want to give him sleeping pills, either. So Malini, Nan, and I took turns stroking his head, his back, and tummy to relax him and make him fall asleep. He enjoyed the attention, but was rather chirpy. When we went to our room, he was up and walking around. I don't know what time he fell asleep. He awoke by 5:00 the next morning, so he had very few hours of sleep.

This morning, the three of them went to Peter Bent Brigham Hospital. Malini had to work at the hospital, and Krish and Nan were going to walk around town. They haven't yet returned.

I am thinking about the inconsistency between his foolish behavior and his wise words on the computer. He writes so eloquently, so philosophically. A couple of days ago, he wrote about attitudes and actions. He writes so deeply. I have been pressuring him to show more connection between his thinking and his behavior. I am trying to create a longing within him that will place some kind of pressure on him to modify his behavior. I believe that we all have some inconsistencies even though we may not be aware of them.

What will make us change our behavior? Nothing but pain. If we become extremely unhappy about the disconnectedness between our thoughts and our actions, we might do something about it. For us to change, the dissatisfaction has to go to the level of intense pain. Only then will we change our behavior.

How can I motivate him to change his sometimes disconnected behavior? He has to feel the intense pain. I know there is a lot of stress involved in changing. Any change is painful. In Krish's case, his destructive tantrums are going to cost him his life. He is so bright; in my opinion, he is almost beyond autism. His angry behavior is going to make him or break him. It has to go.

The price of not changing is much greater than the price paid for changing. The ultimate price of this destructive behavior will be landing in some residential program and not staying home with his family. I have to make him feel the pain. This will control his behavior. I also often tell him that staying home and learning is much more fun than staying in a residential program. I have to give him strong reasons to change. As Archimedes wrote, I have to find a lever long enough:

> Give me a lever long enough,
> And a prop strong enough,
> I can single handedly move the world.

In the afternoon, Krish wanted me to stroke his back to help relax him. I said that he had to wait for fifteen minutes. But he wanted it right away, and was getting frustrated and upset, so I told him:

> I could give you what you wanted. It is easy for me to do that, but it is not right. You have to learn to postpone or delay what you want for some time. This will slowly build up your strength of mind, which is very important for enjoying life. The heavy weightlifting builds the muscles. It is painful, but the result is a magnificent body. In the same way, strength of mind can be acquired by saying no to every wish and want. The mind gets tough when it endures a lot of pain through disappointments and failures. You can't give in to the mind every minute and hope to have a strong mind. Every emotional fiber gets strengthened by delays and denials.

He then waited for fifteen minutes before getting what he wanted. I also explained to him that he did not lose out on what he wanted by waiting for fifteen minutes. Actually, he smiled and was happy when I was explaining how to strengthen the mind. "So, *even* without getting what you wanted, you were happy all because of the mind. If you cultivate your mind like this, step by step, you wouldn't want much to make you happy."

September 18, 1997

Usually, Krishna's behavior changes for the worse in the late evening or just before bedtime. At suppertime, Krish wanted food, and I asked him to wait. He got impatient and frustrated and angry. In his angry mood, he grabbed the soup and started gulping it down in such an impatient and hurried manner that he spilled quite a bit of it on the dining room table, floor, and chair. It took fifteen minutes to clean up the mess. I demanded that he clean up the mess, and he did. I was furious:

> You are insane to do that because you have no reason to do it. You went to Boston. You had a long walk along the Charles River. You had a wonderful breakfast outside. This behavior is unacceptable. It has to stop. Two adults cannot spend their whole lives on you. This can't go on.

He felt very guilty for what he had done, and later he went to the computer and wrote, "Please institutionalize me because I can't control my behavior sometimes. I am trying hard." When his Dad asked, "Do you want to go to a residential program?" He said, "I don't but I don't see any other choice. My behavior is crazy." My heart went out to him. I also felt a great deal of guilt for pushing him that hard. Even though I wanted to hug him, I did not do so, for the fear of being ineffective in disciplining him. I just kept quiet. He saw my serious mood. The rest of the day went beautifully. He studied and worked on his essay. He wrote very poignantly. He is so talented yet so disabled in many ways.

But aren't we all? People like Elvis and Judy Garland were disabled with insecurity. Emotional insecurity is more disabling than physical shortcomings. It culminated in their deaths. So Krishna is not alone. We are all disabled with something or the other.

The whole day, I did not sing, I did not write in my journal, I did not read. I was moping around. I decided to clean the house. And I took a two-hour nap.

In the evening, I heard from Nan that Krish did a good job at MIT. He behaved well. I really don't understand why he cannot behave the same way at home. I somehow feel as though he needs these outbursts at home to behave well outside. They get all his pent-up frustrations out. If he didn't dispel them at home, maybe he would do so elsewhere. That wouldn't be good.

This is the conversation I had with Krishna right before going to bed:

Jalaja:	Our mind is like a monkey. What do you say to that?
Krish:	Maybe.
Jalaja:	It should be tamed.
Krish:	Easy to say, but very difficult for me.

Jalaja:	How do you mean?
Krish:	Your mind is a normal monkey, which is naturally restless. But mine is a restless, drunk monkey, stung by a scorpion on top. It is infinitely tougher for me.

September 19, 1997

Nan went to the bookstore with Krish and bought several math and physics books. Krish was elated with the books. He thought that we were fed up and that he would be going to a residential program. Instead, he saw his Dad buy him books for hundreds of dollars. That means that we are committed to his education, which made him very happy.

The whole of yesterday was a relaxing day for Krish, thus for us, too. I wish I had such days available to me, without any burdensome worries about Krish. I started imagining all that I would be interested in, had I the time. I exercised for the first time in seven or eight months.

Last night, after Krish went to bed, my husband and I were talking about Krish. Do we talk about anything else? When I started blaming God for all of my troubles, he listened very carefully and then said:

> You cannot say God is not right in your case. Do you really know what is good for you? God has been very good to you. Otherwise, he could have given you children like the Menendez brothers, who killed their parents. Would you like to have normal children who commit heinous crimes? Krish's behavior is not violent. All he does is jump up and down and whine once in a while, and that too is due to autism. Once in a while, he grabs your shirt but nothing more. He is a good kid. God knows that to us values are very important. He didn't give us children who lie, cheat, and disrespect people and, above all, feel they are God-given gifts to the world.
>
> In spite of the problem, we have a very good, understanding, loving marriage; we respect each other; we have no financial problems; we have good health. For the grueling life we lead, we should have had heart attacks or strokes due to extreme stress, but we haven't. We haven't had depression or any breakdowns. I did not lose my job because you took care of Krish while I worked. You saved and managed money so we have enough money.

We have a wonderful daughter who respects our wisdom and asks for advice. She went to MIT, and then on to the University of Chicago Medical, and now is going for neurosurgery. She is well married to a cardiologist. Krish is doing extremely well. He has started on the non-linear differential equations in math. Our family, mine and yours, love us both. We have a very good relationship with our sisters and brothers. We do a lot for charity.

In no way do I consider us unlucky. We always keep our minds very strong and cheerful. So in my opinion, God has shown His grace to us. Under the pressure of having Krish at home, we could have lost the aforementioned gifts. But we didn't. Do you know why? Because of God's grace.

He was right and I was wrong. Maybe Krish is good for me. God, in His infinite compassion for me because I think of Him very often during the day, decided that I have to go through the hottest furnace in order to become the finest steel. I have to say that I have become a more mature and less self-centered person because of Krish. We never know God's intentions.

There is a certain law governing the universe. The physical laws are so apparent around us. The earth rotates around the sun in elliptical orbit; energy cannot be destroyed but it can be converted, say, from mechanical to electrical. A human baby takes nine months for its development. Even if I pray incessantly, God will not reduce the duration from nine to three months. It will not happen. Apples will not grow on a pine tree. There are universal laws. There must be similar laws governing the mind also. Just because we don't know what they are doesn't mean they don't exist. For example, gravity existed all along even before Newton's discovery. Similarly, we need to understand the laws of the mind. Nothing is random in creation. Everything is planned and executed.

Do we choose our parents? Do we choose our brothers and sisters? Do we choose our children? Do we choose the way we will exit this earth? Do we choose the length of our stay on earth? What do we choose? We are powerless in big ways. The day the Creator calls us, we have to leave this planet in such a hurry. We are not given time to plan our affairs. We cannot say, "Oh, God, my daughter is graduating. Let me attend that and then I will leave."

The only choice I have is, given the deal, to make the very best use of it or not. I have to give the very best to Krish. But I can't demand

God to make him all right. That's God's province. I have no say in it. But I can live an impeccably moral life. I can choose to improve my character. I can cultivate contentment. Those are in my hands. I guess only trying is in my hands. But will I improve because of my efforts? Or is it again in God's hands? I really don't know.

Total surrender to God's plans is the only way to go about life. Surrender is a magical word and a powerful word. A potent word like "surrender" can transform *my* spirit, and thus *my* life—I just have to do *my* very best and leave the results to God. He is the dispenser of results. The word *surrender* eased the burden from my mind. I don't need to carry my heavy luggage of Krishna on my head while traveling in the train of life. I can put it down, and resume my journey of living with ease and peace.

September 20, 1997

This morning, Krish wrote on the computer, "The life is fast moving. Sad is my state. Behavior bothers me. Behavior teases everything. Behavior saps my energy. Behavior can be controlled by my mind. In my case, behavior *also* snatches my mind away." He looked depressed.

Nan told him that he doesn't need to feel depressed because he is making a lot of improvements. This depressive behavior has been going on since he was a baby. We did not pay much attention to it because we had hundreds of other issues to deal with such as:

Can he crawl?
Can he walk?
Can he chew?
Can he bite?
Can he swallow solid food?
Can he use his hands?
Can he jump?
Can he bicycle?
Can he hear sounds?
Can he comprehend speech?
Can he make sounds?
Can he say words?
Can he be toilet trained?
Can he brush his teeth?

Can he eat by himself?
Can he take a shower and dry his body?
Can he put on and take off his clothes?
Can he play with toys?
Can he communicate?
Can he read?
Can he do math?
Can he write?
Can he tolerate strangers?
Can he handle a public place?
Can he stop his bizarre behaviors?
Can he behave?

I told Krishna, "Since you have overcome the majority of the obstacles in many, many areas, now the behavior problem looks big. This also can be overcome in a few years. So you don't have to worry about it. Think positive. You have done miracles in every area. This area will also see a miracle." Krish felt good and he gave us a big ear-to-ear grin and said, "Thank you."

Today, Krish wrote on the computer, all by himself: "I am sorry. I will behave good. Please be patient." His fear is stopping him from typing fast. He is so unsure of himself; he lacks confidence. This shows in everything he does. The major obstacle is fear. For instance, he makes a fool of himself at the barber's. Although he has been having his hair cut since he was small, he is still gripped with fear; it's as if he were going to the guillotine. This fear accompanies him everywhere. This means he cannot take up any challenges with enthusiasm. He has to be pushed every time to take chances.

How did he become so fearful? One possible source of it is the time he fell from the seat of a shopping cart when he was a baby. For a few days after the incident, his whole body would tremble whenever a stranger picked him up. I have been working all of my life to lessen his fear. Even though it has been tremendously reduced, it still dominates almost everything new he takes up.

The whole day was without incident. He is slowly coming back to his gentle nature. For the last six weeks, he was very tense and was not sleeping well. For the last two days, he has been sleeping soundly from 8:30 p.m. to 5:30 a.m. We feel we are on vacation. Vacationing in Paris, France, or Vail, Colorado, would not make me feel any more relaxed than I do now. It is so delightful to have all this free time in the evening, from 8:00 p.m. to 11:00 p.m., with my husband. I am in bliss.

September 21, 1997

Nan talked to one of our friends today. After hearing about Krish's improvements, Dev said:

> Krishna looks like a person with imagination and creativity. Math and physics are great. They are very logical and analytical. Why don't you introduce him to artificial intelligence? But you should go beyond logic and give him creativity—like an expert system, artificial intelligence. He can be more creative and interact with people on the computer and exchange intellectual ideas, and this will stimulate him. He can be more active, instead of learning alone, passively.

I thought about what he said. It is easy to come up with new ideas. But it takes rigorous thinking to form cognizant, coherent ideas. We need others to bounce ideas back and forth. When we have a discussion with people who have cultivated sharp, deep, analytical thinking, our logical thinking mind is fueled from the discussions. Because Krish has the wonderful habit of reading and enjoying books on history, philosophy, and biography, he should share them with others of similar interest over the Internet. I hope this will happen soon. It will open up a new field of communication for him.

Right now, we as parents give Krish a lot of company in stimulating him with questions and ideas. But he needs more people in his life. The Internet can be a great source for sharing ideas and ideals. It can provide him with very stimulating and energizing conversations with others who share his interests.

I believe that we all need to read books in order to refresh our intellectual potential. Otherwise, the agile, alert, inquisitive mind will wither away. Reading alone, however, is not enough. We need to contemplate what we read. Otherwise, we will become a copy machine with no ideas of our own. Original thinking is very important for inner growth. The books we read prod us to take directions that we would not have taken otherwise. To me personally, the life I see around me is an open book. I devour it with relentless enthusiasm in order to deeply understand and also appreciate what's happening to me as well as others around me. Life's precious lessons are there whether we strive to recognize them or not.

September 22, 1997

We have decided to go to India for Krish's ayurvedic treatment on October 13 for three months. Last year, the treatment yielded excellent results. His nervous system has matured. That shows in his fine motor skills, which is one of his more serious problems. Within the past few months, he has been able to open a single-slice-of-cheese wrapper, open and close a ziplock plastic bag, and lock the bathroom door at MIT.

A couple of days ago, Nan was telling me how he used to feel embarrassed when holding the bathroom door for Krish. Now, for the last few months, Krish is able to lock and unlock the door himself. It is not the concept that Krish did not understand. It is simply that he didn't have the coordination.

The second improvement is that he has started typing on his own since March of this year. That means he feels confident about his ability, which in turn means his fingers are stronger and his eye-hand coordination is better. I expect this newfound independence to spread to other areas that are crucial for his living independently. The third improvement is that his colds are better, and the duration of them shorter. I feel very good about his improvements.

We have had three days without incident. Right now, he is a little frustrated, and he is whining very mildly. The best thing to do right now is to leave him alone. In twenty or thirty minutes, he will be all right.

September 24, 1997

Malini was here yesterday. Krish, Mal, and Nan went for a good breakfast. Then we all went for a walk in Harold State Park. Krish thoroughly enjoyed the walk. In fact, we all did. Malini was telling us all about neurosurgery. It was really fascinating. The most fascinating of all creations is this human brain. Krishna was smiling the whole time. Mal told him that lots of people are affected with speech problems, so he is not alone in this. For some reason, he felt good about his being not alone. He smiled at her and held her hand. That's his way of showing gratitude because Malini was trying to make him feel good. It worked! He was beaming with happiness all day.

They have a very special bond as sister and brother. She always stood by him, gave him support, and felt that he is as smart as she. She is always there to defend him. She is a very, very fine human being.

Because of Krish's autism, we were frequently busy with him, structuring his time. We weren't able to give her one-tenth of the attention that we gave him. She, as a child, understood that most of the time. She was very mature for her age. She never showed jealousy because we were always with Krish. She understood that we were with him so often not because we love him more than her but because he needs us more than she does. He is disabled. How many grownups would have this understanding? In that way, she is very special. This is another grace that God has showered on me. I am so grateful to God.

Malini wanted to go to a Chinese restaurant, but Krish wanted pizza. So we went for pizza. Right after our lunch, we went for our walk in the woods. He is always in a blissful state whenever he is in the state park. On top of it, he had his sister with him. His joy knew no bounds.

We talked about my upcoming trip. Mal insisted that I needed a month of rest, after five years of being with Krish and giving him treatment abroad for months, with very little help. She was adamant that I should go alone for four weeks, without Krish or Nan, and have fun being with my sisters and brothers. Nan also was very stubborn on this issue. They both said that they would make sure Krish has a great time. Krish didn't say a word. But I noticed his face looked forlorn and sad.

Why do I feel bad about going alone? I think I know the reason. I feel that I should always try to ease his pain, no matter what, since I am the cause of his birth. Also he is going through one of the most volatile times of his life.

Krishna wanted to change the subject, so he announced that he wanted ice cream and coffee. So we went to the Tread Mill for ice cream. After having our ice cream, we decided to go home, but Krish wanted to go for a walk again. This time he wanted to walk in the shopping area. After some time, he was ready to go home.

Earlier, when we were walking in the woods, a huge black dog came up to us and started barking. Krishna became upset. He started to walk away from it, but the dog followed after him. When Krish started running, the dog ran after him. The dog's owner wasn't taking charge of him. I told her to get the dog. She said, "He is a nice dog." I thought to myself, if he is nice, why is he chasing a very frightened autistic person? Why does he look so unfriendly, *and* bark without any reason or provocation? But I did not say this to her. We were all bothered by her indifference to what was happening. That dog did not look friendly to us, and Krish was visibly frightened of the dog.

When we came home, I told Krish that I wanted to know his mind about my trip abroad. He should write down what's on his mind for me. He went to the computer room with his Dad.

Nan: How do you feel about Mom going to India first, then coming back in November so that all of us can go together?

Krish: Ecstasy gone. Living alone with Dad is tough, boring. Work, no fun, no chit-chat. Leave me in Shoranur. I can have my treatment. I can live with Dad there. Dad is not alone there. There are lots of people, sages, temple, also Americans who are there for treatment so I will not miss America.

That did it. I changed my mind. I decided that we all should go together and Krish would have his ayurvedic treatment in Shoranur. I will go to Madras for a week or two to attend my nephew's wedding.

Malini was against my decision. She felt that my being away from the family for a full month would do a lot of good for me. I agreed, but at the same time, Krish is fighting for his life. He has no friends except Rich, Richard, and Adam. His life is already restricted because of his ailment. Poor kid! My heart goes out to him. I don't want to put any more pressure on him if I can help it.

All day, Krish was good and happy.

My travel agent got our three tickets confirmed. On October 15, we leave for India. We will return in January, after three months of intense treatment for Krish. Tonight, we have to call my sister, Nan's sister, and the ayurvedic hospital to inform them of our arrival.

In the last three months, I booked and canceled at least two times. This time, I will stick with my plans. No more change!

September 25, 1997

Today, Krish went to MIT, and he did very well with Jennifer. He did speech processing with Jennifer and wrote for her all by himself. When she asked him about his trip to India, he wrote, "India trip is ecstatic and I am excited." She said that he is writing much faster and with more confidence. She also told him, "Speech synthesizer speaks for you when you write." He wrote, "I am fascinated with physics." The speech synthesizer talked. He liked it so much that he wrote, "Teach canned speech."

He also went out with Rich. He did weightlifting for nearly an hour at the YMCA.

Yesterday, at one point when Malini was talking about neuro-surgery, Krish felt despondent. Malini noticed it right away, and she told him that his horoscope is good. In his horoscope, the sun is in his house. So the astrologer said that his mind will be as bright as the sun. One day, his capabilities will emerge out of the eclipse. Then he will shine like a bright sun. Upon hearing this, he grinned from ear to ear.

Nan and I talked about Krish's behavior. Today is the eighth day without an incident. What makes him snap out of it, and what makes his behavior acceptable? Is it chemical? Or is it caused by some short circuit in the brain? Is it due to insensitive remarks we make without knowing? Or is it the combination of everything? If he can behave well for a few days, then why can't he do it for a few months?

If my book ever is sold and I earn some money, I am going to give 20 percent to the Autistic Association here in the United States, and another 40 or 50 percent to setting up a school for the autistic in India.

Right now, there aren't any schools for these children in India. Some autistic children stay at home, and some are in classrooms with other children with disabilities. There are poor families I know of, where the mother must work as well as care for her autistic child at home. I wish I could set up something for these children so that these parents could go to work without worrying about their autistic sons and daughters.

The country is not a wealthy country like the United States. It is a huge country with more than a billion people. Even a rich country like the United States would become poor if it had a populace of a billion people. It is like a family of four, with an annual income of $50,000 versus a family of twelve with the same income. India is like a family with twenty children on an income of $50,000.

This afternoon, I fell asleep for an hour because I did not sleep well last night. When I woke up, the first thought that came to me was where was I the whole hour? When I was sleeping, I was not aware that I was Jalaja. Then who was I? I need not have come back to Jalaja. If I had stayed disconnected to Jalaja, my husband and my children would have assumed that I had died. What is the guarantee that anyone will wake up from his or her sleep and be connected again to his or her presleep state?

This thought was very poignant to me though it was also frightening. It was an experience, not something that I sat down and thought through. This made me realize that death can knock on my door any time. Then there will be no connection to Krish, autism, normalcy, or any of these dichotomies. If my body is not there, then where is my attachment to my family? Everything can be wiped out in a second by one blow from death. Why, then, am I so stupid to worry about anything at all?

September 26, 1997

Why am I writing my journal? What does it achieve? People close to me know who I am and what I have been doing all of my life. The opinion of people I don't know doesn't matter that much to me, anyway. Then why? The drive to achieve for my sake is not there. Certainly, some kind of drive is there. Otherwise, I would not have worked this hard all of my life to improve Krish. If I had invested my intensity, hard work, determination, and tireless enthusiasm for my own self-improvement and my career, I could have done very well.

But I did not choose to do it. Instead, I chose to make Krishna near normal. It is almost like somebody choosing to make a blind person see or a deaf person hear. It is most challenging because of Krish's unpredictability, with his wide range of mood swings, and his many areas of disability. Always anticipating the best possible scenario with Krish has helped me come up with a lot of intuitive ideas.

The stark realization that life is passing me by is a tremendous motivational force for my writing this because I feel I have something to contribute to parents of disabled children. My trials, my disappointments, my stresses, and my ecstasies with Krish over the last two decades are the size of Mount Everest in my bosom. I need to let go of my pent-up emotions.

Right now, I am choking. I can't breathe because I haven't shared this with anybody, not even my own sisters and brothers. Anyone who lived with me, like my mother and my daughter, knew to some extent what I was going through, as did, of course, my beloved husband, who shared the responsibilities of teaching Krish.

I was living my life in anticipation of a crisis, from day to day. Crisis management is what I am good at. Living with the possibility of crisis for more than two decades has made me alert, determined, tough, mentally strong, tireless, goal oriented, resourceful, and above all, dedicated to my dream.

Living with Krish has never been boring. I see many people, including my relatives, complain about boredom. One great thing about our life is that it has been stimulating, exciting, and interesting. There has been no room for boredom. When you have a goal bigger than life, it is all consuming and has made us live life meaningfully. The enriched quality of life, the product of slowly developing a peaceful mind due to intense living—physically, mentally, and spiritually—has become the byproduct of our incredible goal.

I am blessed for knowing this contentment to some degree. Finding happiness and peace when everything is going right is one thing. But finding joy and peace in the middle of chaos and unpredictability needs a strong mind that has lived through intense challenges for years.

I read an article on Michael Landon in *Life* magazine. He once revealed how physically and mentally abusive his parents were. He had a bedwetting problem even when he was in high school, and also had uncontrollable facial tics. He was fearful and insecure. But when he threw the javelin in high school, a miracle occurred. On that day, he found out something he could do better than anyone else, and he grabbed on to it. His coach let him take the javelin home and practice all summer.

He started building his upper body. He got an athletic scholarship to the University of Southern California. In his words, "a mouse had become a lion." The pursuit of a goal made him work hard, believe in himself, show intensity and determination to succeed, and dream of being somebody. Though his vision of being an international track star did not materialize, the other qualities that he developed stood by him to help him achieve stardom.

Similarly, the traits I have developed through dealing with Krish over the years will stay with me forever. Whatever I now take up, I know I will do a thorough job, irrespective of how difficult it might be. All that anyone needs in order to do a thorough job is perseverance, toughness of mind, intensity, hard work, a positive outlook, courage, determination, and relentless pursuit of the goal. These are the qualities I have developed, and they will support me throughout my life. Though there is no doubt in my mind about the importance of having a goal, even more important is how one arrives at the goal.

September 28, 1997

Krish's behavior has been absolutely marvelous. He is so supple. There is no stubbornness or aggression in him for the past week. Above all, he is peaceful. I feel as though he has no inner conflict in him just now. Whatever it was, it seems he got it resolved.

We have another problem cropping up. If it is not Krish, it is something related to him. Lately, DMR has been giving us trouble. I don't want to take up this battle with DMR because we are already fighting a raging war with autism.

When we struggle with DMR, our time, energy, spirit, and mental disposition, all of which are limited, are spent. Who is the ultimate loser? Krishna, of course. I wish we had infinite energy and time, but we do not. We might win a battle with DMR, but what good is it if we lose the war with autism? Nan agreed with me when I mentioned all this to him. He said that he would write a letter to DMR and leave it at that.

DMR tells us, again and again, to place Krish in special programs. There is nothing wrong with going to such schools, where vocational skills are being taught. But Krish doesn't want to go there. He loves physics and math. His enthusiasm and energy level go sky high when he is learning math or physics. As it is, life is an inferno for him. How can we deny him that joy of learning?

Being an autistic, he has so many disabilities that lower his spirit and self-esteem. Is it wrong for Krish to study physics and math and develop self-confidence? Is it wrong for Krish to feel that he is better than many others in math? Is it wrong for Krish to express and get what he wants? Is it wrong for Krish to learn and communicate through the computer? Why doesn't DMR like what we are doing? Why do they think that Krish should organize clothes or sort different nails into their corresponding boxes?

DMR wants him to go to a vocational school, which would mean no time for an academic education. "We are what and where we are because we have first imagined it." Because Krish is autistic, DMR doesn't believe that he can have any capabilities, or if he does, that they would not mean much to him. What a sad state these autistic children are in!

They are the most misunderstood people in the world. They do have capabilities, but nobody even tries to understand them. The world understands the blind, the deaf, the retarded, the people with AIDS, but not the autistic. I sometimes feel that nobody wants to care or tries to understand the autistic because the disease is so baffling. Autism is without logic. People with this syndrome are unpredictable in every area.

Only some climates and only some soils are good for growing tea and coffee. The climate has to be cool, and there has to be plenty of rain. We cannot grow anything in just any climate or in just any soil. If we try to grow tea or coffee in New England, we won't be successful. Krishna has the right soil and climate in him to do math and physics. We want to cultivate them in him, mainly because he shows interest. If his innate interest in math could spread the spark of enthusiasm to other areas, then learning math wouldn't be in vain, it would be therapeutic. I want a beautiful garden in Krishna despite his ailment. I see potential for an exquisite garden, provided I make use of what he has as soil and climate. Our mind and our emotions are the ultimate garden. In the end, our enriched mind and our balanced emotions are the ultimate goal.

When you aim high, your interest and energy get kindled. Why do I want to put him in some special program and smother his flame of interest in academics with a woolen blanket? That is very dumb. I don't agree with DMR. Period!

September 29, 1997

Krish was excited and making noise. I told him that he has all the ingredients necessary for acceptable behavior. He has the desire to behave normally. He has the intelligence, motivation, logical mind, support from us, and ayurvedic treatment. Above all, his desire to improve is there in him. It is like having all the ingredients—spices, vegetables, oil, and rice—for an Indian dish. All one has to do is put forth the effort to make Indian curry rice. In the same way, all he has to put forth is a little effort. He has everything he needs to make good behavior. Upon hearing this, he calmed down and stopped his whining. He became serious and attentive.

Right after lunch, Krishna wrote about the stock market:

> Stocks are rather reasonably volatile. The volatility of the market makes me nervous; the trouble is the trashed stocks seldom go up; the market venom can kill you. Rather buy real estate. The real estate will increase in value. The rest, offer to charity. There are therapy centers that need help.

Krishna sometimes isn't inclined to write on the computer. Focusing is very tough for him. Writing on his own takes every ounce of energy he has. But he is doing it independently. This skill has been developing since the second week in April of this year. He takes nearly thirty minutes for typing a five- or six-line paragraph.

I told him about a movie in which an autistic child in a residential program was sexually abused by one of the case workers. The autistic child's sleeplessness and other behavior problems worsened after the incident. Through facilitated communication, the child convinced the jury to find his abuser guilty.

The power of writing came through in the movie even though the child's hand was held by the teacher. Through facilitated communication on the computer, a mute, autistic child is able to convince a jury of several men and women, without a trace of doubt, that his caretaker abused him sexually.

As I told him, writing skill is like a piece of wood in the water when you are about to drown. It gives you the hope to try harder. It will take you to shore safely. You should cling on to the wood of writing and save yourself. You have to shed the fear of writing before strangers. You too must learn to protect yourself. You must practice writing regularly, no matter what.

September 30, 1997

Today, Nan took Krish to see Dr. Jones, a neurologist. He is a very kind man. I did not go with Krish to see Dr. Jones this time. Last time, I went and came away feeling that he is a caring man, ready to help us with Krish. Dr. Jones sincerely complimented us on our dedication to our son. He was also impressed with Krish's writing. He suggested that Krish undergo an MRI and an EEG in order to rule out any seizure activity in his brain. When Nan asked him whether Krish's sudden outbursts could be due to seizures, the doctor said that the EEG will clearly show any such activities.

October 1997

October 1, 1997

Krish's behavior is very good. There are no angry outbursts. He is calm and obedient, and his study habits are coming back. He wants to improve his speed in independent writing, so he is working on that. We are happy with his behavior, his motivation, and his energy level. No longer is he telling us that he is tired all day long.

Nan told me a story about a prisoner who committed a terrible crime. He was given a life sentence and confined to a maximum security prison. He was watched day and night. After a few years, he realized the enormity of what he had done and started repenting. Slowly, this changed his behavior. He started praying and reading his scriptures. He also contemplated what he read. He made those scriptural passages his own by thinking deeply about them. In time, he became a model prisoner. The guards started noticing a tremendous change in his character, and the warden was impressed by his sincerity. This went on for some years.

In spite of the prisoner's newfound attitude and behavior changes, nobody could do anything about his release or parole because he was sentenced to serve twenty years before any parole was possible. So this changed convict had to serve another ten years before he was paroled. However, he was transferred from a maximum security to a minimum security prison. He was also given more freedom and more responsibility.

I was listening intently. My husband stopped the story for a few seconds and then continued:

> We must have done something wrong, knowingly or unknowingly. So we are now living like that prisoner, with our freedom terribly curtailed. We cannot do things like others. Because we pray a lot and give to charity and try to live an extremely disciplined, God-fearing life with enormous dedication to better Krish's life, we have been transferred from a maximum security prison to a minimum security one. We are able to have fun and joy with him because of his improvements. We are enjoying his essay writing and communications. But we are not yet paroled. That will happen *only* when he becomes independent. Now we are enjoying life to some extent because his autism is on the decline. But still, when we go out with him, we are always keeping an eye on him, and we can never forget his needs and just enjoy.

You may think that it is outrageous to compare my husband and me to a criminal in prison, but that is how I feel. I have seen what autism has brought upon our family and other families. I really don't know whether the real crime is keeping our autistic children at home or giving them up to, say, residential programs. Either way, the parents of an autistic child are given very tough punishment. The lifetime prison term imposed by autism is real and unrelenting.

A successful engineer earning a six-figure salary moved to Massachusetts from California for better educational opportunities for his autistic son. Because he moved during a recession and couldn't find a suitable engineering job, he had to take a menial job to support his family.

A Harvard-trained tax lawyer with a very successful law practice was forced to neglect and ultimately give up his practice because of the chaos created by his son's autism. He couldn't uphold the responsibilities of his career because he was consumed by the battle to help his son. When I saw him last, he had incurred so much debt that he will likely be penniless for the rest of his life.

Another friend of mine who wanted her autistic child at home when her husband wanted the child put into a residential program got a divorce in order to keep her child at home.

In another family, a depressed father killed himself and his wife. I am sure it was because of the stress of having an autistic son at home.

I haven't suffered as much as some of these families even though I have been stripped of friends because the challenge of autism leaves no room for them. In my case, I have become a total recluse. That is the price I paid. If a handful of people attend my funeral, I may jump out of the coffin from sheer surprise.

The only difference between the criminal and Nan and me is that we don't know what we did wrong. Regarding that, Nan said, "In nature, nothing is random. Doesn't our scripture say that every effect has a cause, whether or not we are aware of it."

Cause and effect permeates the universe. Otherwise, God becomes cruel to some people and nice to others. I guess reincarnation originated from such a theory. Why do some people live in utter poverty, whereas others live in luxury? How can some live to the age of eighty or ninety, whereas others die young? Where is the justice for those good people who suffer if there is only one life? I know for sure that the God that we all believe in is extremely compassionate. Then why do I see so much disparity around me?

Although I don't necessarily know the cause, that doesn't mean I bore an autistic son out of the blue, for no reason. There is a reason for my life. Just because I don't see electricity with my naked eyes doesn't mean it does not exist.

October 2, 1997

Malini came home for a day. We went out to eat in a restaurant in the afternoon. Later that evening, we went out for coffee and ice cream. We really had a lot of fun. Krish had a wonderful time with Malini. The love between them is very touching. Whenever she talks about her residency in neurosurgery, she makes sure that she does not offend him. She is always eyeing his reactions, and she makes sure to mention how smart he is. When Krish did an equation in physics, she said, "Krish, I don't know how to do that. You have gone far beyond me in physics. Just like you, I am also interested in physics. Can you teach me physics someday?" Krish grinned from ear to ear on hearing that. Malini meant every word she said. Such a fine girl, always thinking of Krishna, always trying to be sensitive to him. I am prouder of her character than I am of her academic achievements.

Later that day, Krishna looked sad and dejected. In order to cheer him up, I gave him a speech on how lucky he is to be so smart, so handsome, and overall, so healthy. I also reminded him of how lucky he is to have a sensitive, smart sister who adores him.

He wrote in response:

My future kindles strange emotions. The future is uncertain; the life is boring; the perception of yours (meaning mine) messes up sad facts; no amount of reasoning can convince me. The reason for quite a large camouflage strengthening statements does not measure up to reality; the nature of autism restrains normalcy.

October 4, 1997

Yesterday, Krish went to Children's Hospital to have an EEG. He was extremely nervous about the test. The room in which the EEG was done was very small. He gets claustrophobic in crowded, small rooms. The second big concern he had was about being touched on his head. He used to be very sensitive about his head area, and he still is to some extent. For this test, he needed twenty-three probes stuck to his head with paste. In the beginning, he did not let the nurse apply the ointment to various areas of his head. He simply wouldn't let her. The time was passing by. The way it was going, we all felt that he would come home without having the test done. That would have been disappointing to everyone concerned.

When Nan asked Krishna what would make him let the nurse apply ointment, he wrote on the pocket computer, "Read to me." So Nan read to him. The nurse was successful in applying the cream. She also stuck three of the probes on his head. Suddenly, Krish moved, and all three probes came unglued. Again, Nan explained to him that if he kept on getting up, we would never leave the hospital. One thing is for sure, Krish did not want to spend the whole day in the hospital. He also started becoming interested in the book. While the nurse worked on the probes, Krish did not make much fuss. He was asked to lie down quietly. He did that.

Malini came to see him. That cheered him up quite a bit. She was stroking him so that he would be relaxed. He was so relaxed that he fell asleep for a few minutes. That pleased the nurse because she preferred that Krish be asleep during the test. He did very well during the test. When the ordeal was over, he was elated.

Krish then started talking: "I want to go to the bathroom. I am thirsty. I want to go home." The nurse couldn't believe that Krish could talk so well. She had been seeing a lot of disabled children, including autistic children. She also witnessed his writing on the computer. She felt that Krish is one of the highest-functioning autistic kids she has ever seen. She praised us for our dedication and the way we handled Krish during the EEG.

Next week, Krish is having his MRI. We don't know how that will go. I have to do a lot of praying until then. Living with Krishna has done one thing for me: it has made me a praying, God-loving person. I have no other alternative. Not a single day goes by without my asking God for help regarding Krish. Every day is unpredictable. The unpredictability of Krishna's problem has made me surrender to God. If Krish had been normal, I doubt whether I would be praying this sincerely. Of course, there would be less need for God, and more need for enjoyment. But I am happy God got me with the bait called Krishna. I am very thankful to God for letting me feel His presence.

October 5, 1997

Krish wrote a few lines about Lyndon Johnson this morning. He also wrote about Princess Diana's death:

> The tragedy of late Diana's death coverage overshadows her death; it recreates the same old scenes; it is highly melodramatic; the funeral coverage enumerated redundant themes. It was manipulated way too much.

Krish has strong views on everything. I remember the days when I used to wonder if Krish would ever form his own opinions about the world around him. I feared he might grow up to mimic whatever we or others say. Now, he is a man with his own thoughts, ideas, and values.

Today, I saw a show in which they talked about self-mutilation or self-abuse—about how some young people cut themselves with a needle or knife to make themselves feel better. They had so much tension building up inside them that, when it became too much to handle, these kids resorted to self-abuse. This actually gave release to their anger, frustration, tension, and other pent-up negative feelings inside them.

When I heard them talk, I was reminded of Krish's self-abusive behavior when he was two or three years old. I remembered how he used to hit his head on the wall while rocking in a corner. He looked very tense and intense while doing this act. I used to hold his frail, little body close to my body, against his will, so that he could not do it. Today's show shed light on the fact that Krish was self-abusive in those days in order to release his unbearable internal tension. Maybe hitting his head on the wall helped relieve him of his tension and actually made him feel better. What a concept! How little we know about our minds! Who knows how many of his bizarre behaviors also provide him relief!

October 6, 1997

Krishna has been behaving exceptionally well over the last two weeks. He is loving, caring, listening, and above all, helping around the house. He is a gentleman. My heart is so swollen with pride that it might burst and cause my death. But not now, especially after so many years of heartbreak and endless rounds of anxiety over his bizarre behavior, oh God, please not now! Though I promised God once that I would trade my life for his behavior to be normal, now I would do anything to get out of this deal. Right now, it is very hard to understand the urgency of my need to bribe God because he is behaving well. But when I was cornered and going crazy, I had nowhere to go but to our Savior. But don't we all go to Him when we are desperate?

If this good fortune continues, who knows, maybe he will marry someday and have a family of his own. My intense addiction to my dream may be like trying to get the moon as my golden cup, from which I want to drink my morning coffee. I may never come to a maturity level to realize that it is an impossible dream. Why should I be that practical anyway? Who could say that the dream that sparks a flame of enthusiasm in me for my existence is stupid, or meaningless, or impractical?

October 8, 1997

Today, we took Krish to Dr. Jones. When we arrived in his office, he saw us right away. This pleased me because Krish cannot deal with long waiting.

After studying his EEG and MRI, this is what he said:

> In the right frontal area in the temporal region there is a spontaneous firing. This shows as generalized spikes in the EEG. This is very abnormal. The effect of this is that the brain will be irritable. This is not a seizure, but in seizure patients, you will see these spikes also. *Now we know what is causing his restlessness.* The treatment for this is Depakote, a medicine that has been in use for twenty years. We know a lot about this medicine. It gives emotional stability and is an anticonvulsion drug. It will help to calm him. It is also good for depression. It will induce sleep also, like Haldol. His MRI is very normal.

Dr. Jones spoke of another patient who is taking eight times Krish's dosage. That patient seems to like the medicine, but the doctor wants to observe Krish before increasing the dosage in order to make sure that this medicine suits Krish.

Dr. Jones read what Krishna had written on MRI:

> High on nurse's mind was my behavior. High on Dad's mind was my behavior. The nurse was quite worried. The life was tense. The uppermost in my mind was freedom from hell. The life was miserable. The choice was either run away or control my mind. Running does not provide long-term solution. The only choice was mind control. The mind is tough to control. The very mind is a devil and savior. Periodic lecture is necessary. The first lecture came from Dad. Answered was Dad's prayer. The mind became calm. Relaxation started the minute I lied down. The alignment was perfect and hence no problem with the head mask. Head control was made easy by chanting "Om." The control was neat and perfect because of God's grace. I felt enormous relief when the nurse announced the end.

Dr. Jones is very puzzled about Krish's speech problem. If he can write so well, then what is preventing him from talking? His brain seems to understand language, so the problem must be localized. He also mentioned that another behavioral neurologist from Harvard is very interested in Krish's case. He, too, wants to observe Krish's neurological functions as well as his behavior.

This evening, Krishna looked totally wiped out, emotionally drained. He took his shower and ate supper, and then he went to bed by 8:00. Right now, he is listening to the tape about Alexander the Great. He seems to enjoy that tape very much.

Before going to bed, he wrote this comment about his visit to Dr. Jones:

> The visit was good. The mood of Mom has changed. The mood changed because careful analysis of the EEG has shown that frontal firing is causing behavior problems. The treatment offers hope. The visit was great. Drastic mood changes takes place all the time. The mood changes rob me of mental peace. Therapy in India gives calmness. Given ayurvedic treatment, behavior is somewhat controlled. The restlessness is reduced. The restlessness throws my mind off balance. The restlessness exists all day. The Kizhi massage gives the best relief. The western medicines produce far too many side effects. Given Haldol, great useless movement is manifested. The Haldol dulls the intellect.

Later that evening, Nancy Johnson called me. She is very concerned about Joe. He is acting more aggressive than usual, and so his residential program is giving him strong doses of Respirodol and some other medicine. The medication is making him a zombie. He is not active during the day. Nancy has decided to bring him home once a week. I think this will do some good. I told her that she should get a tape recorder and put on some stimulating audiotapes, such as those by or about Nelson Mandella, American history, and Mother Theresa, for him to listen to before bedtime. This will reduce his boredom and keep his mind alert. Learning is always important. She agreed.

October 9, 1997

Nan: Any thoughts for today?

Krish: Education nurtures the brain. The connection between physics and math is fascinating. By Coulomb's law (physics), one must derive Laplace's equation. Noting the relationship between calculus (math) and Gauss's law, one can derive the Laplace's equation. The Laplace's equation provides rather drastic and complete three-dimensional solution to a system consisting of charges and conductors. The Coulomb's is a simple one-dimensional law between two charges. Both the Coulomb's law and calculus are great in their sphere of knowledge.

As I listened, I was astonished at his knowledge. I understood nothing, zilch. I said that to him. He gave me a big grin. Just the thought that he has come from simple arithmetic to this level in the last four years simply boggles my mind! Can you comprehend his brilliance? It is not that he studies all day. He studies for two hours on math, physics, and electrical engineering. He cannot work more than three hours a day because of his illness. Yet with only two hours of daily study time, he has come this far in four years. *That is a miracle.*

I believe in God and His miracles. I also believe that they happen every day, all around us. That a virtually invisible sperm and an egg can create a beautiful human being is miraculous. Compared to that, my son's becoming normal must seem commonplace. So, my dream for him is not an unrealistic one. My undaunted faith in God and His miracles has made me focus on what Krish can do and not what he cannot do. I attend to what he cannot do only in order to set goals for him.

October 10, 1997

This afternoon, I talked to Dr. Jones. I started giving Krish the new medicine on Friday. I wanted to give him my observations of the last two days. I told him how well he sleeps. His speech has increased. His cooperation is better. His outbursts and irritability are reduced. Upon hearing this, the doctor was happy. He said he will write a case study on him. He was simply elated. He wants to see Krish before we leave for India.

Nan is an electrical engineer with a Ph.D. The following is his explanation or interpretation of the EEG results. He actually is elated about the connection between brain signals and electrical signals:

> In electrical circuitry, A emits electromagnetic signals. Another circuitry, B may not function properly if the signals from A interferes with it. I wonder whether two nerve signals interfere with each other in Krishna's brain. Maybe the frontal lobe misfiring shown in the EEG is due to interference.
>
> There are two ways to attack the problem. If we know where this noise is coming from and how to reduce it, then the unwanted noise can be eliminated, and the brain will function properly or let the noise be there, but shield the rest of the brain from the noise. In the electrical circuitry, you enclose the circuitry in a properly designed metallic box to shield the circuitry from the interference. This is one of the methods we use. In Krish's brain, if we know for sure where these noise signals are produced, maybe that part can be shielded.

Ayurevedic treatment improves Krish's abilities and behavior by at least 20 percent. If the Depakote improves him by another 10 percent, then together he may improve, not by 30 percent, but by 50 or 60 percent. That's synergy. We have heard about chemical explosions. I want such an explosion, such a synergetic creation to occur in Krish.

Yesterday, Krishna didn't do much. He slept a lot. He had a very bad cold, and he is on Depakote. I don't know which made him sleepy. But today, he seems much better. He wrote: "The new medicine is quite all right. The medicine helps in speech. The speech is coming because I am calmer. The mind is less restless. The Haldol is far too neurotic. It makes me a zombie."

October 30, 1997

We landed in India on October 17. It took Krish nearly a week to get over his jet lag. Since our arrival, Krishna hasn't been writing his essay on the computer. But he is using the pocket computer for communication. He is also undergoing intense ayurvedic treatments, which is tiring him quite easily. He is much calmer, and his behavior has improved. We are delighted with his progress. He looks much happier because the tidal waves of anxiety are receding, thanks to the medicated fomentation treatment called Kizhi.

November 1997

November 1, 1997

The day before our travel to India for the treatment, I was on pins and needles with worries, all day. I couldn't fall asleep that night. From Boston to Madras, India, it was more than twenty-four hours of travel. I was visualizing who Krish is and how the slightest disruption would make him lose his equilibrium and send him crashing into the proverbial wall.

That night, I was thinking about one particular day in the Bahrain airport some twelve years back. I still remember it as if it were yesterday. Every detail of that particular day is so vivid in my mind, I don't think that I will ever forget it, unless I were to receive electric shock treatment to kill those particular memory cells in the brain.

Our flight from New York to London got delayed by a few hours, which created a chain reaction of delays from London to Bahrain and Bahrain to Madras. From the time we left Boston, by the time we arrived in Bahrain, we had been traveling for nearly twenty-four hours. Krish was totally wiped out with exhaustion. Though he got on the plane in Boston with lots of cheer, when we landed in Bahrain, he was on the edge, but was under control. He tried very hard to be well behaved and cheerful. But then, unfortunately, the Bahrain airport terminal was not a spacious one and on top of that, it was overcrowded, with no seats available to sit down or lie down. Too many flights got delayed on that particular day, and so there were too many weary and unhappy travelers with very little patience.

Krish was sleeping when they served food on the London to Bahrain flight, so it was understandable that he was hungry when we landed. The restaurant was mobbed, and there was a mile-long queue. I stood in line while Krish and Nan were walking in circles, due to lack of space to move around in. It looked as if it would be an eternity before I could get a chance to order. While I was buying the food, I heard the last call for boarding the plane. I had no choice but to buy. I was well aware that on the plane dinner would be served only an hour after the take off. Krish couldn't or wouldn't survive without food for that long, and the stewardesses wouldn't care to understand him. Explaining autism to them would be like explaining a flash of lightning to a totally blind person.

When I got out of the restaurant and couldn't find Krishna or Nan, I went berserk. By this time, our names were announced over the PA system to board the plane. I was in a burning dilemma. So many questions were oozing out of my brain. Have they already left for the plane? In that case, should I proceed to the gate or stick with our agreement to meet and proceed together? What if I wait for them, and in the meantime, the plane leaves without me? I was freaking out. Worrying had sapped the little energy I had left in me.

Around this time, Nan and Krishna emerged from the men's room. They were unaware of the announcement. Krish announced clearly that he wanted to sit and eat since, to his astonishment, he found lots of seats empty because many had left to board their planes. All this time, he had been a model traveler, putting up with all kinds of stresses at the basic level, forgoing eating and sleeping. It was extremely heartwrenching to tell him, "Krish, we have to proceed to the gate. We have to go through the security check and so on. Why don't you eat on the plane?" I didn't expect hell to break loose at that point. But that's what happened. The exhaustion of traveling without adequate sleep for twenty-four hours and waiting for hours in the crowded transit lounge without a place to sit or eat did break the camel's back. He got out of control, more than I ever could have anticipated in a million years. At that point, nothing I could do or say would change the angry mood he got into.

Before we knew what had happened, he started running wildly through the security check. Krish was in the full throes of his autism, with all its true colors of unpredictability and unreasonable impulsiveness. Momentarily fleeing from the scene with aimless running without any regard for the resulting consequences was the ultimate response of the unbearable, explosive tension he was feeling at that very moment. He must have felt so claustrophobic that doing anything, no matter how thoughtless and stupid it may be, was better than the uncontrollable feeling of being boxed in. He wanted relief. He has always been known to run like an Olympic sprinter under such stressful times. Here also, I guess, his desperate mood demanded a desperate move from him.

I saw Krish running at the speed of light with three or four security guards holding guns chasing him. Everything happened so fast I could scarcely digest what was going on. We have been traveling all of our lives. But nothing like this ever happened before. My hands were tied. The security guards must have thought that Krish was a hijacker with a bomb running to get on a plane. In a few seconds, a dozen of them with guns in their hands were running after him. They were ready to rain bullets down on him. Here, in a Middle Eastern airport, an Indian American kid was running like a bolt of lightning through the security check into the open area where our plane was getting ready for takeoff. I saw a gaping, black tunnel of horror as my future, and my family's, at that terrifying moment.

I saw some ten people surround him and take him down. At that moment, I hadn't expected to see my gentle, sweet, innocent son alive. I never imagined in my life until that moment that autism could cost him his life. But it was happening before my own eyes and I couldn't do a thing to stop that from happening. My hands were tied. When they surrounded him, Krish being in the middle, I had no idea what was happening. Were they gunning him down or what? But even at that time, I was ferociously praying and having a mental dialogue with God. Please God, after all this hard work and human sacrifice, are we going to lose him to a violent death? Even if he died, his death would be in vain, for there is no real good cause. The world wouldn't blame the people who killed him, for they would be doing their job, which was to protect the other passengers. On top, the question on many people's minds would be, "Who asked that kid to run wild through the security area? Where were the parents and what were they doing? Why weren't they taking better care of him?" Please God, don't make us look like uncaring and irresponsible parents, which would feel like my very own death. I knew in my heart for some unknown reason that God wouldn't ditch me. It was "the survival of the fittest" time. "Kill or to be killed" time. When a couple of security guards came to take Nan and me to where Krishna was, I thought that they were taking us to the gallows. I felt very alone in that Middle Eastern airport. My whole existence was dangling in their hands.

When I saw him brought in, alive, I felt relieved. My pent up emotions got released in a floodgate of tears. I was sobbing uncontrollably, while Nan was trying to comfort me, and at the same time telling them that Krishna was autistic and could not talk well. When my emotions got under control, I asked Krishna to apologize for the scene he had created. Krishna obliged my request by saying, "I am sorry," to them.

Those security guards were very kind to him, and they felt sorry for what they had done. One of them actually got very emotional. He apologized over and over to me. I ended up comforting him by saying it was not his fault and he was doing only his duty, which is to protect the passengers. He couldn't have known Krish's problem. When I was asked, what can we do now so we can get on the plane without further incident, I said, "He should eat something before he boards the plane since the crew will be busy preparing for the takeoff. He will be given food only after they serve the other passengers, and also, they serve according to seat numbers. If he were to sit at the end in back, he would be served very late."

They telephoned the pilot of our plane to wait so that Krish could eat. Actually, they ordered ice cream for him. Krish was treated like a prince, and he was enjoying all the attention he was getting. When he left for the plane, he shook hands with them and even hugged one of them.

When we got on the plane, we were getting looks from stewardesses and the passengers. The plane got delayed by half an hour because of us, and the crew was indirectly letting us know. They made us feel guilty. When we got on the plane, the stewardess literally slammed the airplane door on my heels.

As I sat down and fastened my seatbelt, I had finally run out of puff. My blood sugar was totally used up. I felt as though I was trying so hard to keep my body engine running without any gas in the tank.

When dinner was served, I didn't eat much. I felt so weak from the frightening incident, I couldn't move my hand with a spoon to my mouth. It was too much of an effort. Nan was trying to feed me. But just chewing and swallowing was taking too much out of me again. I felt like a flat tire. I couldn't move any part of my body. I was trying so hard to keep my head above the water, but with no luck. I was virtually drowning in sorrow and the aftermath of the shock. How I was wishing to be all alone in an airless, windowless fortress in Siberia rather than being on that crowded flight, surrounded by a mass of people. I requested that Nan leave me alone.

After a couple of hours of melancholy, Nan was trying to console me:

Nan:	It must be tearing you apart. But you will get over the shock.
Jalaja:	Will I ever be? What if they had showered bullets on him?
Nan:	But they didn't. He is very much alive. Look at him, how much he is enjoying his dinner while listening to the

music. He is not suffering. Please try hard to get over it. Please think about something else.

Jalaja: This is very personal. I am an involved party here. I am not a reporter. I can't jump from one incidental news item to another.

I was in such a rotten mood, I didn't care whether Nan understood what I was going through or not. I was cutting off the hand that was trying to support me. Poor Nan! It is amazing how he put up with my mood at that time.

November 3, 1997

What will make Krish motivated to use the computer for his essay writing? Why this sudden allergy to writing? Am I to be blamed? Why can't I help him become motivated? Maybe I am pestering him too much; that may be the reason he is turned off. A skill like using the computer for writing will help him communicate with the world around him. He should be joyful, not unmotivated, to use the computer. Maybe I am not offering enough images to suggest the picture of success or quality of life that he would realize by using and improving his computer skills. He is somehow missing the point. How can an intelligent, logical person like Krish, though autistic, not know that having computer skills is sure to enhance his quality of life?

It is not that I am just trying to be positive about this skill. It is the truth. The fort called autism is his home, and it is pitch dark inside. He has been unable to find the exit to get out. All these years, we did not even know that there was a door to get out. But I do know now that there is a door, and that there is a world of opportunity beyond this door. I have been hammering that idea every day, relentlessly. Yet he is so afraid to open it. The excuse? "The door is too heavy. I can't do it." How can I motivate him to open the door and get out?

What can I do to convince him that the computer will give him access to the world outside, which will open up new possibilities for him? I cannot allow him to ignore this skill. He has to spend more time on the keyboard and more time on his communication, as well as his essays. There is always unpleasantness when it comes to using the computer. Letting him not do it lest he become unpleasant is tantamount to fostering his reluctance to do it.

I know the reason for his unwillingness to use the computer. His lack of coordination means his independent writing on the computer exhausts him in thirty minutes. But I believe the practice will help him improve his coordination. To him, the avoidance of the immediate pain is more important than any long-term gain. Though he has a legitimate reason, he must realize that the reason for practicing on the computer is far more logical. That is where I come in—to motivate him and make him strong enough to transcend the immediate obstacles.

I heard a man on television say, "Always *focus on* good behavior to cheer them up." He went on to say how a whale is trained to jump twenty feet over the water. First the trainer puts a rope underwater, and if the whale goes under the rope, he ignores it. But when the whale swims over it, the good behavior is rewarded with food. There ensues a relationship between the trainer and the whale after a while. The trainer slowly increases the height of the rope, and the whale responds by jumping over the rope, whereupon the trainer rewards the whale with food.

Is it that I am not letting him know that I am observing his good work and praising him enough? When we do the cheering, it creates positiveness, happiness, and a feeling of success in the person. Maybe that's the answer. I will keep score of his progress on his computer skills and give him positive feedback more often.

Once, Krish wrote that he wants to be a writer. He has eloquent written English, as well as great ideas. Too many of us say no too often to our children. I don't want to say to him, "You are autistic, and you have many fine motor problems and speech problems. So I don't think you can become a writer and publish a book." Building up his confidence is especially important. Yet he is unable just now to sustain much interest in using the computer for his writing. Still, if he has a dream to be a writer, I want to inspire him to be passionate about what he wants to do.

Anthony Mark Hankins, a fashion designer with a $50 million company, said that his mother not only let him use the sewing machine for the first time to make a dress for her when he was sixteen, she wore that dress to a wedding, also. She has no idea what kind of an encouragement she gave her boy by doing that. I was touched by her inspiring act. I told Krish that I will publish his work, no matter what it takes. It is a promise I have given him. What a smile he gave me when I uttered those words!

December 1997

December 8, 1997

Because he has been sick with the flu for the whole week, the treatment has come to a screeching halt. I feel terribly guilty. I didn't listen to the doctors. I was told time and again that Krishna should not sit in front of the fan right after his treatment. But Krish insisted on doing so. And I was not strict enough to disallow him. Now we are paying in a big way: no treatment for a full week.

December 14, 1997

Am I living the right life? If so, why am I not always happy? My happiness seems to rest on some achievement. I have got everything I worked for: enough money, a good marriage, good health, and kind, achieving children. Malini is studying neurosurgery at Harvard, and Krish is battling against autism. I believe that what Krish is accomplishing with his autism is as wonderful and difficult as what Malini is accomplishing in neurosurgery. Yet I don't feel that I have done the best in life. What's wrong? I am complaining that living with autism is stressful. It is stressful, but since Nan left his full-time job a year ago, I have a lot more freedom. Why don't I recognize and cherish the freedom that I have? Maybe I am putting too much importance on achievement. Perhaps I am equating it with peace of mind and happiness. My faith has taught me that happiness is now, and it is here. A reflective life, not a materialistic one, will bring happiness.

When I was young, I thought if I got married to an educated man, I would be happy. Then, when I got married, I thought if I had children, I would be happy. Then, when I had children, I thought if I had money in the bank, I would be happy. Then, when I had financial security, I thought if my daughter got married, I would be happy. Then, when she got married to a cardiologist, I thought if she became a physician, I would be happy. Now she is a doctor. But am I happy? No.

Now, why can't Krish be normal? I have worked hard with him. I have to think through everything in life with Krish. Nothing is easy and on the spot. It has to be well planned. No detail can be omitted. My thinking is that since my relatives and friends have spontaneous lives, I should also have one. So is it my birthright that he should be normal? Does any of this make sense? What I am saying is that my happiness is going to depend on Krishna's becoming normal. That means if he doesn't, I will die a sad, broken-hearted, unhappy person. Because he is autistic, he may never be normal, in spite of his brilliant mind. Thus, it is virtually guaranteed I will die a sad person. Is there any logic to my thinking? I thought I was smart. But I guess I am not. My brain is in a convulsion.

How can my happiness solely depend on Krishna? Does that mean that, though I say I am a devout Hindu, I am not? My religion tells me to accept whatever is given to me as a gift from God, and God knows best. I should surrender totally to Him. But am I doing that? I am questioning His wisdom in having given me an autistic son.

Why can't I appreciate life as it is? That is where happiness lies; in accepting what life is and not what it could be. If I ask, "What if Krish had been born normal, where would my life be?" It is a stupid question. It is like saying, "If I had been born as a white male, in America, in a middle-class family, and had a future from having a good education, I would have become president." Or it is like saying, "If I had been born in the place of Princess Diana, I would have become the wife of Prince Charles, and I would have become a queen if and when Charles became a king. Or if England changes the constitution, maybe, who knows, if and when Charles, my husband, dies, I will become the ruler of the country." All this amounts to nothing.

What is real is I have an autistic son who is growing well, but there is no guarantee that I will see him grow to be normal before I die. I have to accept the reality and move on. Happiness is not in the future; it is now and here. "What if?" is the dumbest question any intelligent person can ask. If I want to be happy, I have to stop now, where I stand, and find happiness. I need nothing more to be happy. In spite of everything, I should be happy. In this changing world, nothing is certain.

Look at Christopher Reeve; in the prime of his life, he lost everything in one spill. He lost all of his motor functions. Now, he is totally dependent on others for his basic needs. He can't even breathe on his own; he is hooked up to a ventilator. Anything can happen to anybody, at any time. Nobody is necessarily free from tragedy. President Kennedy was shot to death by a crazy man. Neither his position, his power, nor his wealth protected him. The United Nations secretary general died in a restaurant. The cause? Choking on a fish bone. A plane crash, a diving accident, a stroke, a heart attack, any one of them can alter a life. Our life is so flimsy. I better make the best use of my life.

I was inspired by the courage of Christopher Reeve. While I was thinking of him admiringly, a flash of thought came: "Wait a minute. I admire him. Do I admire my own son for the war he is waging against autism?" It was really overwhelming. What strength Krish is displaying against overwhelming odds! He has been persevering, day after day, for more than twenty years, on very simple tasks that we all take for granted. What is the source for his energy and strength of mind for the relentless pursuit to learn simple skills? His trying is the proof that he hasn't given up.

These thoughts melted my heart. I started sobbing. I have no right to be unhappy. If Krish can be this strong, then in the eyes of God, I am sinning for being unhappy and complaining. I am blessed because Krish hasn't given up on life. This is good enough reason for me to be happy for the rest of my life.

December 29, 1997

Today Krishna's ayurvedic doctor said:

> Body and mind are one and the same. When the body is sick, the mind gets weak and restless and doesn't perform at its peak. When the mind is anxious, fearful, and worried, the body is affected. It is like when a pot is boiling hot, the cold water you pour in that pot will get hot, and thus the temperature of the water is affected. When the boiling hot water is poured into a cold pot, the pot loses its coolness. That's the way the mind and body are connected. In western medicine, the physicians don't look at the whole human being. They treat part by part.

In ayurvedam, the physician prays deeply before he starts the treatment. In his praying, the physician acknowledges that he is only the instrument in the hands of God. Only He can heal the body, not the physician. The physician prays that he never become arrogant because of the knowledge he possesses, which is given to him by His Grace. The physician also instructs us to pray for recovery. Right before every new treatment, he prays with the family for the success of the treatment.

According to ayurvedic doctors, medicine teaches humility in the practitioner. The more a doctor knows, the more the doctor feels he doesn't know. Sometimes one doesn't even know that he doesn't know. There is no way he can know it all. The doctor always tells us that we have to trust our inner self to heal our ailing body.

The ayurvedic hospital is set on the riverbanks with lots of trees; coconut, mango, palm, cashew and so on; very rustic looking. Peace permeates the whole place. One doesn't need to sit in meditation. Just being there will envelope you in the warm, cozy blanket of meditation. For Krishna, who is pestered with anxieties, penetrated with uncertainties, and pivoted by unreal worries, this quiet, tranquil, serene place with nonthreatening, mild-natured staff and doctors is a haven from autism. He could keep his distance from people and at the same time is not lonely. The hospital is in a small, poor town that offers very little in terms of entertainment. Anyway, Krish loves to read books, go for long, pensive walks, listen to classical music and tapes on books. He doesn't care for parties or noisy entertainments. His syndrome with his malfunctioning senses wouldn't let him. I don't think my daughter could survive for a week in such a place. She would call it "boring."

Along with the doctors, the hospital employs around fifty people, who work with the fifty patients, so they have plenty of time to spend with each and every patient. They are very kind and caring and very much involved with the treatment of the patients. The place is buzzing with activities. Each ward has a veranda, bedroom, kitchen, and massage room. Usually we are given an independent house with three bedrooms and two bathrooms, a big kitchen, and a huge porch enclosed with mosquito net.

Krish has been undergoing ayurvedic treatment for the last five years. In those five years, his progress has been nothing short of a miracle.

January 1998

January 17, 1998

Scientists are trying to come up with a vaccine for melanoma, a type of skin cancer. If this vaccine works, maybe they will also come up with vaccines for other forms of cancers. I wish someone would discover a vaccine for autism. Who knows, maybe the next generation of scientists and researchers will find a cure for autism. In the 1920s, people were dying of anemia, but not any more; vitamin B12 cured the deficiency. Streptomycin, in the 1950s, saved the lives of people who had tuberculosis. A few decades ago, we came up with antibiotics. Infection following surgery was the number-one killer. But now, it is controllable, thanks to antibiotics. Even the scourge of AIDS may soon be contained.

Perhaps, in a few decades or so, we will have a U.S. president diagnosed with autism, who needs to take only a couple of pills a day to control the symptoms. We may not have a cure for autism, but it will be controllable, in the same way that high blood pressure and diabetes are now controllable.

January 18, 1998

Today, we were talking about having goals in life. Krish was listening with all ears, and at one point, he started to breathe hard:

Jalaja: Do you want to say something on the subject?

Krish: I want to write.

He went to the computer and wrote:

Goal kindles the purpose in life and thus kindles joy of life. Joy of life kindles my interest in learning. In fact, emotions and learning are coupled. The learning offers hope when life is emotionally soothing.

My goal of learning math and physics, which I love, builds up my sagging confidence. The building of confidence eliminates terrible negative thinking. My negative thoughts are "I am autistic." Far cry is normalcy for an autistic. Far removed is the territory of autism from normalcy. High on people's mind is the funny behavior of mine.

On the other hand, my goal of learning math or physics creates positive thoughts, such as, "I am improving. My parents are dedicated to me.

I am intelligent and almost brilliant." As my mother says, the world will see me for who I am, despite autism.

January 19, 1998

Living with an autistic can be very tough. I recently was thinking about a friend of mine who has an autistic child. Debbie is divorced and alone takes care of her son. She was once audited by the IRS and had to meet with an agent. Along with her records, she took her autistic son. Before very long, the agent was asking too many questions, and she had had it.

She wanted to make him realize how tough life could be with an autistic son, so she went to use the restroom, leaving her son with the agent. When she returned, the agent was disheveled and out of control. In fact, the whole room was a mess. Papers and books were strewn all over the place. Upon seeing her, he said, "Take him away. I'm glad you are back. I can't do a thing with him. How do you live sanely with a kid like that?" She was so happy he learned his lesson. Never did the IRS agent bother her again. She got her point across.

Here, I want to stress a point, that it is unfair to compare my son's behavior to that of my friend's son. Krishna is far better and has come a long way in every area, including behavior.

Life with an autistic person always brings out the intensity in others around him. My life has always been tense as well as intense. It is ridiculous to think that one can have an autistic at home and have a relaxed, easygoing life.

With Krish, there is no halfway. Either you give all or you walk away. Krish, with his autism, is all consuming. Whatever I do, whatever I think, whatever I feel revolves around him. My total being centers on him. Krishna is the nucleus of my existence. The undaunted spirit in me has driven me to defy all the odds against autism. "Prosperity is a great teacher; adversity is a greater teacher. Possessions pamper the mind; privation trains and strengthens it."

When Krish was young, I tried to explain to our relatives and friends why it was so necessary to be exclusively focused on Krish. I told them that without Nan and me, Krish has been given a death sentence. Still, they would ask why I couldn't get away to take care of myself for an hour or two in a day.

I often try to convince my relatives and friends of my situation with the following allegory, in order to shed some light on my decision to live a life of intensity:

> A man purchased an egg, and he wanted to preserve it until it hatched. So he obtained a chick. But at the same time, he wanted to eat it, too. So he thought, "Let me keep one half of the egg for hatching and eat the other half." He went on to implement his plan. The result was disastrous. He neither had the egg for hatching nor the whole egg for eating. Either way, he was a loser.

January 20, 1998

At times, I wonder whether my life was spent in vain. Perhaps I could have become a successful professional with my intensity, dedication, and tireless work toward a goal. I feel a woman in a gray suit is very much appreciated for juggling a career along with motherhood. Many of us think of it as a big deal. On the other hand, a mother with a disabled child at home is like a mirage, almost unreal. She is the most unrecognized and the most unappreciated person because she never seems to do anything big in the world's eyes. But in reality, she is so involved with a bigger than life challenge that she doesn't even have time to take care of her basic needs. She is so left out in a society where there is no glamour and no value attached to her work. At times, this desperate loneliness is excruciatingly unbearable for me. Is it all worth it?

However, I often try to remind myself that nobody's life is trivial, and no one action is worthless—certainly not a life spent for the love of one's child. Doesn't love make the world go around? As George Bernard Shaw wrote, "Perhaps the greatest social service that can be rendered by anybody to the country and to mankind is to bring up a family." This kind of thinking always restores my equilibrium, without fail.

Whether I live long or die soon, my love for my son will be immortalized in this diary. As Keats wrote in "Ode to a Nightingale":

> *Thou was not born for death, immortal bird!*
> *No hungry generations tread thee down;*
> *The voice I hear this passing night was heard*
> *In ancient days by emperor and clown.*

February 1998

February 10, 1998

This morning, he was restless and again, despondent. I spent nearly two hours talking to him in the morning.

After my talk, he studied well. He then reminded Nan to get yogurt from the shop while coming back from the library. For the first time in a long time, he listened to the television news attentively.

Later in the day, Krish initiated a conversation on death. He wrote, "I'm scared of death. Need to talk about death." This is what I said to him:

Jalaja:	You cannot worry about death. Death is something nobody can escape from. Sooner or later, we all succumb to death. It is following us like our shadow. It is like saying I am afraid of my shadow. You tell me, can we try to escape death? Is it possible?
Krish:	As possible as trying to bury one's shadow.
Jalaja:	Exactly. There is one glaring truth about life, that is, we all die. The only thing is, we don't know the exact date or time.
Krish:	I'm scared of cancer.
Jalaja:	Why cancer? You can worry about a car crash, plane crash, drowning in the pool, and so on. You start worrying like this, you will never be able to get on a plane or go in a car. Do you want to live in constant fear?
Krish:	No.
Jalaja:	Because nobody is singled out in death, why worry about something that happens to every living thing? From the time of birth, the decay starts. The baby grows to become a boy, a teenager, an adult, an old man, and ultimately, dies. We have to accept growth, decay, and death. Once we accept death, we become free of fear.
Krish:	Easy to say, but very difficult to practice.
Jalaja:	You are right. Unfortunately, we are given no choice in regard to our death. All I can say is that by fearing death, you are dying inside every day. A fearless person will have a joyous life. So don't worry about cancer or death. That fear will cripple your healthy mind. That is a can-

cer of the mind. Actually, it is worse than any cancer. To be fear-free, you have to accept reality.

Krishna: But, can't help worrying.

Jalaja: If worry and fear can give you a good life, make you happy, by all means you should cultivate fear and worry. But does fear make you feel good?

Krish: No, not at all.

Jalaja: So why worry to inherit unhappiness? Fear and worry rob us of our vitality, our motivation, our zest for life, and ultimately, our happiness. Right now, there is no reason to worry. Are you diagnosed with cancer?

Krish: Certainly not.

Jalaja: Then there is zero reason to worry. So stop this useless, stupid worry. It is very destructive.

Krishna looked very serious while we were talking, then he came over to me and took my hand and said, looking into my eyes, "I love you, my best friend."

February 15, 1998

This morning, he is peevish, unhappy, and not in the mood for doing anything. All he wants to do is lie down. I am wondering if he is depressed. Maybe he needs a psychiatrist to treat his lack of motivation and unusual feeling of tiredness. I don't know much about depression. From what I have read, it is not that uncommon. Unusual tiredness and lack of motivation are a few of the characteristics of depression.

I also wonder if all autistic children have depression. If you look at these kids when they are occupied with their self-stimulating behaviors, like chin tapping or rocking, they look so confused. They don't look very cheerful or free of anxiety. Those self-stimulating activities exhibit a lot of anxiety and tension in most children. Chin tapping and rocking are not very happy, creative activities. While engaged in such behaviors, autistics seem to be preoccupied with one thought and one thought only; they are oblivious to the world around them. So they cannot be distracted from their repetitive activities.

The same destructive, painful theme is being played over and over in their minds, and they don't know how to escape.

What kind of a mind would allow itself to have such destructive, uncontrollable, negative thoughts? I am sure it must be a very unhappy, frightened, sick mind. To me, that is depression. I feel that these children should be treated for depression. Perhaps that could reduce their sadness and anxiety, which in turn, might reduce the behaviors that stem from having such an imbalanced mind.

For the last two years, I have been plagued by these thoughts. I saw, on television, how Prozac can help mild depression. I called my family doctor right away and got the prescription. I gave Krish one 5-mg pill, and I noticed marked improvement in his mood swings. The doctor said that the dosage was so minuscule that he was amazed to see any change in him. Because the doctor had little information on the prolonged use of the medication, I stopped giving Krish the Prozac after a month for fear of doing him permanent damage.

Every day, after I talk to him, he studies and behaves well. But it takes so much out of me, as well as out of him. Can a simple pill from a psychiatrist help him? If so, maybe I won't need to spend so much time realigning his mind in the right course every day.

This morning, I told Krish that his sister called and that she said something that made sense to me. Malini said:

Mom, Krish is so bright. He can learn in one week what I can learn in a month. Yet he is not making use of his brilliant mind and working hard to become all right. He doesn't need to talk since he can communicate through the computer. Look at Dr. Hawkins. He is physically a lot more disabled than Krish. But his mind is positive, strong, and tough, whereas Krish's mind is weak. If his mind got strong, Krish would make it in life, in spite of his coordination and speech problems.

I told him this and still more:

Krish, you get up every morning with peevishness, frustrations, lethargy, negative attitudes, and unhappiness. It takes so much energy and time to set you right. I have to thank God for at least making my words work for you. But it takes an hour to two hours before you smile and become all right. I cannot keep on giving you pep talks, a couple of times a day, throughout my life. At some point, you have to store them in your memory and rehearse them periodically and get strength from them.

Right now, I am going to give you a vivid picture of what we are going to do. First, we both are going to collect all of your insecurities, anxieties, fears, bad attitudes, anger, and so on, and get them out of your body. Remember, your body is sacred, and it is the temple of your soul. So we cannot contaminate it with all the negative emotions. We take out all those and pile them up in front of us, pour a lot of the gasoline of logic on them, and ignite the wood sticks of unwanted fears and anxieties. Now the bundle is burning ferociously. We are both watching the huge flames rising taller than we are. We are watching, watching. Still watching. Now, suddenly, the ferocity is slowing down. The height of the fire is getting shorter and shorter. At last, we see no flames. Instead, we see a heap of ashes. Now, Krish is free of anxiety, fears, stress, tensions, insecurities, and negative attitudes.

I turned to Krish and said, "Now, are you ready to study and concentrate on learning and enjoying life?" He let out a big laugh. He took my hand and started massaging it. "You are too nice, too *nice*. I love you," he said, and he gave me a kiss on the cheek.

At that point, I said, "Nobody can mend their behavior, including me, the way you can after listening to me talk. That is what smartness is all about—being flexible enough to change instantaneously when you see logic. I am so proud of you, Krish."

Krishna wrote on the computer with an impish smile on his face, "I have a great therapist at home." After that, he went upstairs to study.

February 20, 1998

A couple of weeks ago, a small incident that happened to my eighty-four-year-old mother—she slipped and broke her ankle—bothered him. Krish loves my mother dearly, so he became a little depressed when he heard about this. Nan and I, however, did not know he was upset over this incident. We noticed the symptoms, such as reluctance to write his essay, lack of motivation, and lack of concentration, but we failed to notice the cause. If we had given him a small dose of Prozac right away, he might have come out of it.

Once on the Prozac, he was back to normal, again writing on the computer. But he was still feeling tired in the mornings. We wanted to overcome this unusual tiredness. My desire for him to become normal is so intense that I want to take chances with medicines. We cover up the glaring facts, such as Krish's near normal behavior, with other facts, such as he is more tired than usual and sleeps a couple of hours more. So, we went to Dr. Jones. As usual, we wanted to improve the situation. This attitude is always with us. This is what made us travel to Tokyo for his schooling; to India for his treatment; to New York, twice a year, for his megavitamin therapy; to Philadelphia, for his sensory integration therapy. It made Nan give up a six-figure salary and take chances with his career. It made me give up my graduate course work when I was getting A's. We have given up a great deal over the years.

Usually, we no longer go to neurologists, who have been, in the past, of little or no help. Once, when he was thirteen, he was given Melleril, which made him behave like a zombie. He slept all day and did very little. When he was forced to work, he became uncontrollable. To us, it seemed as though he became even more autistic. So we stopped the Melleril within a few days. After that experience, we never went back to any doctors for medications until six months ago. We felt the medications did more harm than good. But when his EEG indicated spikes in the central lobe area, Dr. Jones gave him Depakote before bedtime. This medicine is supposed to be good for sleep, but it did not change his peevish behavior.

A few days ago, Dr. Jones wanted to try Neurontin for his spikes. The devastation it did to him in two days cannot be comprehended by the human mind. Krish became neurotic and extremely anxious, which manifested itself as hyperactivity. His group of unwanted bizarre behaviors came back, after years of absence. He started flushing the toilet every few minutes. He would brush his teeth every few hours. He went haywire. A lot of obsessive-compulsive behaviors started cropping up in him. He couldn't sit still for more than a couple of minutes to study or write. The medicine certainly must have stimulated that part of his brain.

Last night, he was awake and anxious all night. He was going to the bathroom every fifteen minutes. He was breathing hard, restless, and tense. At last, he fell asleep at 4:00 a.m. He woke up at 7:00 a.m., still restless. He took a shower and started walking in the damp basement. The restlessness is continuing even though Neurontin was given at 6:00 p.m. yesterday. We also gave him Depakote, 250 mg, at 8:00 p.m. for his sleep, and 1 mg of Haldol at 9:00 p.m. to calm him down. All this was done under the doctor's supervision. But they were of no use. His anxiety was unmitigated and going strong until 1:30 p.m. So I gave him another Depakote. Usually I give him Depakote, 1 pill, at 8:00 p.m. every day, for sleep. That will knock him out in thirty minutes. But yesterday, thanks to Neurontin, Depakote was useless.

The conclusion we came to is never to use Neurontin again because it triggers the very basic element of autism, which is anxiety. That is what we have been trying to eliminate all of his life. The structuring is aimed at mitigating anxiety. The ayurvedic treatment is powerful in the sense that it has drastically reduced his anxiety level over the years. Now this new medicine has destroyed the progress of years of hard work in a few small pills, like an earthquake demolishing an entire city.

The most precious lesson from this ordeal is to be contented with what you have. I wanted more, more, more. That is why I risked what I had with Krish's improvement and made it worse. It was a painful lesson I learned yesterday. I did virtually nothing. That doesn't mean I was having a good time, with a movie or a book. I was overworked and overwhelmed with worry and constant supervision. I didn't want to fall asleep. I wanted to know what this medicine was doing to him. So I made sure I didn't fall asleep so that I could witness all the results of this medicine. They were not pleasant. They made my stomach turn inside out.

My research gave clarity to my mind. I need to stop giving him any and every medicine. Every few years, we want to try new medications to improve him. But so often his reactions to them are so bad that I blame myself for trying, and I feel guilty for knocking him off balance. I always, without fail, find him worse off after taking medications. The neurologist wanted us to continue with the medicine for a few more days. Sometimes, these reactions to new medications would clear up. Thus, he reasoned. But I didn't want to listen to him because I was becoming more autistic than Krishna. The doctor is not living with him; we are. Right now, living with him is becoming a nightmare.

The other lesson I learned is that we have to tell doctors that any medicine that triggers anxiety cannot be given. Unfortunately, the doctors don't know which medicine gives what side effects to an autistic person like Krish. He is like an alien from outer space in the realm of chemical imbalance. Rarely does a medicine suit him. The core of autism is anxiety. All the unwanted, bizarre behaviors are produced by intense anxiety. Anxiety also causes lack of attention and lack of motivation. Anxiety is the basic foundation of autism. This revelation came to me in the middle of the night. Always, the research is done by us. But it is Krishna who ultimately pays the price.

No medicine is available to improve willpower. Krish, alone, must resolve to strengthen his mind. He has to trust God and say prayers regularly for a strong mind. He has enough command of the written English language. He must start writing about his feelings and insecurities. He needs some form of relief.

Right now, what he needs is more control over his mind. In the last four years, he has learned a lot, read a lot, and listened to a lot of educational tapes. Now, the next step is control of mind and motivation, without which there is no life for him. Our energy should go toward helping him strengthening his mind. *But how?*

February 21, 1998

Four years ago, we gave him thakra dhara continuously for three months. After that, his reading, his education, his concentration, and his behavior all improved. We were elated. Once, Nan took him to the symphony. Can you imagine an autistic sitting through the performance without attracting attention to himself? Our joy knew no bounds. He looked normal wherever he went. As long as no one turned around to see him or stare at him, he was normal to me. But we, in our anxiety for his growth, completely forgot about the effects of this treatment. If by some miracle his anxiety can be eradicated and calmness restored, as it was in 1994, he will shine like a star with his God-given strength.

This morning, Krish is miserable, and he is crying. I have just had it. He woke up at 5:00 a.m. He had his shower by 5:30 a.m. If he is up, everybody is up. He started coughing like a maniac. When he coughs, it is not a normal cough. He coughs from his guts, very powerfully; it is an earth-shaking cough. That scares me to death. I can never deal with that kind of a cough. I always worry for his lungs. What if his lungs collapse? I have to go to a doctor and find out if such a deep, gut-level cough can puncture his lungs. Krish doesn't care, no matter how many times I tell him to cough normally. On top of it, he always wants to go to the damp, cold cellar to walk. This always aggravates his cough. Again, he doesn't get it. His skull must be so hard, it doesn't let any good messages get in.

This morning, I was furious. I screamed at him:

> You are so stupid. Either you should know what's good for you or listen to someone who is right. You have neither discrimination nor obedience. You are smart, but you are not using your smartness to come out of autism. Your mind is your enemy now. You are listening to your fickle, weak mind, and not to your strong intellect. Slaughter your stupid, fickle, negative mind with your God-given, strong, logical intellect. That brain of yours is your armor. Use it to shield yourself from your jumping-jack mind. Don't choose negativism over positivism. It is very easy to be negative initially, rather than positive. Only initially. Later, it takes hours and days, even years, of work to undo the harm. So cultivate positive habits. Initially, they are hard, but later, it pays enormous dividends in life. Negative emotions, negative habits, and negative actions are like walking in quicksand. You only totally ruin yourself. So stop being so negative.

He started crying so loudly, I had to leave the room for my own sanity. As I was leaving, I heard him say, "Stop giving me medicine. I can't take it." I reassured him that I would never give Neurontin to him again.

February 22, 1998

Krish is so talented, brilliant, logical, analytical, and above average when he is communicating over the computer. But why is his behavior so unintelligent, virtually stupid, and on the verge of insanity at times? Why? Why?

For instance, he opened a loaf of bread in the evening. How did he do it? He tore it open. Nobody does it that way. I thought about his cousins, his sister, his brother-in-law. Would they do it that way, tear it open? A couple of pieces fell on the floor. Did he pick up the bread that fell? Did he put it back in the plastic bag? No! I don't think he even noticed the bread on the floor. He grabbed a couple of pieces and went away. No meaning to reality. Reality is bread all over the floor and a torn bag.

In another instance, he went into the bathroom to brush his teeth. He spent only a couple of seconds on brushing, and he rinsed his mouth right away. That incident told me that he was not brushing to clean his teeth, but that it was an obsessive-compulsive behavior. What did it achieve? He came out with the same dirty teeth. He did not clean his teeth. It is like his flushing the toilet aimlessly. But if you sit him down and let him talk on the computer, he will give perfectly intellectual answers about his obsessive-compulsive behavior. This is how he behaves unreasonably when he is plagued with hyperactivity and sleeplessness.

At such times, there is no connection between his intellect and his action. It is like a person's asking me, "How do you turn off the light?" And I respond, "Every lamp comes with a switch to turn it on and turn it off. You simply turn the switch in a particular direction to turn it off. It is as simple as that." Then, the same person requests that I demonstrate turning the light off. In response, I simply touch the lamp, and then walk away.

It takes a methodical, relaxed approach with some intensity. First, you must find the switch by feeling with your hand or by looking under the lamp. Once you locate the switch, try to turn it off. Try one way, and if it does not work, try another way; try pulling, pushing, turning, pressing. You need patience and mental control to do this. The major thing is to control the mind. Patience comes from mind control.

Last night, I was thinking, why does Krishna behave almost stupidly, in spite of his brilliance that is known *only* to his family? I had a tough night; I could not sleep at all. Finally, around 12:30 a.m. I did fall asleep. Then, around 2:10 a.m., I woke up. The first thought I had was, "Control. Control." It was a revelation in the middle of the night.

It dawned on me that Krish's problem is nothing but a lack of control. I always felt structuring gave him some control. He looks normal when he writes on the computer. In every activity, structured and supervised, he looks normal. Whenever someone is with him, making him accomplish something, he looks normal. When he brushes his teeth on his own, he is in a hurry to get it over with. There is no control of mind. But when someone else stands by the bathroom door, he does a good job. He has the brushing skill, but not the patience to do it for a longer time. He knows the skill of brushing as well as anyone else. But when he does it, his patience disintegrates. Why? When someone else stands by, looking at him, he does a decent job.

To finish any job, big or small, you need patience. For that, you need mind control. So patience and mind control are interrelated. My method of structuring his time has given him lots of skills and has reduced lots of his bizarre behaviors. But my method has not gotten him out of autism. Why?

Then a thought came to my mind. What did Haldol do? I have seen, whenever I give him Haldol, it gives him *some* patience; his obedience, listening, and mental control all improve dramatically. We are so lucky that he can improve so dramatically on such a small dose. Moreover, I see stability in his mood swings. On top of it, he becomes a pussycat with little or no aggression at all. All this for 2 mg of Haldol for the entire day. Then why are we not giving it to him? Because we are so damn stupid!

We choose aggression, nonlistening, obsessive behavior, weak mindedness, all this and more because we are afraid the Haldol makes him a zombie. And Krishna also *refuses* to take it. According to him, the medication turns him into a moron. We always said, "It cures symptoms, but not the underlying cause." We are struggling to keep him from aggression, to encourage him to work on the computer, to make him listen, to keep him away from the basement with his wild cough. Dr. O'Shea, the allergy specialist, told us when Krishna was eight years old that Krish will get liver problems later on if he continues to use Haldol. I got scared and stopped it. But we still use it during plane trips or long car rides.

Once I had a conversation with Krishna about the medication.

Jalaja:	How is Haldol?
Krishna:	I simply hate it. Makes me a zombie.
Jalaja (jokingly):	Are you in thoughtless awareness like one is in meditation?
Krishna:	Thoughtless? Yes. Awareness? None.

We all laughed.

I strongly believe that Haldol can give him some control. It doesn't let him jump off the cliff when his autism is at its peak. The ayurvedic treatment helps reduce the side effects of Haldol—the hand stiffness, sleepiness, and drooling. The treatment also keeps the dosage small and stimulates the brain.

When I was talking to Krish about the benefits of Haldol as well as counseling by a practitioner, he said, "Love. Love can cure. It is already improving me. Love is very powerful."

It triggered an entirely new approach to this issue. I couldn't help admiring his perceptive, thoughtful answer. Life can be led if one person loves you for who you are, unconditionally. You can face life's sorrows and difficulties undaunted. Life's disappointments and tragedies won't turn you into a bitter human being if you love and are loved. Love is very powerful. Here I am, talking about counseling, when he is coming up with a better and deeper answer to the problem. He is absolutely right.

I know a young woman, my friend's daughter, who had deep-seated wounds that interfered with her reaching her potential. She got married. Her husband and his family gave her so much love and acceptance that she was able to come to terms with her father's rejection and her mother's death. Now, she is a shining star in her career. The transformation was brought about by pure love. This is what Krish is talking about.

In my own case, when I was in my early thirties, I was plagued by my sadness over Krish's condition, by my despair over my father's premature death when I was eight, by my baseless worry about something terrible happening to Nan, and by my constant anxiety over saving money for Krish's future needs. The love of my guru, my spiritual guide, healed the scars and gave me enormous hope and courage to go on with life in a positive manner. His love and concern for me made me grow into a deeper-thinking person who can withstand the trials of life like a blade of grass in a storm. I never needed therapy because I am insulated with love. Love allows me to face the tough realities of life.

In the morning, Krish was laughing so much that we asked him what the joke is. He said, "You guys love me so much that nothing bothers you. I am giving hell to you guys. *But you don't give up.*"

February 23, 1998

Today, we drove to New Jersey. It is a five-and-a-half-hour journey. We were talking about how our success in life depends on the choices we make. Choices are everything. Some people are in the maximum security prisons because early in life, they chose to be in the wrong group and to be influenced by the members of that group. Later, they ended up in a situation where they committed armed robbery or some other crime, and now, they are in the prison. Likewise, Clinton wanted to become president of the United States, and he chose a path that would lead him to the White House. I said:

> There is nothing a person cannot achieve when he puts his mind to it. Look at Gandhi, Lincoln, Mother Theresa. Why go that far? Look at Krishna. What he has achieved is nothing less than a miracle, for an autistic. Against all odds, he is improving.

Then I wanted to find out what Krish thought about making choices:

Jalaja:	Do you think, Krish, you came this far due to the choices you made?
Krish:	Yes.
Jalaja:	What choices?
Krish:	Learn more and stimulate the brain.

I was very happy to hear those words from him. They were music to my ears.

February 26, 1998

This morning, right after his shower and breakfast, Krish said that he is tired and doesn't want to work. I got upset and said the following:

> After ten hours of sleep, nobody can be that tired. It is the mind that is playing tricks. Do you think anybody wants to work? Not me! Early in the morning, I have to make your ayurvedic medicine, at 5:45 a.m. Do you think that I am thrilled to do hard work? Believe me, I am doing it because I have to do it. Do you think the people who drive in the early morning rush hours to go to work love the driving in the traffic? They do it because they have to feed their families. It is out of responsibility that people do what they don't like to do. You cannot always do things you like. Most of the time, you do what you don't like, but have to do. So

now, go up and study. Don't waste your precious mornings. The whole afternoon, from 12:00 p.m. to 5:00 p.m., you do nothing but have fun with Rich. After 5:00 p.m., you are too tired to do serious studying. Please don't do work based on what you like and what you don't like, but go by what is good for you in the long run.

Right away, upon hearing me, he got up from the couch and went upstairs to his study room. I am fortunate in that no matter what I say, he sees some logic in it and changes his mind. My tough advice doesn't seem to bother him. My talk is his Haldol, his Respiradol, his Depakote.

Again, in forty minutes, he was back in the family room, which is like a football stadium, 26 feet by 26 feet. He has ample space to walk around. On seeing him waste away his precious morning, because he is leaving around 11:00 a.m. to go to Boston, I again started my lecture. At that time, I was practicing my music. Though I was upset, I didn't want to reveal my anger to him.

I said very casually:

You know, Krish, it is very important for your happy existence to learn. The process of learning gives freedom from worries, sorrows, tension, and wrong emotions. Learning takes away your mind from mundane, day-to-day worries. That is the only reason I put an hour aside for classical music. It takes my mind away even from you. It doesn't have to be done for the sake of earning money. You are thinking, what am I going to do with this much physics, math, and electrical engineering if I cannot earn money? Besides earning money, learning stimulates your mind and refines it. It develops thinking, concentration, and deeper insights. It gives purpose to life. You can never underestimate knowledge. It is very powerful. Knowledge is like a sharp-edged sword with which you can cut your ignorance into pieces. It can do wonders to the mind and soul. Don't stop learning. Learning is oxygen to the mind. Never let your mind get bored and monotonous. Life becomes a bore without the challenges of learning.

He listened to me carefully. At the end of my talk, he left again for his study room. This morning, he seems to need a lot of lecturing from me. That, for now, seems to motivate him to study. I don't really understand why he is so unmotivated when he is so bright. Sometimes I feel he is overwhelmed with his disability of being autistic. He loses sight of the purpose in living. I cannot blame him for the way he feels, so hopeless and helpless.

Krish cannot communicate orally very well. He needs a computer to be able to communicate. But because of his coordination problem, his fingers don't move fast enough to match his racing mind. Sometimes, he is hyper, and sometimes he feels very tired. With medication, he sleeps, but he gets easily tired in the daytime. Any wrong food—like coffee, coke, artificial coloring or flavoring—affects his behavior. Changes in the weather also affect his health; he continually gets colds, which in turn affect his motivation level. He is fighting every battle in every corner, constantly, day after day. Not just for a year. This is the fight he has been waging ever since he was a baby. It is relentless. The payoff for such hard work is so very little. As if all this were not enough, he has to fight the misconceptions and perceptions of the world around him.

Not too many autistic adults live at home. That puts even more pressure on him because his paranoid mother doesn't let him be autistic. If I were he, I would have been dead by now from the burden of trying so hard. He is a very tough kid. I have to take my hats off to him. The disease, though, is tougher; it is relentless. He is tired of fighting all of his waking hours. Autism does not give him a reprieve—not even for a day. What's more, I lecture him constantly. For him, it must be very hard to hear my lectures, day after day, week after week. My talk is not very sympathetic to his needs; I am always pushing him. I do not say to him, "You poor thing, it is okay if you don't feel like doing anything." I am a fighter. I am also waging a war against his autism. Only time will tell whether this family will finally win or lose this Trojan War.

February 27, 1998

Today, no matter what I said, Krish was adamant about not writing on the computer. He had a fight with his Dad. I was furious at Krish. At one point, he wrote that, "Mom is very caring. She is very unselfish." But I was so angry, I told him:

> If I am that caring, how come you don't care to do much for me? Have you ever tried hard to make me happy? But on the other hand, I am

breathing only for you. I think, day and night, about you, day after day, all of your life. Have you thought one minute about me? This morning I virtually begged you to do computer. You refused flatly. You didn't write more than a few lines. Do you think I want to live the way I am living because I like it? I have chosen to live like this because it is good for you, not for me. Why can't you do a few things, even when you don't like to do them, for other's sake? You have to think about what I said. Simply saying nice things about me is not enough. You have to show me that you care, as I do.

He left and went into his study room. He studied for an hour and a half without a break.

February 28, 1998

This morning, Krish got up at 5:00, crying wildly. I went to his room and put my arms around him to console him. But he rejected my love. Instead, he started crying even louder. So I decided to let him cry out loud and exhaust his sadness for a few minutes. When I came back, after five minutes, his crying spell had subsided. I sat next to him on his bed and stroked his back and face. So I wanted to talk to him about what had been bothering him: I asked him in a soft, kind voice:

Jalaja:	What is the matter, Krish? Did I do anything wrong?
Krish:	I had a terrible dream.
Jalaja:	Can you tell me more about it? Dreams reveal a lot about your inner conflicts.

Krish went to the computer and started writing.

Krish:	Washed away in floods.
Jalaja:	What were you doing, when you were washed away?
Krish:	I was sleeping.
Jalaja:	So the dream bothers you?
Krish:	Yes. It scares me. No more writing.
Jalaja:	You are doing very well. Don't be stubborn and block the flow of communication. Don't let your autism dictate.

Krish:	You are blaming me. I am axed for telling.
Jalaja:	I am sorry. I apologize for my insensitive remarks. Can you please tell me more? Did my talking at breakfast in any way give you this terrible nightmare?
Krish:	Maybe.
Jalaja:	Be frank. Don't protect me.
Krish:	It bothered me; autism kills the joy of life.
Jalaja:	I am really sorry about what I said. I didn't mean it to hurt you. I said something without thinking how my words will affect others around me. It was very wrong on my part not to be thinking of you when I narrated yesterday the story of an autistic boy. This demonstrates how loosely I am using my tongue, even though I am well aware of the power of words. They can make or break one's spirits. Will you forgive me?
Krishna:	It's okay. I cried like a baby for a stupid reason.
Jalaja:	Don't feel bad about your crying, either, because we would never have had this talk without it. It also shows how well you are growing and how beautifully you communicated your feelings to me. So this dream has really brought out the best for both of us.

Yesterday, Nan and I were having coffee at the kitchen table while Krish was walking in the adjoining family room, around the furniture. We were talking about some of our friends who are also parents of autistic children. At one point, I recalled reading a book a very long time ago that was written by a father about his autistic son. All I can remember is that the book was written in a diary form. Except for one incident, I have forgotten most of the book though I vividly remember this man's intense love for his autistic son. This one incident stands out in my memory. One day, he writes, out of immense frustration, how much he wants his son dead. He writes how he could take his son in a boat and fake an accident, how he could swim back to shore while his son drowns. Everything will look like an accident, he assures himself.

How poignant this portion of the diary was. How much I cried and laughed at the same time! It is one of the most touching sections of the entire book. I was able to relate to the father's words and feelings.

Like the father, I also feel as though I can never put him away. That means I can never have a normal life with Krish at home.

Krish was listening to our conversation, as usual. Though he did not show any disapproval at that time, he must have felt very sad. I am sure his terrible dream was a reaction to an emotional state brought on by my talk with Nan. *How guilty I feel, beyond words! How miserable I feel, beyond hope!*

March 1998

March 1, 1998

We wanted Krishna's opinion because he is very much tuned in to his medications:

Jalaja:	What combination of medicines would you like?
Krish:	Haldol, .75 mg, in the morning. Depakote, one pill, at night. Prozac, one 10-mg pill, in the afternoon.
Jalaja:	Why?
Krish:	Good mix.
Jalaja:	Why is it a good mix?
Krish:	Haldol, over 1.5 mg, makes me a zombie. Depakote needed for frontal lobe firings. Prozac, one 10 mg, is for depression.
Jalaja:	Why Haldol at all if it makes you a zombie?
Krish:	Less aggression. Often depression comes with higher dosage. A lot of worry. I mourn my life.

We are also constantly pushing him to the next step so that he can become more normalized and lead a quality life. Our motive for pushing him to improve, is out of love for him. We would never want him to go to a residential program when both of us are dead, where nobody will do graduate-level math and physics. No person will believe, as we do, that despite his autism, if something like physics gives him joy, he should spend time on it so as to stimulate his intellect and so that he is not bored with life. That is the reason we push him so hard to improve in his behavior, communication skills, and other skills—to keep himself busy in life, without boredom. We will never give up on education because he is lacking in living skills.

When Nan and I die, we want Krish to live with his sister, without being a burden to her. He should be able to live with her or next to her in a guest house on the same lot, and at the same time have a very stimulating life, as he has now. He can read plenty of books, go out with people, and have a family life. This is our goal, if this is okay with Malini and her husband.

Before applying for neurosurgery, which she very much wanted to do, she asked me:

Malini:	My career as a neurosurgeon, will it affect Krish's life? Will I be able to give time to Krish?
Jalaja:	He will be okay by then, or he will be so improved that you don't have to give any time to him. Even if he needs help, he can live with you. We have saved enough money for his lifetime that you can get people for him, to live with him.

I encouraged her to go after her dreams, and not to worry about Krish. I also relieved her worry by telling her that she is not being selfish.

I went to Krish and told him what I had written today about living with his sister, and asked his opinion. He replied, "The point as mentioned, often discussed by us, has become hackneyed. As discussed, we need to focus on behavior, centered around communication."

This morning, we gave him Depakote because the neurologist wanted to see the effects of Depakote in the daytime. An hour later, he complained about his writing. He wanted to have another shower. He totally refused to write. Nan went after him and asked him how he is feeling:

Nan:	Why do you want another shower?
Krish:	Depakote.
Nan:	What does it do?
Krish:	Sleepiness.
Nan:	How sleepy are you?
Krish:	As sleepy as night.
Nan:	How about Haldol?
Krish:	No sleepiness. But zombie.
Nan:	What do you mean by zombie?
Krish:	Peevishness, tiredness, no energy. Passivity, no motivation, total withdrawal. Awesome, drastic depression.

We have been trying medications on him, but nothing seems to work favorably.

March 3, 1998

Krish looked different this morning. He was more normal looking than he usually appears with all of his idiosyncrasies. He was looking for a sweater very calmly. There was no tension or restlessness.

The mornings are usually chaotic, and it takes a couple of hours before he settles down. But after an hour of math or physics, he becomes a different person altogether. Very serious education in the morning sets the tone for the rest of the day. His behavior gets hit with the hammer of concentrated work. This morning, he was calmly looking for a sweater with no prior academic study:

Nan:	Hey, I have an idea for a second book.
Jalaja:	Krish has not even written his first book! You are talking about the second?

Krishna, upon hearing us, started laughing.

Krish:	Good joke. Good laugh.

As we started asking more questions about his medications, he ran away. When I chided him for his irresponsible behavior, he came back and wrote:

Krish:	Hate computer. You are treating me like a baby. Lousy, mindless questions.
Jalaja:	I don't need to ask lousy questions if your behavior is not lousy with autism. Do you know Newton's Law of Motion? For every action, there is an equal and opposite reaction. Here I am, doing research on your medicines. How can I know what's happening inside your body? Only you can assist me in this area. I seek your help, and you don't back me up with your remarks. We don't want to drug you, and at the same time, we want to keep your behavior under

control so that you can learn, not be lethargic and drowsy. In this endeavor, I need your cooperation.

He heard me out and promised to be cooperative.

March 4, 1998

Again today, we had a tug of war with his computer practice. He is constantly looking for ways to get out of any skill that is difficult:

Jalaja:	What is the problem?
Krish:	I don't like computer. Alphabet arrangement on keyboard stupid. Hard to remember.
Jalaja:	That may be true. But don't evade the work with excuses. Everybody does it, with or without complaints. If you spend enough time practicing, that will help. We will also try to find out whether we can have a keyboard made the way you want it. Okay?

I again went on to give a speech:

I don't like the excuse you give me, "I don't like it. I don't want to do it." Your actions should not be dictated by your likes and dislikes. Do you really think I like cooking every day, or cleaning the kitchen and the rest of the house every day? If I go by your method, I should stop doing these things because, like you, I hate doing the work. It is boring, not very stimulating to make beds, fold clothes, wash dishes, etc. But I don't think in those terms, "liking and hating." Certain things have to be done. That is that. Maybe I will not cook because I am bored. How is that? I will give you some sandwiches today. If I start saying, like you, "I hate, I don't like," our home will be in a mess, with no food to eat, either. If Daddy says, "I don't like to send bills, it is boring," we will be thrown out of this home in no time. Your good life will come to a screeching halt. You remember this. Some things you have to do. You can never say, "I don't want to do it."

He listened to me very carefully. He looked as if he understood what I said. So I asked him, "Are you ready to write your response to my lecture?" He said, "No."

In that case, this is the deal. Because you are too bored to write, I am too bored to cook and wash dishes. I hate doing them, like you hate writing. So today, we will have no spicy Indian food; instead, we will have some soup and sandwiches. You make up your mind. You want good food, you have to produce. It is fine with me, whether you write or not, because if you don't, then I will have a vacation from cooking today. It is up to you.

Before I finished my statement, he started walking toward the computer. In no time, he was ready to punch those keys. I almost expected this, in response to what I said. He loves good, spicy food. He is an excellent eater. Further, I know that he is a gut-level person. I said we both don't have to work, but the only catch is he will not have the yummy, spicy Indian curry. When I presented it at the gut level, the message came to him very clearly that this is the way it will be from now on. He knew I meant it. It worked.

He wrote beautifully after this speech. When I read what he wrote, it brought tears to my eyes. He did not lash out at me; he did not retaliate. Instead, he saw the logic in my statement. He wrote even better than I did about what I said. He is a remarkable kid. I really, really mean it!

March 5, 1998

Krishna's aversion to the computer is mind-boggling. He's uninterested and refuses to use it for communication. He would rather not communicate than work on the computer. If I were he, without much ability to speak communicatively, I would do the computer all day because I have an enormous desire to communicate. Maybe he doesn't have the intense desire to communicate.

He seems happy with his life as it is. He lives in a big house, eats good food, and has a couple of young men who take him out. He travels abroad for a couple of months for his treatment. He has a family who dotes on him, a father and mother totally dedicated to him. His sister adores him. Even his brother-in-law, a new addition to the family, really loves him and shows a lot of affection to him. He has no money problems. He has mental stimulation from studying physics, math, and electrical engineering. He seems happy with the way his life is structured.

Another point is that maybe he doesn't want to share all of his inner feelings and emotions with us, or others. Isn't autism all about staying in one's shell? He doesn't want that shell cracked open by his own communication. Then the mystery of autism would no longer be a mystery. It could be very painful and unbearable for him to open up, to share his thoughts and emotions. The autistic are not supposed to be open and people oriented; on the contrary, the autistic are supposed to be withdrawn and people allergic. Maybe I am asking too much from him.

The autistic have many problems dealing with people. That may be the reason Krish shrinks from typing his feelings and emotions on the computer. I have been thinking about the hours I have spent trying to coax him into writing about himself. Hereafter, I will ask him to write something else, something not involving himself, something about the world. I will ask him to write about Indonesia. How is the collapse of the Indonesian economy affecting other Asian economies; how is it affecting the world economy? Maybe he will be interested in writing about that since it is not personal. I cannot push him this relentlessly about his computer communication. My pushing could create a psychological hatred for the computer and make him not want to ever achieve that skill. What's more, it is killing my spirit and making me depressed. This is not good for the family in the long run.

I am always worried about how much catching up he has to do. But it is irrelevant. I know that too many people stop learning by the time they are twenty-two or so. He can learn all of his life if he wants to; that is another fifty years. Look at Venus Williams, the black tennis player. She did not play many junior tournaments, as other pros did. She worked at home on her tennis skills. She came to the finals or semifinals in the first years of Wimbledon. Turning pro without playing the junior circuit is not the norm, but she did it successfully. Krishna also can learn at his pace (which is very fast, astronomically so). He is learning every day, in every area. He is trying, and we are trying; that's all that matters. It doesn't make sense if I get frustrated and get him frustrated. It does no good to anyone in the family, especially Krish. I have to back off from bugging him about the computer.

Another thought. Maybe his eyes are bad and he needs glasses. Nan and I both wear glasses. I want Krish to see an opthamologist in case all he needs is glasses. Suppose difficulty in seeing the computer keys is the problem. That would be great. Why am I always wishing some problem or another to be detected? Truly such a thought makes me feel elated.

The amount of time that Krish spends in bed has been considerably reduced. He is also more obedient, except regarding his use of the computer.

March 6, 1998

Since Nan quit his full-time job, I have been able to take up classical music to keep my mind sane. I lead a very intense life with Krish, so I spend at least an hour a day on my music practice. I need to do something for myself in order to take my mind away from Krish. Krish's autism is all consuming. Music takes my mind away from the prosaic practical issues of life with an autistic. Without music, or writing this journal, or my prayers, my life seems on some days, though not all days, pointless and meaningless. I believe it is of utmost importance to keep oneself involved in some form of creative activity like music, dancing, painting, or writing.

Writing gives me a place to vent my feelings. Music also relieves me of my tensions. It is so fulfilling, it makes me soar high with creativity and good feelings. Singing gives me joy and fulfillment in life. With music, I can be alone yet not feel lonely or empty. To the contrary, I feel enriched, blessed, and joyous. I thank God for bestowing that gift on me.

I was considered a shining star in classical music (South Indian sitar) when I was a teenager. With marriage and autism, other realities of life took over. There was no time for music when Krish was young. Now, I make sure to find time. I really encourage all the parents of autistic sons and daughters to have some creative outlet in order to have sanity in their lives. Music and writing give me sanity, sharpness of intellect, and fulfillment in life. People come and go in one's life, but something like music will stay faithfully with me as long as I live. It will not demand, exploit, insult, or desert me. It will be my joy in sickness, old age, and loneliness. It is a precious gift from God that will act as my friend, my soulmate, during my odyssey.

March 7, 1998

We have been swimming against the currents and powerful, gigantic waves of autism. Some days, I wonder and wonder, when will all this end? Is there an end in sight for the ocean to be without waves? Is there a finish line for the rotating earth? Right now, I understand Lord Tennyson's anguish in his lines:

> *I love not hollow cheek or faded eye*
> *Yet, O my friend, I will not have thee die!*
> *Ask me no more, lest I should bid thee live;*
> *Ask me no more; thy fate and mine are sealed.*
> *I strove against the stream all in vain;*
> *Let the great river take me to the main;*
> *No more, dear love, for at a touch, I yield;*
> *Ask me no more.*

I have been thinking constantly about giving medication to Krish. But I have a conflict in this area. The medications always make him drowsy and sleepy. We want him to learn, not vegetate in a comatose state. We don't want to sacrifice his learning with an alert mind to good but dull behavior. We want alertness, learning, and good behavior. Is it too much to ask? I guess it is, with autism.

If autism were an uncomplicated syndrome, the researchers would have found a cure for it. They haven't. What does that say? It is still considered the most baffling condition, out of all the childhood disorders. If that is so, how can a layperson, a homemaker, cure this one? The only medication I have in my pocket is enormous love for my son, intense hard work, utter dedication, incredible desire to improve him, unswerving belief in his abilities, and total blind faith in our Creator. Are these ingredients enough to make him better and ultimately all right?

My husband sees autism very simply. On the contrary, I feel autism is anything but simple. Everything about it is complicated and mind-boggling.

Today, I find myself trying to handle Krish's behavior while trying to convince Nan of the value of what I am doing with Krish. It takes everything out of me because I am not only dealing with Krish's behavior, I am also making sure that Nan does not send out contradictory signals to Krish. As it is, Krish is already confused at those times. On top of that, he has to deal with two parents with opposing views on handling his misbehavior. This certainly is too much for an autistic.

I could leave the discipline of Krish totally in his father's hands, but I don't trust Nan in this area. I may not be perfect, but I am definitely better than his father. Nan is better than I am in teaching him math and physics. Why can't he accept that I am better in dealing with Krish's behavior?

Sometimes I wonder, is it worth all this stress? Is he making enough progress to justify our efforts, or am I walking in quicksand, working feverishly to get out? The more fiercely I try, the deeper I sink. What should I do? Should I abort my efforts and call it quits? Or should I try until the last minute, until my head is submerged in the quicksand?

Today is one of those bad, depressing days. Once in a while, I get these doubts. Are they valid? Or am I making a mountain out of a molehill with my discontented mind?

I am well aware that this mindset of mine is no good and very unproductive. This thinking will sap my energy and enthusiasm for living and lead me to a hole called self-pity. I cannot encourage my mind to destroy me. I have to think that I am not alone in my mental anguish. So many tragedies are happening around me.

My life is not a tragedy, but it is very stress ridden. In mudslides, in earthquakes, and so on, whole families are wiped out. A plane crash or a car accident can take away a loved one. Cancer can snatch away a child. When you think of all the bad things that can happen to any one of us, it is a miracle we are still living.

No more negative thinking.

March 9, 1998

Krishna wrote the other day, "Depression comes out of worry over the future. I moan my life." When Nan started studying physics, Krish said, "boring." That day, he was not in the mood for studying, so his father said:

Nan: If you think it is boring, it is boring. On the other hand, if you think it is interesting, it becomes interesting. Your

way of looking at it changes the way you feel about it.
Physics doesn't say either, "I am boring, don't read me"
or "I am challenging, so please read me." The book is
there. It is you who experience boredom or stimulation,
according to your mind. I can say, bringing you up is either challenging or boring. Either one is true. I take it to
be challenging. So it is interesting.

Krishna: Got the point. No more elaboration needed.

After this talk, Krish started studying physics. He didn't say a
word about boredom.

March 15, 1998

I saw Oprah's show the other day. A guest on the show said that she
was given some anesthetic before her abdominal surgery, which put
her to sleep right away. But she woke up even before the actual
surgery started. She wanted to let the doctors know that she was
awake and aware of the surgery. But she was totally unable to speak
or move any part of her body because of the muscle relaxant that was
given to her. She was screaming and moving in her mind, but nothing, no words or sounds, came out. All of her shouting was inside her.
Nobody in that operation theater knew what was going on in her
mind. They were totally unaware of her unbearable suffering on that
operating table during her entire surgery. Suddenly, the connection
between this woman in the operation theater and Krish became obvious to me, like an object on the table. I couldn't miss it.

Last year, Krish wrote on the computer that he gets all the words
for communication in his head. For some unknown reason, they don't
come out. Even when they come out, there is no resemblance to the
words he had in his mind. Maybe something chemically equivalent
to a muscle relaxant is produced by his brain? He wrote to us that his
problem is with the defect in the output area.

Krish thinks and talks in his mind like everybody else. So the
brain is okay, but something goes wrong in the output. Can it be
due to slow muscles? Maybe, when the brain sends out the signal, the
muscles are not responding fast enough. By the time they start responding, the brain has already sent out more signals in succession.

So when the word finally comes out of his mouth, there is no correlation between the question and the answer. Or is it that something else is wrong in the output? I have been telling doctors that Krish seems to understand a lot of things, but he is unable to recall the words for some unknown reason. First, he cannot say what he wants to say. Second, even when he is able to speak, it comes out wrong.

He was hypotonic when he was a baby. The muscles in his hands are still weak. The skill involved in writing is *still* difficult for him. Anyone can see him struggle with speech. When he was young, he didn't have any eye contact with others. His gaze was always away and unfocused. Was it due to lethargic eye muscles? The doctors were attributing it to avoidance of people. Maybe he was physically too strained to focus.

To me, it seems the part of his brain that deals with output is terribly hurt. How can we rule out the possibility that his brain is secreting some chemical similar to the muscle relaxant that is used in surgery? It could be this or something else in his body that is putting the muscles to sleep. Who knows, he may be screaming and shouting words internally, which are not heard by us. Krish always says that he has a lot of language in his head and that he, too, is very shocked to see the words not come out. Instead, they come out as strange, unintelligible sounds.

I like to think that Krish is under the influence of some sort of muscle relaxant because to my mind it simplifies the problem, whereas autism sounds ominous and scary. When I went to a few neurologists and tried to explain my theory, nobody seemed to understand me. How can they find a cure for a problem they can't even comprehend?

This speechlessness is affecting his moods, his behavior, and his mental state. He would take a giant step toward normalcy if he could express himself orally.

March 20, 1998

As I near the end of this journal, a question has been raised. What have I gotten from this whole ordeal?

In life, you are either a victim or a survivor. Once upon a time, I felt I was a total victim of autism. I didn't know whom to turn to for help. I still don't know. I feel so lonely at times. I used to feel so angry and resentful that I had been wronged by God. Why didn't He prepare me in gradual steps for such a huge, life-consuming trauma? He could have hit me first with a pebble, then a bigger stone, still later with a granite rock, and at last, with a huge boulder to knock me down. I was not ready at such a young age, in my twenties, to face such a huge challenge. Yet I was forced to face it.

I never lacked for teachers in how to handle life's trials and tribulations. God provided me with competent teachers all around me. Nature to me is our teacher; our experiences in life are our lessons; learning from those experiences is our wisdom. The container of that wisdom is our body. Krishna's autism gave me lessons in quick succession. I was panting for breath, being the mother of a severely autistic child; I had to learn the lessons so fast, at such a young age. Otherwise, my existence, as well as my family's existence, was at risk. I learned so many lessons, pearls of wisdom, during this ordeal.

No matter what, life goes on. That is one of the major lessons I have learned. As Wordsworth says in "The Brook":

Sans teeth, sans eyes, sans taste, sans everything.
Men may come and men may go, but I go forever.

Whether you are lucky or not, healthy or not, rich or not, successful or not, happy or not, married or not, young or not, it doesn't matter. Our houses will stand longer than we will. We better learn some humility from this.

Another important message is, God has plans for every one of us, including me, whether we approve of His plans or not. It doesn't matter to God. From an unknown source, "Deep in your quoted instruction, your creator has placed a very special job that only you can do . . . you are patented and copyrighted in heaven."

It is obviously God's will that I should be in the war zone of autism. I am in the battlefield of family relations, and the raging war against autism has been going on for years. Like a soldier furiously fighting the enemy while wanting a peaceful, serene existence, without the worry of being killed or captured by the enemy, I am fighting to make Krish a normal person, while trying to stay calm and happy.

Yet another precious lesson is how we cope with our daily problems, big or small, for this makes a difference in the quality of our lives. The ordeal often has made me wonder, who is not beset with problems in life? Every day is a day of challenge for every one of us. The happiness and the peace we want so desperately depend on our coping mechanisms. If the coping mechanism is strong, vibrant, and ever-present, our hardships and obstacles will never be insurmountable. This kind of reflection on life has given me the mental strength to evolve to where I am now, as a human being. In the end, I became not a survivor but a conqueror of my life's circumstances.

My intense love for God has not made me a bitter person, but a better person. To me, this is the real grace of God. To me, grace is not being successful and powerful like a corporate CEO, or being an author with a million copies sold, or being a talk show host or a sports celebrity.

We cannot stop tragedies, adversities, or mishaps. God decides those. But one thing is in our hands: what we do with our lives with whatever we have. That choice is solely ours. Early on in life, I decided to be a winner. That's what I am now, with or without autism. My limitation is not autism but my attitude toward autism. I can either think that I am fettered by autism or that I am unfettered, an all-expansive spirit that will guide this body, mind, and intellectual entity named Jalaja, my physical existence.

One of the great saints of India says that with shoes, one can walk even over thorny bushes and stony slopes. You are protected from it all. We don't need to cover the whole world with leather in order for us to walk safely. Similarly, I don't need to make Krish's autism go away for me to be happy. All I need is a pair of shoes to walk over the thorny fields; that is, I need a change of attitude, a strong, controlled, poised mind.

To win the mind is to win all, just as to one who is wearing shoes, the whole world is covered with leather. If you change, the whole world will change.

Epilogue

In this book, I have talked extensively about the conflict we were having with the DMR. Our viewpoint clearly differed from theirs. The DMR felt that Krish would greatly benefit from programs like ASA, designed for the autistic. Whereas Nan and I did not agree with them since, in our opinion, he would be very poorly served by such programs because of his higher level of functioning. He would be bored, hence his anxiety-induced behavior would worsen.

He is unique among the autistic. He doesn't belong with the low functioning autistic because of his academics and other skills. He doesn't belong with the high functioning either because he lacks speech. Speech defines the line between the higher and the lower functioning in autism, I guess. We have designed a tailor-made program for Krish by taking into account all of his strengths as well as his weaknesses, or limitations.

The DMR did not believe in what we were doing. People from the DMR made us feel enormous stress by freezing their funding and so on. We always came home angry from the meetings with them. To resolve this conflict, we decided to get an independent evaluation from a professional in this area. That was our sole motivation in going to Neuro-Psychology Associates of Western Massachusetts. Our wish, fortunately, coincided with that of the DMR. We wanted them off our backs.

On June 18, 1998, we took Krish to see Dr. Deborah Fein to assess his current functioning level and also to find out whether what we are doing for Krish as parents is the right thing to do. Even though I knew all along that we were doing the very best for our son, I wanted a professional to reassure me and at the same time, tell the DMR to stop breathing down our necks.

As usual, Krish was extremely anxious in the new place; especially with the testing atmosphere, his fear and anxiety increased exponentially. His ability to concentrate declined rapidly. Numerous times, he let the doctors know that he was "tensed up" by writing on the portable computer. A couple of days later, Krish wrote that he felt as if he failed the tests even before he actually got started. He was certain that Dr. Fein was going to support the DMR in their beliefs. His fear of being sent to a program for the autistic at the expense of his academics was intense. On the contrary, Dr. Fein was extremely kind to Krish. Her empathy and kindness started to relax him. At the end of the day, he started to trust her; that is, when he did some simultaneous equations for her. He typed in some answers to her questions. If he had been in that frame of mind from the beginning, he could have done a lot more. But unfortunately, he was very anxious.

Here is the neuropsychological evaluation of Krish by Dr. Deborah Fein:

Krishna was quite anxious throughout most of the evaluation session. His parents report that he is typically anxious when in new situations and his ability to attend, process information and formulate responses declines as his anxiety increases. He was able to type "tensed up" several times on his hand-held keyboard and was helped to relax by taking brief walks in the hall with his father. He is able to communicate basic needs and answer questions orally in single words or brief telegraphic phrases. His independently typed work shows a much broader vocabulary use, understanding of grammar and syntax, and symbolic thought.

The Peabody Picture Vocabulary Test was administered to assess Krishna's single word expressive vocabulary. Each of the four pictures was pointed out to him to make sure he looked at each of the pictures before making his choice. Otherwise, he would anxiously respond randomly. With the structure to look at all of the options, he was able to identify pictures. After each response, he would look at the examiner to confirm the correctness of his response. He needed calm reassurance from his father and several breaks during this particular test to complete the items, but, despite these attempts to calm him, the test was discontinued before reaching a ceiling score because of his level of anxiety. Therefore, a formal score was not obtainable. However, before testing was discontinued because of his anxiety, he successfully identified words such as "foundation," "wailing," "dilapidated," "isolation," and "adapter," which clearly show a higher level of receptive understanding than he is able to demonstrate orally. Throughout the testing, his anxiety was barely contained and would erupt through after about 5 minutes of testing. When he did not know an answer, he became very agitated. At these times, he would shout, "I don't know," he would pace the floor, vocalize, rock and breathe heavily. Some hand posturing was noted. Going for a walk temporarily dissipated his anxiety.

Other non-verbal testing was attempted, but Krishna's high level of anxiety precluded a successful demonstration of skills.

He is able to read and can answer questions about the content of what he has read. He does not read aloud. His parents brought in handwritten examples of his ability to respond to written questions about current events and common information. When asked to type an answer for a few of the Comprehension items from the Standford-Binet Intelligence Scale: Fourth Edition, Krishna was able to successfully type a simple answer to each of the questions. When complimented with "That was beautifully written," Krishna typed "Thanks." He was also able to type in correct answers to multiplication problems presented orally and he could write the answer to two problems involving simultaneous equations. Krishna is able to correctly respond to Yes/No questions.

Krishna is a 27-year-old young man who clearly meets the criteria for the diagnosis of Autistic Disorder, but with an unusual profile of skills. His social and pragmatic communication abilities are significantly impaired, and he shows repetitive sensory and motor behaviors, but through the independent use of written and typed communication, he has shown higher levels of cognitive processing and insight. It was not possible to formally assess his cognitive abilities because of his high level of anxiety in an unfamiliar setting. This anxiety interfered with his ability to sustain his attention to test materials and to formulate a response verbally or through written communication. However, an informal demonstration of his math skills, knowledge of current events, knowledge of vocabulary meaning and self-descriptions of his affective state showed cognitive abilities well beyond those expected of a man with such severe autistic behaviors.

It is strongly recommended that Krishna continue his current program of daily tutoring in areas of interest to him and the social experience opportunities with the workers who now take him on daily outings. Because of his higher level of cognitive functioning and his emotional insight, he would be poorly served in a day activity program with low functioning autistic adults. Vocational programming with higher functioning autistic adults would severely strain his limited communication abilities. Programming for Krishna should focus on quality of life issues. He is calmest and happiest when involved in cognitive pursuits (math, history, art, classical music) and he is developing social relationships (to the best of his ability) with the workers who currently work with him. Krishna is extremely fortunate in having parents who can provide for his current needs. Realistic vocational planning does not seem feasible unless and until Krishna's anxiety is under control and he can stay with a task and his communication is more speedy and efficient.

In addition to the academic activities now carried out with Krishna, he should also continue to be involved in some vigorous physical activities every day to help dissipate some of his debilitating anxiety and for his overall health.

Krishna should also be seen by an occupational therapist with experience in autism who can assess Krishna's sensory processing and his fine motor coordination. He will need specific suggestions for helping to self-monitor his affective state, activities to help normalize sensory processing and integration, and for improving his fine motor control and speed. The occupational therapist may have suggestions for therapeutic motor activities that can be worked into Krishna's daily exercise program with his aide.

Krishna's high levels of anxiety interfere with his ability to process information and to formulate verbal or written responses. He and his family may want to explore the use of anti-depressant, anti-anxiety medication to help alleviate some of this anxiety. A psychopharmacology consult is recommended.

The DMR contributed in a great way by asking us to seek a professional opinion. Further, the conflict between us got resolved when the DMR accepted the verdict from Dr. Fein and released the money. Before going to the neuropsychological evaluation, we felt very much alone in our endeavor with Krish. We had no professional support for what we were doing with him. Now, we came out with the conviction that what we have been doing for our son is the very best any parent can do. The support we received from Dr. Fein was morally uplifting and emotionally fulfilling.

The harvest of peace we are reaping with pleasure and gratitude now is due to the three seeds we planted in the last two years. They are: changing the course of the ayurvedic treatment by focusing on good, acceptable behavior; going to Dr. Deborah Fein for the neuropsychological evaluation; and finally, going to see a psychiatrist named Dr. Katic, who has some knowledge of autism.

The ayurvedic doctors don't know who Krish is, whereas we, the parents, know him extremely well. I am his soulmate, with my laser beams constantly scanning him and his moods. Previously, the treatment was aimed at improving his concentration, memory, and his brain function overall. I had a very serious discussion with the doctors on how he needs to improve his behavior. I told them that he is a lost soul without a predictable behavior that we can live with. That can be achieved only by reducing his anxiety, which is caused by tension, which in turn will improve his overall brain function, including his concentration. The ayurvedic doctors were very sympathetic to my cause, and they were humble enough to listen to me, a layperson in medicine, and take me in as a member of the team.

The new ayurvedic treatment was aimed at eliminating the constant firing in the frontal lobe area of Krishna's brain. The doctors felt that his erratic behavior, along with his peevish moods, is due to this firing. According to them, it indicates a silent seizure activity in his brain. We saw instantaneous results in his mood swings. They became more normalized. Recently, in July of this year, under the insistence of our ayurvedic doctors, we had an EEG done on Krish's brain at Boston's Children's Hospital. We were extremely thrilled to hear from one of the world's best minds in EEG that Krishna's EEG looks normal and he doesn't see any firing in his brain. The same hospital told us in November 1997 that Krishna's EEG showed firing in the frontal lobe area. All I can say is that it is one of God's miracles.

We really don't know what twists and turns our journey through life may take, and no one is bestowed with the power to predict. What we viewed as a bad period with the DMR turned out in the end to be the best thing for our family. Without the constant pinpricks from them, we wouldn't be where we are as a family today. We wouldn't have gone to Dr. Deborah Fein without the motivation of getting the DMR off our backs.

It was Dr. Fein who convinced me that I need not go through Krish's anxiety-ridden, angry outbursts all alone, without any professional help. I can get medications from Dr. Katic to reduce it, if not eliminate it completely. Even though I was convinced, I didn't go to Dr. Katic for a year because of the failure of previous trials with medications. Even in our thinking we need God's intervention, I guess.

There would be no Dr. Katic for us without Dr. Deborah Fein. Dr. Katic's patience and deliberate approach to introducing new medications have done wonders in reducing Krish's impulsive, aggressive behavior. His constant sleeplessness, enormous anger, uncontrollable restlessness, and incurable frustrations are, though not totally eliminated, very much controllable. Under Dr. Katic's care, Krish's depression and lack of motivation are minimized. This doesn't mean Krish is cured of autism; he still displays some amount of anxiety. From time to time, Krishna's brain seems wired. That is the innate nature of the syndrome he is suffering from. Otherwise, with all of his intelligence, he would be normal by now. But he isn't; he is still very much autistic. The difference is that now we can live with him peacefully, not from crisis to crisis. The medications we give to him are Prozac, Buspar, and Melatonin, along with lots of vitamins.

Here is a portion of the psychopharmacologic evaluation of Krishna from Dr. Katic of the Cambridge Hospital.

MENTAL STATUS EXAMINATION: Krishna was seen on June 30, 1999. He presents as a well-developed 28-year-old young man. He makes poor eye contact and is clearly anxious upon entering the office. He is hyperventilating, holds his body in a rather rigid and tense manner, as well as having his eyes wide open. At times, he engages in moaning sounds. Otherwise, his spoken language is rather rare, except for requests for leaving the office or to go get food when he is hungry. He tends to type the remainder of his responses on a computer. His face is generally held in a smiling, strained type of grimace. At times, he will sit and type answers to my questions. At other times, he will begin spontaneously to hyperventilate, complain of tension, and will stand up, as well as pacing about the office in a circular manner. He engages in stereotypical behaviors, such as finger tapping and various other finger movements. Krishna typed out that he is "tense all day." He did describe this tension as being a mixture of anger and nervousness. He complained of feeling sad, and typed the "future makes me sad," as well as, "I am going nowhere." He expressed wishes of becoming a math professor and expressed wishes that the examiner could help him, specifically in reducing his tension.

ASSESSMENT: Krishna is a 28-year-old young man with a long-standing diagnosis of autism. He presents with symptoms that are consistent with both depression and anxiety disorder. He clearly experiences anxiety, given the significant physical tension and hyperventilating behaviors that he displayed in the office, and unfortunately these can escalate at times to aggressive behaviors. At this juncture, it is my impression that his current medication treatment is subtherapeutic, and I discussed with his parents attempting to maximize his antidepressant trial.

I must also give credit to Krishna for putting up a brave, fierce fight all of his life. He had and still has every reason to give up on life and not to cooperate with us or the doctors. But he chose to take the shot, listen, obey our commands, and try to overcome his negativity regarding autism. Above all, he decided not to be an invisible writer by just having a dream, but doing something about it. He has a way of rising from the ashes. The resilient spirit in him is astounding.

Now, I feel in my heart that his wanting to be a writer shouldn't be a fleeting dream for him. From time to time when I encountered those most daunting, difficult periods of my life with his bad behavior, I felt that his dream might be way beyond his horizon. I shuddered at the thought of his dream bubble bursting. His senses, his coordination, his mind, his concentration, his speech, his social awareness, even his basic life lines like sleep and a partner in his life, which are taken for granted, are robbed from him against his will and wishes.

In Francis Bacon's words, "We rise to great heights by a winding staircase." If that is true, Krish has been relentlessly climbing one of the most winding staircases of all for years, and so he is bound to succeed. The time is ripe, with his unacceptable behavior under control, his low self-esteem on the decline, and his motivation on the rise, for his inner talent to sprout like a seedling in waiting, with training and hard work. My surging desire to make my son almost normal is no longer waning, but waxing.

Coping with Autism

Perish the thought of normalcy sought
By ways beyond destined lot
Let rightful thinking guide my wish
For my beloved son called Krish.

Expectations bring no joy but strife
Such is the true nature of our life
Ponder thus on the blatant truth
Receive in abundance, peace beyond wealth.

Time steals dire poverty and glorious presidency
Time robs incurable autism and cherished normalcy
Time destroys all worldly things in sight
So cast off desire for a son perfectly right.

In all things, I must see equality
To enter the world of tranquility
Perceive not senseless, sinful divisions
For they dispel the treasure of vision.

However much I long for a normal son
However fearful I become of autism
And thus chained in its gory grip
Thy Sheer Glance can disperse my grief.

Oh merciful Lord, vanquish my sorrow.
Bestow me, the frail mortal with
Infinite peace and inner awareness,
Exquisite serenity and eternal bliss.

Afterword

From a Mother's Heart: A Journal of Survival, Challenge and Hope is a moving account of one mother's journey of love. As professionals we need to appreciate first-hand the true meaning of such a dedication and sacrifice entailed in the day to day care of individuals who need our special attention. Jalaja Narayanan invites us to witness this journey of fulfillment through a simple act of sharing which she has so aptly termed as "sharing as a healing force."

We are enriched by Mrs. Narayanan's experience: as parents, family members, caregivers and professionals. We learn about the reality of living with her son with autism brought forth in this book as a "one year snap shot" diary that also captures Krish's past 25 years.

Although a book for parents, this work stands also to contribute significantly to the training of professionals engaged in services for persons with special needs. As I read Mrs. Narayanan's account I became more self-aware of my professional development. One of my early supervisors during psychiatric residency training, then at the Massachusetts General Hospital in Boston, routinely called upon our ability to understand and diagnose ourselves through "autognosis." This self-reflective process helped us to capture the meaning of our therapeutic roles within the context of our own personal experience and remembrances. In so doing it facilitated our recognition of the transformations within ourselves in our daily work with our patients. It was an inspiring process that was often difficult but enriching in so many ways. Like the book *For the Love of Anne,* that has given so much strength to Jalaja Narayanan, this was "my candle in total darkness."

Such inward looking perspectives helps us to discover ourselves as we discover others. In his book *Bitter Lemons*, Lawrence Durrell (1) wrote, "Journeys, like artists are born and not made. A thousand differing circumstances contribute to them, few of them willed or determined by the will—whatever we may think. They flower spontaneously out of the demand of our natures—and the best of them lead us not only outwards in space, but inwards as well."

More is learned if we are touched directly by a person and a family affected by autism. It is in this light that I remembered first-hand my own experience of knowing a child with autism born of a family now considered among our best friends. The "roller coaster of emotions" that Jalaja Narayanan describes blends easily with that mother's experience. There is a lot to be shared and much more to be discovered.

However the process of sharing as a therapeutic and educational tool will empower and strengthen us all.

This diary indeed represents a "pair of shoes" for us to travel across those "thorny fields." In its structure the book contains many themes and dilemmas that families will find familiar. The reader will also derive much pleasure in the book's metaphor and poetry. Poems, it is often said, amplify our appreiation of those qualities that we may take for granted. It's not only the ideas and thoughts, but also the patterns and syntheses of words that give meaning to them. In this respect, this *Journey* is healing not only of our thoughts, but also of our character. The symbols create a backcloth, a mood and a personal communication that speaks directly to our *whole personhood,* a term once used by an influential psychiatrist Adolph Meyer in his integrated psychobiology (2).

It is on this topic that I would like to further expand. The road to personhood is through education. That is what makes us distinctly human. It's all "education, education and education" a former esteemed headmaster once retorted. Yet, like him, I also despair of the effects of our current system. Neither our health nor our educational care represents a high-yield, low-cost commodity. So much is left to parents and families to shoulder: too many hurdles, many points of assessment and too many "thorns" on the road. This book helps us to manage these challenges and not ever to give up.

In the face of caring for children and especially those with special needs, the parents need our support to stick to their guns, and to maintain their identity, dignity and sense of purpose. All those nights the parents have to stay up to shepherd their children, all that planning and preparation required for each daily eventuality. Yes, so much hard work and responsibility!

The science is full of jargon: many publications too technical and often conflicting and the road to care a complex one. In the atmosphere of our postmodern world, this book rewards us all for bearing the burdens, for taking on the responsibility. It is indeed not too old-fashioned to do one's best, simply as a matter of principle. It is not out of date to parent a child to one's full capacity. This book speaks to our inner strengths as we travel our paths as parents.

Our system of health, educational and rehabilitative services need to aspire to *support* such a system of "total [parental] care." We need to reward good parenting, not because it is economical for governments for them to exist in the long run, but because stronger parents behave instinctively with good sense and great kindness. They support one another magnificently. They are quiet and generous and, where they feel able, they always manage to smile.

As a physician working with children, I know that parents, in the broadest means possible, are our key. I salute the Narayanans for sharing the days past and present and for many more days of fulfillment in the inspiring life of Krish.

References:

(1) Durrell L. Bitter Lemons. New York: E.P. Hutton, 1957, p. 15
(2) Meyer A. The rise to person and the concept of wholes or integrates. Am J Psychiatry 1944;100:100–106

Kerim M. Munir, M.D., D.Sc.
Director of Psychiatry
Institute for Community Inclusion
Division of General Pediatrics
Harvard Medical School
Children's Hospital

ORDER INFORMATION

Telephone orders:
> BookMasters   1-(800)-247-6553 toll free
> *Please have your credit card ready*

E-mail your request to:
> order@bookmaster.com
> OR
> http://www.atlasbooks.com/marktplc/

Postal orders:
> BookMasters
> 30 Amberwood Parkway
> Ashland, OH 44805
> *Please enclose check, money order, or credit card information*

Please send the following number of books: _____
I may return any of them for a full refund—for any reason, no questions asked.

Name:_____

Address: _____

City:_____State: ___ Zip: _____

Telephone: _____

Sales tax: MA and OH residents include applicable sales tax
Shipping: within the United States $4.00 per single book
Inquire about quantity discounts for large orders.

Payment: □ Check   □ Credit card:

□ Visa   □ Master Card   □ AMEX   □ Discover

Card number: _____

Name on Card:_____ Exp. Date ___/___

ORDER INFORMATION

Telephone orders:
BookMasters   1-(800)-247-6553 toll free
Please have your credit card ready

E-mail your request to:
order@bookmaster.com
OR
http://www.atlasbooks.com/marktplc/

Postal orders:
Bookmasters
30 Amberwood Parkway
Ashland, OH 44805
Please enclose check, money order, or credit card information

Please send the following number of books: _____
I may return any of them for a full refund—for any reason, no questions asked.

Name:_____

Address: _____

City: _____State: _____ Zip: _____

Telephone: _____

Sales tax: MA and OH residents include applicable sales tax
Shipping: within the United States $4.00 per single book
Inquire about quantity discounts for large orders.

Payment: ☐ Check   ☐ Credit card:

☐ Visa   ☐ Master Card   ☐ AMEX   ☐ Discover

Card number: _____

Name on Card:_____ Exp. Date ___/___